PSYCHOLOGY OF EMOTIONS, MOTIVATIONS AND ACTIONS

PSYCHOLOGY OF IMPULSIVITY

NEW RESEARCH

Psychology of Emotions, Motivations and Actions

Additional books in this series can be found on Nova's website under the Series tab.

Additional e-books in this series can be found on Nova's website under the e-book tab.

PSYCHOLOGY OF EMOTIONS, MOTIVATIONS AND ACTIONS

PSYCHOLOGY OF IMPULSIVITY:

NEW RESEARCH

MARY C. OLMSTEAD
EDITOR

nova publishers
New York

For permission to use material from this book please contact us:
Telephone 631-231-7269; Fax 631-231-8175
Web Site: http://www.novapublishers.com

Library of Congress Cataloging-in-Publication Data

Psychology of impulsivity : new research / editors: Mary C. Olmstead (Department of Psychology, Dept. of Biomedical and Molecular Sciences, Centre for Neuroscience Studies, Queen's University, Kingston, ON, Canada).
pages cm. -- (Psychology of emotions, motivations and actions)
Includes index.
ISBN: 978-1-63321-879-6 (hardcover)
1. Impulse. 2. Problem solving. 3. Impulse control disorders. I. Olmstead, Mary C.
BF575.I46P792 2014
153.8--dc23

2014033509

Published by Nova Science Publishers, Inc. † New York

CONTENTS

Preface		**vii**
Chapter 1	Impulsivity, Problem-Solving, and Suicide: Assessment and Treatment Considerations in the Context of Scientific Literature *Kari Koss, Laura L. Neely, Jennifer Tucker, Marcus VanSickle and Marjan Ghahramanlou-Holloway*	**1**
Chapter 2	Halo Effect of Student Misbehavior on Teacher Ratings of Impulsivity and Other Executive Function Deficits *David Álvarez-García, Trinidad García and Paloma González-Castro*	**21**
Chapter 3	DAPP-BQ Personality Prototypes in a General Psychiatric Inpatient Population: Associations with Symptom Expression and Treatment Indicators *Tim Bastiaens, Laurence Claes, Eva Ceulemans, Dominique Vanwalleghem and Marc De Hert*	**33**
Chapter 4	Differential Role of Impulsivity in Adolescents' Suicidal Behavior with Borderline Personality Disorder and Major Depression *Daniel Serrani Azcurra*	**49**
Chapter 5	Impulsive Behaviors that Distract from Distress: Non-Suicidal Self-Injury *Elizabeth N. Riley, Jessica L. Combs, Heather A. Davis and Gregory T. Smith*	**61**
Chapter 6	Impulsive Action and Impulsive Inaction: Toward an Integrative Theory of Impulsivity *Leila Guller, Lauren Boyle, Nichea S. Spillane and Gregory T. Smith*	**77**

Chapter 7 Biomarkers of Impulsivity **93**
Dubravka Svob Strac, Matea Nikolac Perkovic, Gordana Nedic Erjavec, Evelyn Kiive, Katarina Dodig Curkovic, Mario Curkovic, Dubravka Kocijan Hercigonja, Jaanus Harro, Dorotea Muck-Seler and Nela Pivac

Chapter 8 Impulse Control Disorders: Prospect for Treatment Using Noninvasive Brain Stimulation **141**
Maya Dickler, Antoine Hone-Blanchet and Shirley Fecteau

Editor Contact Information **159**

Index **161**

PREFACE

Impulsivity is a primary feature of many psychiatric conditions and often leads to maladaptive behaviors in nonclinical populations. This predisposition to rapid, unplanned actions and a disregard for future, negative consequences leads to seemingly irrational and self-defeating behaviours including substance abuse, pathological gambling, binge eating, and self-harm. Even in young children, impulsivity can have detrimental and long-lasting effects: deficits in impulse control predict poor academic performance and are correlated with behavioural, social, and emotional problems. This book provides an up-to-date overview of research in impulsivity from personality theories through cognitive and biological mechanisms to genetic markers. It also reviews current theories on factors that precipitate the emergence of impulsive behaviors, such as early adversity or learned contingencies. Topics include the development of assessment tools to identify impulsivity in vulnerable populations, conceptualization of impulsivity within a personality prototype model, and identification of disorders in which impulsivity leads to suicide-related behaviors. This broad psychosocial perspective helps to explain how impulsive tendencies develop and how these are exacerbated in certain conditions. Most importantly, factors that mediate the relationship between impulsivity and maladaptive behaviors such as aggression, excessive drug use, or self-injury are discussed throughout the book. Many of the authors present new ideas for the remediation and therapy of impulse control disorders; the final chapter discusses exciting advances from proof of concept studies exploring non invasive brain stimulation as a treatment for neurocognitive impairments associated with impulsivity. Overall, the integration of data from behavioural, biological, social, and environmental studies takes research in impulsivity to a new level. For the reader, the novel theoretical perspectives presented in this book will lead to a more thorough understanding of the relationship between impulsivity and behavioural disorders.

Chapter 1 – Impulsivity is a predisposition toward rapid, unplanned actions to internal or external stimuli without regard to the negative consequences of these for self and/or others (Moeller et al., 2001). Clinically, impulsivity is a personality characteristic that is commonly observed in suicidal individuals based on both self-report and laboratory measures (Gorlyn, 2005; Horesh, 2001). Therefore, empirically driven risk assessment protocols often mention impulsivity as a risk indicator for suicide. Of course, impulsivity can serve as a symptom for psychiatric conditions such as bipolar disorder, borderline personality disorder, and substance-related disorders – all of which have also been recognized as risk factors for suicide. Given the strong empirical link between impulsivity and suicide, one may assume that all suicidal acts are impulsive in nature, yet to date, there is evidence to the contrary. For example, Witte and colleagues (2008) have shown that only less than a quarter of those attempting suicide do so impulsively (i.e., without prior planning). Therefore, some have argued that the link between impulsivity and suicide may be indirect (Bender et al., 2011). One possible explanation for such an indirect path may be related to problem-solving. An individual who is characteristically impulsive may consequently engage in impulsive and careless problem-solving, particularly during stressful life circumstances. Such deficits in problem-solving may have a biopsychosocial underpinning. For example, an individual may have had the biological predisposition to an impulsive nature and subsequently learned over time to make careless decisions to cope with life stressors. The relationship between impulsive and careless problem-solving and suicide-related behaviors has also been shown in the scientific literature. Simply stated, an individual with an impulsive and careless problem-solving style moves quickly from facing a problem to taking action without considering the consequences of such actions and/or repeatedly engages in many careless and unsuccessful attempts at solving the same problem. The objectives of the proposed chapter are threefold. First, a brief summary of the scientific literature on the relationship between impulsivity, problem-solving, and suicide will be presented. Second, clinical advantages of assessment and treatment of impulsivity and problem-solving are explored, and a list of psychometrically sound psychological assessments for the measurement of impulsivity and problem-solving will be presented. Finally, a series of assessment and treatment recommendations will be provided to address impulsivity and problem-solving among suicidal individuals.

Chapter 2 – *Introduction.* Student problem behaviors at school have a multicausal origin. Among the proposed causes are deficits in impulsivity control and other executive functions. Behavior rating scales are one of the most extensively used techniques to identify such deficits. They provide advantages, but they also have potential drawbacks. The *halo effect* is a possible response bias of these scales. Goals. a) To identify the executive function deficits that best predict student misbehavior, b) to analyze the possible negative halo effect of students´ misbehavior on teacher ratings of executive functioning using behavior rating scales, and c) to identify reasons for the halo effect when it occurs. *Method. Participants.* The authors assessed 179 Primary Education students from 3rd to 6th grade (8-13 years). *Assessment instruments.* The teacher who had more contact with the students completed two behavior rating scales: *Alteración del Comportamiento en la Escuela [Misbehavior at School]* (ACE; Arias, Ayuso, Gil, & González, 2006), reflecting the frequency of students' aggressive and disruptive behavior; and the *Escala de Funcionamiento Ejecutivo para Profesorado [Executive Functioning Scale for Teachers]* (EFE-P; García, Álvarez-García, González-Castro, Álvarez, & Segurola, 2013b), measuring the frequency of children's behaviors indicative of executive function deficits. Specifically, this scale measures students´ behavior related to impulsivity control, activity regulation, emotional control, working memory, planning, organization, flexibility, concentration and attentional focus. High scores in these components are indicative of executive function deficits. The parallel version of the EFE-P *Escala de Funcionamiento Ejecutivo para Familias [Family Executive Functioning Scale for Families]* (EFE-F; García, Álvarez-García, González-Castro, Álvarez, & Cueli, 2013a) was administered to the assessed students' parents to compare their responses with those of the teachers. *Results.* Stepwise multiple linear regression analysis showed that the executive function deficits that statistically and significantly predicted students´ misbehavior were those based in impulsivity control, activity regulation, and emotional control. The ANOVAs showed that, according to the teachers, students with the worse behavior emitted significantly more behaviors indicative of deficits in impulsivity control. They also seemed to have more problems with the rest of executive functions assessed. In contrast, parents' rating only yielded statistically significant differences in impulsivity control, activity regulation, and organization, with notably lower effect sizes. *Conclusion.* Impulsivity and hyperactivity are factors closely related to misbehavior at school. In this sample, the authors confirmed that misbehavior at school can have a negative halo effect on teacher ratings of executive function deficits. Psychometric, clinical, and educational implications arising from these results are discussed.

Chapter 3 – The present chapter contributes to the study of Impulsivity as it sets out to demonstrate evidence for an impulsive cluster of personality functioning (labelled Undercontrolled) overarching a heterogeneous clinical population. Conceptualizing Impulsivity as a combination of high Neuroticism, low Agreeableness and low Conscientiousness, the authors' study makes use of a clustering approach as opposed to a dimensional one. They investigated personality prototypes using the personality dimensions of the Dimensional Assessment of Personality Pathology Basic Questionnaire (DAPP-BQ; Livesley & Jackson, 2009). One hundred and ten psychiatric inpatients filled out the DAPP-BQ and the MMPI-2. The number of personality prototypes was determined by means of a model-based cluster analysis, which yielded three distinct personality clusters. Patients in cluster 1 (labelled Overcontrollers) were identified by higher scores on emotional dysregulation and compulsiveness. Patients in cluster 2 (labelled Resilients) were characterized by lower scores on the emotional dysregulation and the dissocial dimensions. Patients in cluster 3 (the impulsive cluster, labelled Undercontrollers) were identified by higher scores on the dissocial dimension and lower scores on the compulsiveness dimension. The clusters were validated by means of the MMPI-2 scales. Resilients reported being less overwhelmed by problems (MMPI-2 K scale), presented themselves more well-adjusted (MMPI-2 S scale), showed no MMPI-2 Content scale elevations, and presented themselves with significantly more tolerance for confrontation, self-confidence, responsibility and good reality testing (MMPI-2 Es, Do and Re scales) compared to Overcontrollers and Undercontrollers. Overcontrollers showed significantly more hypochondriac concerns (MMPI-2 Hs scale), depression related problems (MMPI-2 D scale) and social introversion (MMPI-2 Si scale) than Resilients, but did not differ from Undercontrollers on these dimensions. Undercontrollers displayed distinctively higher levels of Antisocial Practices (MMPI-2 ASP) and acting-out (MMPI-2 Pd and Ma scales) than Overcontrollers as well as Resilients, differences which were not attributable to state-dependent demoralization (MMPI-2 DEM) but represented valid trait-like features (MMPI-2 RC4 and RC9 scales). While Undercontrollers specifically reported the highest levels of psychopathology and expressed need for help (MMPI-2 F and Fb scales), they nevertheless displayed the least positive attitude towards treatment (MMPI-2 TRT scale). In conclusion, current results demonstrate evidence for the existence and clinical relevance of an Impulsive cluster of personality functioning (labelled Undercontrolled) overarching a heterogeneous clinical population. With the Undercontrolled cluster representing the opposite of the Overcontrolled cluster in terms of Compulsivity, two of the three personality prototypes center around (the inverse of) Impulsivity. Implications for further research and clinical practice are discussed.

Chapter 4 – The objective of the study was to examine the differential role of impulsivity in suicidal behavior attempts among adolescents with borderline personality disorder (BPD) and major depressive disorder (MDD). Seventy eight adolescents were recruited for the research, of whom thirty-nine had BPD and the rest had MDD. Among participants who had exhibited a recent suicidal attempt, 18 belonged to the BPD group and 16 to the MDD. Assessments were made with the Barratt Impulsiveness Scale, the Diagnostic Interview Schedule for Children, the Deliberate Self-harm Inventory, the Beck Depression Inventory, the Beck Hopelessness Scale, the Beck Hopelessness Scale, the Multidimensional Anger Inventory and the Lifetime History of Aggression Results showed that the adolescents with BPD had more anger, aggression, and impulsiveness than those with MDD, but similar levels of depression and hopelessness. Suicidal versus non-suicidal adolescents were more depressed, hopeless, and aggressive, but not more angry or impulsive. There were no significant differences in impulsiveness for the MDD suicidal group versus the MDD non-suicidal group, but the suicidal BPD adolescents were significantly more impulsive than the non-suicidal BPD adolescents. In the participants with BPD, impulsiveness and aggression correlated significantly and positively with suicidal behavior, but no such associations were found in the participants with MDD. In both diagnostic groups, depression and hopelessness, but not anger, had a positive association with suicidal behavior. The suicidal participants with MDD had significantly higher suicidal intent scores than the suicidal adolescents with BPD. As a conclusion it seems that suicidal behavior in adolescents with BPD and MDD shares a common basis related to hopelessness but impulsivity trait plays a differential role in those participants with BPD, apart from those with MDD. These features may help to differentiate suicidal risk behavior in adolescents with BPD and MDD, and implement predictive and protective measures.

Chapter 5 – There appear to be a set of behaviors that belong to a common response class, which are characterized by rash, impulsive actions that provide immediate relief from intense negative affect. First, the authors will review evidence identifying several behaviors as members of this "impulsive behavior for negative reinforcement" response class, including heavy drinking, smoking, and binge eating/purging. Second, they will review emerging evidence that identifies non-suicidal self-injury (NSSI) as an additional member of this response class. NSSI refers to the direct, deliberate destruction of bodily tissue without suicidal intent (American Psychiatric Association, 2013). Third, the authors highlight the role of negative urgency, the personality disposition to act rashly when distressed, as a personality trait precursor to all behaviors in the response class, including NSSI. Fourth, they review a model designed to help understand why an individual would choose to engage in one behavior in the response class over another. This model emphasizes psychosocial learning, measured as expectancies for reinforcement from a given behavior. Expectancies are understood to reflect summaries of an individual's psychosocial learning history concerning anticipated reinforcement from behaviors. Individuals tend to choose behaviors that are likely to provide reinforcement. Prediction from expectancies is disorder-specific: for example, alcohol expectancies predict drinking problems and eating and thinness expectancies predict bulimia nervosa. The use of measures that assess individuals' expectancies for reinforcement from NSSI will (a) test the basic model of NSSI (American Psychiatric Association, 2013); (b) clarify further the risk process for behaviors in this response class; and (c) test the hypothesis that risk for NSSI is a function of both personality traits and psychosocial learning.

Chapter 6 – Historically, the construct of impulsivity, also referred to as disinhibition or behavioral undercontrol, has been understood to reflect the tendency to act in rash, ill-advised ways. In recent years, theory and research have moved toward a different and broader understanding of impulsivity. Carver, Johnson, and Joorman (2008) defined a construct called reflexive responsivity to emotion (RRE), which refers to the tendency to respond to intense negative emotions in an immediate way, with the goal of distracting oneself from, reducing, or avoiding subjective distress. From their perspective, the traditional conceptualization of impulsive action is only one form of RRE. The impulsive actions of heavy drinking, disordered eating, smoking, and gambling (as well as other behaviors) often serve the function of distracting one from the distress one was in prior to the impulsive act. The second form of RRE is referred to as impulsive inaction. Impulsive inaction refers to a tendency not to act, when acting would better serve one's interests. At times, inaction helps one avoid intense subjective distress. Examples include not asking one's boss for a raise or not asking a date to the prom. Those two forms of inaction are impulsive in the sense that they are often not chosen because, after careful consideration, one believes they meet one's ongoing needs and goals. Rather, they are chosen without reflection because they provide immediate relief from distress, even though they are inconsistent with one's needs and goals. This chapter reviews these recent advances in the context of the traditional conceptualization of externalizing and internalizing psychopathology, and addresses several questions: (1) Is there empirical evidence that there are common risk factors for impulsive action and impulsive inaction? (2) What are the neurobiological underpinnings of RRE? To what degree do the same brain systems underlie impulsive action and impulsive inaction? (3) What factors influence whether a given person is more disposed toward impulsive action or impulsive inaction? (4) How can we understand RRE in the context of development?

Chapter 7 – Impulsivity represents a complex human behavior characterized by little or no forethought, reflection, or consideration of the consequences. The definitions of impulsivity include a number of subtraits, such as risk taking, lack of planning, making up one's mind quickly, acting on the spur of the moment (motor activation), not focusing on the task at hand (attention), and not planning and thinking carefully (lack of planning). Evidence from different genetic and neuroimaging studies suggest that biopsychosocial factors and their interaction affect the development of impulsivity; however the underlying biological substrates are not yet fully defined. Biological factors are greatly influenced by a variety of genetic and non-genetic factors. Although impulsivity represents one of the diagnostic criteria for several psychiatric disorders, its complex role is still not fully clarified. There is a large body of behavioral, personality, psychological, biological and neurological research on impulsivity, with a great interest in identifying biomarkers associated with this trait. Impulsivity is moderated through a network of different cortical regions such as medial and dorsolateral prefrontal cortices, and the subcortical ventral striatum. These results suggest that structures mediating reward related decision-making are associated with impulsivity. Biomarkers are objective, quantifiable characteristics of biological processes. As impulsive behavior has been associated, primarily, with functional changes in serotonergic, dopaminergic, and noradrenergic systems, the authors' aim was to investigate the biological and genetic markers of impulsivity, especially those related to dopaminergic and serotonergic systems in children and adolescents. In this chapter they have presented the results regarding association of impulsivity with peripheral biochemical markers such as platelet serotonin (5-HT) concentration and platelet monoamine oxidase (MAO-B) activity. Moreover, they have investigated the potential genetic markers of impulsivity, such as different variants of the genes encoding catechol-o-methyl transferase (COMT), dopamine-beta-hydroxylase (DBH), monoamine oxidase type B (MAO-B), dopamine receptor type 4 (DRD4) and serotonin transporter (5-HTT). The authors' findings might contribute to a more complete understanding of the etiology of impulsive behavior and lead to improvements in the treatment of a variety of psychiatric disorders.

Chapter 8 – Impulse control disorders (ICD) are defined by an impaired ability to resist urges and impulses leading to deleterious long-term consequences. ICD affect the general population but may also develop in Parkinson's disease (PD). Indeed, dopaminergic treatments can improve motor symptoms but may also cause ICD, such as hypersexuality and pathological gambling. There is a need for other treatment approaches for ICD as current alternatives still lack conclusive results in terms on long-term treatment efficacy. Conversely, noninvasive brain stimulation (NIBS) is currently studied as an alternative treatment for several psychiatric disorders. The aim of this review is to explore if NIBS may represent an alternative treatment for ICD. Two lines of work are discussed. First, the authors describe neurocognitive impairments that have been reported in patients with ICD. They mainly focus on risk taking, reward seeking and impulsivity, which have been found to be abnormally higher in patients with ICD with and without PD as compared to healthy subjects. These distinct impairments have been associated with abnormal activity of the prefrontal cortex among other brain regions. Second, the authors present two NIBS techniques, transcranial magnetic and electric stimulation, and their current use to alleviate symptoms in various neuropsychiatric disorders, including depression and substance use disorders, when targeting the prefrontal cortex. They also discuss proof-of-concept studies modulating cognitive processes such as risk taking, rewars seeking and impulsivity when applying NIBS over the prefrontal cortex in healthy subjects. Although additional studies will be needed on the specific issue of ICD, this short review provides theoretical support for a possible alternative approach to reduce ICD with NIBS.

In: Psychology of Impulsivity
Editor: Mary C. Olmstead

ISBN: 978-1-63321-879-6

Chapter 1

IMPULSIVITY, PROBLEM-SOLVING, AND SUICIDE: ASSESSMENT AND TREATMENT CONSIDERATIONS IN THE CONTEXT OF SCIENTIFIC LITERATURE

Kari Koss, Laura L. Neely, Jennifer Tucker, Marcus VanSickle and Marjan Ghahramanlou-Holloway*

Uniformed Services University of the Health Sciences (USUHS), Department of Medical & Clinical Psychology, Laboratory for the Treatment of Suicide-Related Ideation and Behavior, MD, US

ABSTRACT

Impulsivity is a predisposition toward rapid, unplanned actions to internal or external stimuli without regard to the negative consequences of these for self and/or others (Moeller et al., 2001). Clinically, impulsivity is a personality characteristic that is commonly observed in suicidal individuals based on both self-report and laboratory measures (Gorlyn, 2005; Horesh, 2001). Therefore, empirically driven risk assessment protocols often mention impulsivity as a risk indicator for suicide. Of course, impulsivity can serve as a symptom for psychiatric conditions such as bipolar disorder, borderline personality disorder, and substance-related disorders – all of which have also been recognized as risk factors for suicide. Given the strong empirical link between impulsivity and suicide, one may assume that all suicidal acts are impulsive in nature, yet to date, there is evidence to the contrary. For example, Witte and colleagues (2008) have shown that only less than a quarter of those attempting suicide do so impulsively (i.e., without prior planning). Therefore, some have argued that the link between impulsivity and suicide may be indirect (Bender et al., 2011). One possible explanation for such an indirect path may be related to problem-solving. An individual who is characteristically impulsive may consequently engage in impulsive and careless problem-solving, particularly during stressful life circumstances. Such deficits in problem-solving may have a biopsychosocial underpinning. For example, an individual may have had the biological predisposition to an impulsive nature and subsequently learned

* Corresponding author: Dr. Marjan Ghahramanlou-Holloway, Associate Professor and Director of Laboratory for the Treatment of Suicide-Related Ideation and Behavior, Uniformed Services University of the Health Sciences, Department of Medical and Clinical Psychology, 4301 Jones Bridge Road, Bethesda, Maryland 20814-4799 (marjan.holloway@usuhs.edu).

over time to make careless decisions to cope with life stressors. The relationship between impulsive and careless problem-solving and suicide-related behaviors has also been shown in the scientific literature. Simply stated, an individual with an impulsive and careless problem-solving style moves quickly from facing a problem to taking action without considering the consequences of such actions and/or repeatedly engages in many careless and unsuccessful attempts at solving the same problem. The objectives of the proposed chapter are threefold. First, a brief summary of the scientific literature on the relationship between impulsivity, problem-solving, and suicide will be presented. Second, clinical advantages of assessment and treatment of impulsivity and problem-solving are explored, and a list of psychometrically sound psychological assessments for the measurement of impulsivity and problem-solving will be presented. Finally, a series of assessment and treatment recommendations will be provided to address impulsivity and problem-solving among suicidal individuals.

INTRODUCTION

Public Health Significance of Suicide

Suicide remains a significant global public health problem with both emotional and economic costs. According to the World Health Organization (WHO, 2011), there is approximately one death by suicide every 40 seconds. Within the United States (U.S.), suicide is the 10th leading cause of death for all ages, the 3rd leading cause of death for ages 10-24, and the 2nd leading cause of death for ages 25-34 (CDCP, 2011). Death by suicide can occur as a complex interplay between environmental, psychological, cultural, social, and biological factors. One such factor is impulsivity, which according to the WHO contributes to suicides in Asian countries. Mental disorders such as depression and alcohol use disorders (which also may reflect some degree of impulsivity) contribute to suicides in Europe and North America.

Definition of Impulsivity

Impulsivity is a predisposition toward rapid, unplanned actions to internal or external stimuli without regard to the negative consequences of these for self and/or others (Moeller et al., 2001). Impulsivity can be viewed as a state and/or trait characteristic that facilitates the progression of an individual from thinking about suicide to inflicting suicidal self-directed violence. In *state* form, impulsivity may be experienced at a particular time and subsequently directly contribute to suicide risk. For example, in the midst of a heated argument with a cheating spouse, one may point a gun to his head with the stated intention to die and then pull the trigger. In *trait* form, impulsivity may be experienced throughout a person's life due to a biological vulnerability or diathesis (refer to diathesis stress model of suicide) (Mann et al., 1999). For example, a person, due to such vulnerability, may engage in risk-taking and impulsive behaviors (e.g., overspending, substance abuse) as well as problematic problem-solving throughout his or her lifetime – all of which consequently result in the trajectory toward death by suicide.

Definition of Problem-Solving

Problem-solving is conceptualized as the process of generating alternative solutions to a given problem and then selecting the most effective choice out of the alternatives. The process of problem-solving allows for an individual to adapt to internal and/or external challenges or demands (Heppner & Petersen, 1982), and is considered to have cognitive, affective, and behavioral elements that are learned over time. The term "problem-solving" has been viewed as synonymous with coping because of the continuous situational problems that arise in daily living, which must be handled in an effective manner in order for a person to maintain an adequate level of effective functioning.

Impulsivity, Problem-Solving, and Suicide: Brief Review of Scientific Literature

Impulsivity and Suicide

Overall, while the association between impulsivity and suicide has been well-established in the field of suicidology, the pathways and mechanisms for this relationship remain unclear. In a review of the literature, Bryan & Rudd (2006) identified impulsivity and lack of self-control as clinically meaningful predictors of suicidal self-directed violence. However, scientific debate is currently focused on whether suicidal actions are for the most part impulsive or planned – and ways in which impulsive versus planned suicide attempts can be best differentiated. For instance, interviews of suicide survivors, from medically serious and nearly-lethal suicide attempts, indicate that 1 in 4 individuals deliberated the action of suicide for less than 5 minutes and 9 out of 10 deliberated the action of suicide for less than a day (Simon et al., 2002). Similarly, in an Australian study, approximately 48% of those who had attempted suicide reported a span of 10 minutes or less from the first thought of suicide to actual attempt behavior (Deisenhammer et al., 2009).

On the other hand, impulsivity does not characterize all suicide deaths as there is scientific evidence to suggest that some individuals who attempt suicide prepare specific plans for the suicidal self-directed violence. In fact, Witte and colleagues (2008) reported that less than a quarter of those attempting suicide did so impulsively (i.e., without planning ahead). Those who had made a suicide attempt without prior planning actually scored lower on measures of impulsivity than those who had planned and attempted suicide. An inverse relationship between impulsivity and lethality of the attempt has been shown repeatedly in several research studies (Baca-Garcia et al., 2001, 2005; Wingate, 2004). These findings suggest that impulsive attempts tend to be less lethal, with some of strongest predictors for death by suicide to include an increased duration of suicidal ideation, greater specificity of a plan for suicide, and preparations for making the attempt (Wingate, 2004).

To gain more clarity on the relationship between impulsivity and suicide, self-report and laboratory measures of impulsivity have been used. Brodsky and colleagues (1997) examined the relationship between Borderline Personality Disorder and suicide, and reported that impulsivity was the only characteristic of this disorder associated with a higher number of previous suicide attempts (after controlling for lifetime diagnosis of depression and substance abuse). Similarly, impulsivity has been found as an important factor, independent of depression, when examining adolescent suicide attempts by overdose (Kingsbury, 1999). These authors, as well as many others in the field, postulate that impulsivity may mediate the relationship between depression, subjective stress levels, and suicide behaviors. High levels of impulsivity may predispose individuals to engage in suicidal thoughts and behaviors prior to considering the potential benefits of social support and problem-solving strategies. In summary, the relationship between impulsivity and suicide is complex and multidimensional. A brief review of theoretical models of impulsivity and suicide is provided in the following section.

Brief review of theoretical models of impulsivity and suicide. In 1990, Baumeister explained that suicide may result from a number of psychological processes, one of which would be escape from meaningful awareness of negative thoughts about oneself and associated painful emotions. The earliest theoretical framework for understanding the role of escape in suicide was provided by Baechler (1979, 1980) who viewed suicide as one strategy for solving life problems. Baumeister provided an elaboration of the theory by suggesting that suicide occurs because an individual's standards are "unrealistically high" and/or because the events experienced by the individual are "unusually bad." One or both of these states result in negative affect such as a state of depression, anxiety, or both. When one is attempting to avoid these psychologically aversive states, cognitive deconstruction occurs which refers to low levels of engagement in self-awareness and thinking. This deterioration in cognitive functions results in passive handling of actions, random as well as aimless activity, as well as impulsivity. The basic argument is that cognitive deconstruction removes "inhibitors and internal restraints" associated with suicidal self-directed violence. In this model, impulsivity is considered a result of deconstructed state of cognition, and suicide is considered a *state* characteristic (as opposed to a stable personality trait) that results in suicides carried out "on a whim" or "on the spur of the moment."

In contrast, impulsivity has also been viewed as a relatively stable personality trait that leaves individuals more prone to engaging in suicidal self-directed violence. The stress-diathesis model of suicide proposed by Mann and colleagues (1999) posits that the occurrence of suicidal self-directed violence is dependent on the existence of both a stressor (e.g., unemployment) and a diathesis (e.g., impulsive personality). One way in which impulsivity is hypothesized to increase one's risk for suicide is through simply making an individual more apt to act quickly on suicidal thoughts without considering all available options. A second way that impulsivity could increase suicide risk is by increasing one's susceptibility for head injuries, which can be associated with disinhibition and aggression, which could compound the harmful effects of an impulsive personality style.

Other models view the link between the trait of impulsivity and suicide as more indirect. For example, the Interpersonal Theory of Suicide (IPT) (Joiner, 2005; Van Orden et al., 2010) maintains that highly lethal suicide attempts are preceded by: (1) suicidal desire born of a sense of thwarted belongingness (with respect to social groups) and/or perceived burdensomeness (in relation to others) and (2) an acquired capability to carry out painful and fear-inducing suicidal self-directed violence. Impulsive individuals are considered more vulnerable to engaging in painful and risky behaviors (e.g., drug use, physical altercations) throughout their lifetimes, possibly because they fail to think through the potential consequences and outcomes of their behaviors prior to engaging in them. This increased exposure to pain, both physical and emotional, is believed to lead an impulsive individual to become habituated or desensitized to pain, which is a precursor to acquiring the capability to make a suicide attempt. Thus, in the IPT model, impulsivity contributes to suicide risk through the indirect path of increasing one's habituation to pain and thereby increasing one's capability for inflicting violence on the self.

In the cognitive model of suicide, impulsivity is understood in the context of problem-solving associated with one's life problems (Beck, 1976; Ghahramanlou-Holloway et al., 2012; Rudd et al., 2001; Wenzel et al., 2008). Suicidal individuals, either due to state or trait problem-solving deficits, experience what Beck referred to as the suicide mode. When a suicidal individual has an activated suicide mode, he or she experiences thoughts and emotions associated with suicide, is motivated to plan for suicide, experiences attentional fixation, and subsequently behaves impulsively on urges to inflict suicidal self-directed violence. Suicide is viewed as the only solution to one's life problems while other potential solutions are not even considered. Because problem-solving is impaired, cognitive rigidity takes hold where the suicidal individual becomes fixated on implementing an immediate solution to one's life problem(s), and an impulsive decision to kill oneself is put into action. Therefore, a cognitive therapy clinical strategy for suicide prevention is to teach patients the skill of "procrastinating" suicide such that the urge to act immediately on one's suicide mode is delayed and other options to one's life problems may be considered. The relationship between impulsivity, problem-solving, and suicide is complex – and much research in this area is still needed for best understanding pathways to suicide. A brief review to explore the role of impulsive problem-solving in suicide is provided in the following section.

Problem-Solving and Suicide

Deficits in problem-solving have been found to have serious implications for mental health. An individual (1) may struggle in identifying problems, (2) may experience challenges in generating potential solutions to identified problems, and/or (3) may select one or more maladaptive response(s) to identified problems, given the possible available options. Suicidal self-directed violence can be viewed as a manifestation of ineffective or poor coping, particularly during times of stress (Schotte & Clum, 1982, 1987). A suicidal individual may be incapable of generating or considering all available options, and may therefore mistakenly conclude that suicide is the best solution to a problem.

In the diathesis distress model (Schotte & Clum, 1982) mentioned earlier, external stressors are conceptualized as having a more significant impact on poor problem-solvers. Specifically, when these individuals are faced with life stressors, they become more easily overwhelmed and progressively more hopeless because they are unable to generate effective solutions to resolve the stressors. In fact, suicidal psychiatric inpatients have shown deficiencies in interpersonal problem-solving skills when compared to their non-suicidal counterparts (Schotte & Clum, 1987). More specifically, suicidal patients use fewer, less relevant means to solve interpersonal problems, and evaluate proposed solutions more negatively. In addition, there is a strong association between problem-solving appraisal, stress, and hopelessness among suicidal individuals. Schotte and Clum's (1982, 1987) diathesis-stress-hopelessness model of suicide views problem-solving as both a mediator and moderator of the relationship between stress and hopelessness – two factors predictive of suicidal self-directed violence. Individuals with a history of suicidal self-directed violence and hopelessness appear to generate only half the number of possible solutions to their own interpersonal problems (Dixon et al., 1991, 1994; Rudd et al., 1994). Furthermore, individuals who appraise their own problem-solving ability as inadequate appear to be significantly more likely to endorse depressive symptoms (Nezu, 1986). Depressed individuals report their problem-solving as less effective and less systematic and feel that they have less control in problematic situations (Nezu, 1986). In samples of both college students as well as individuals diagnosed with depression, problem-solving appraisal (Heppner & Petersen, 1982; Heppner, 1988) is significantly predictive of depressive symptoms.

A strong correlation between poor problem-solving ability and suicidal self-directed violence has been supported by the scientific literature. Ghahramanlou-Holloway and colleagues (2011) found that individuals with attempted suicide demonstrate significantly lower scores on problem-solving appraisal when compared to a normative sample (D'Zurilla, Nezu, & Maydeu-Olivares, 2002). More specifically, higher ratings for negative problem orientation (i.e., perceived poor self-efficacy in solving life's problems), impulsive/careless as well as avoidant problem-solving styles, and lower ratings on positive problem orientation (i.e., perceived effective self-efficacy in solving life's problems) were found for those with attempted suicide in comparison with those in the normative sample. These findings suggest that individuals who attempt suicide are more likely than a normative sample to either avoid problems altogether or approach them in a careless or impulsive manner. Those who attempt suicide were also more likely to view their problems as insurmountable challenges, which likely increased feelings of hopelessness. Further research supports the relationship between problem-solving style and suicidal self-directed violence. For example, Rotheram-Borus and colleagues (1990) found that adolescent females who had attempted suicide, compared with controls, generated significantly fewer alternatives to problems. Gibbs and colleagues (2009) found that those with suicide attempts, compared to those without, appraised themselves at a lower level of rational problem-solving and a higher level of avoidant problem-solving.

Assessing Impulsivity and Problem-Solving among Individuals at Risk for Suicide

The scientific literature, as described above, suggests a link between impulsivity, poor problem-solving, and suicide; however, the precise nature of this relationship remains largely unknown. What is known is that treatments aimed at remediating deficits in impulsivity and problem-solving, such as Cognitive Behavior Therapy and Dialectic Behavior Therapy have demonstrated efficacy in reducing suicidal self-directed violence. But before implementing such effective interventions, mental health providers who work with individuals at risk for suicide are strongly encouraged to directly assess for the constructs of impulsivity and problem-solving. The use of psychometrically validated assessments for measuring impulsivity and problem-solving is instrumental for the early identification of potential problem areas within these domains as well as treatment conceptualization and planning. Identified skills deficits in impulsivity and problem-solving can subsequently be directly targeted in treatment and tracked on an ongoing basis along with well-established suicide risk factors such as depression, hopelessness, and suicide ideation. See Table 1 for a summary of the clinical advantages of utilizing formal assessments by treatment stage.

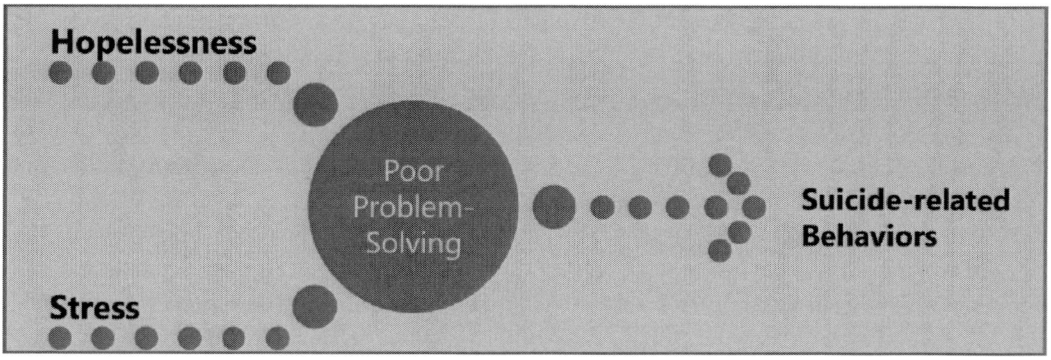

Figure 1. Problem-Solving as a Mediator and Moderator for Suicide.

Table 1. Clinical advantages of utilizing formal assessments by treatment stage

Treatment Stage	Clinical Advantages to Utilizing Formal Assessments
Information-Gathering	• Expands patient's psychological horizons • Engages patient in treatment • Creates opportunities for dialogue, increased motivation, and possibly change
Treatment Planning	• Increases speed and efficiency of treatment planning • Provides objective support for treatment strategies • Protects and strengthens collaborative working relationship
Treatment	• Maintains focus on treatment goals • Measures progress toward goals

Information-Gathering on Impulsivity and Problem-Solving

Several of the clinical advantages of psychological assessment involve expanding the psychological horizons of the patient, engaging the patient in treatment, and creating opportunities for dialogue between the patient and clinician. Assessment tools can serve to broaden a patient's psychological horizons by introducing a new construct or by presenting a known construct from a different perspective. After completion of certain psychological instruments, patients may comment, "I never thought of things that way," or "Seeing everything together like that makes me see myself differently." These types of patient remarks are not only invitations to participate in further exploration, but they also add valuable subjective data, such as relevant personal experiences, to the objective data captured by the specific assessment tool.

While psychological assessments can work in many ways to engage a patient in treatment, some of the more basic mechanisms that engage suicidal patients include the following: (1) satisfaction associated with completing tasks in a timely manner; (2) increased curiosity stemming from considering different aspects of one's life experiences; and (3) a feeling of support (and possibly increased hopefulness) associated with forming a working relationship with an interested professional. The nascent working relationship between the patient and the clinician can be solidified by eliciting feedback from the patient and providing the patient with feedback regarding completed assessments in a timely manner.

The information-gathering sessions are also beneficial for the therapeutic alliance through the creation of opportunities for casual dialogue about difficult topics. For example, a clinician may inquire about a patient's verbal (e.g., "I don't like this one.") and nonverbal (e.g., slowed completion, frustrated countenance) reactions to measures as a way of initiating informal conversations with the patient. For patients who display few to no reactions to the assessments presented, the clinician is advised to ask for "comments, questions, and criticisms" after a patient completes each of several key measures in the assessment battery. By asking for feedback, the clinician communicates to the patient the importance of the patient's opinions and experiences as well as the importance of thinking critically about both the content of the measures and one's emotional reactions to that content. It is important to note here that while psychological assessments are very valuable in understanding constructs such as impulsivity and problem-solving, these initial information gathering sessions also provide an opportunity to make direct observations of the patient's style in problem-solving and decision making in session, such that impulsive and careless errors can be tracked while in action. Clinicians may use this opportunity to assess for insight and inquire about ways in which the patient views his or her style of approaching decision making and problem-solving.

Assessment and Treatment Considerations for Suicidal Patients with Impulsivity and/or Problem-Solving Deficits

Once the results of psychological assessment have been understood and shared with the patient, the treatment planning stage will begin. Advantages to clinical assessment during this stage include increased speed and efficiency of treatment planning, the provision of objective support for treatment strategies, and increased strength of the collaborative working relationship through a reduction in the perceived threat of the clinician. First, the data presented in well-organized assessment reports allow the clinician to quickly and easily identify the relative strengths and weaknesses of a particular patient. Although impulsivity and problem-solving assessments require some time for selection, administration, and scoring, the data yielded in that given amount of time is generally considered more precise and nuanced than similar data obtained via interviewing techniques. Hence, assessments are believed to speed up the treatment planning process through concise presentations of pertinent data.

The provision of objective support for treatment strategies is another advantage that assessments present during treatment planning. After reviewing a patient's score profile and noting the relative strengths and weaknesses therein, the clinician can link the patient's noted weaknesses to his or her maladaptive thought(s), emotion(s), or behavior(s). This allows the clinician to identify treatment strategies that can potentially remediate the noted weaknesses. The clinician then presents the findings and associated action plan to the patient, citing the assessment scores as objective data in support of the treatment plan. Consider a situation in which a clinician notes that a patient scored highly on a scale of impulsivity and also had detailed several accounts of reckless or dangerous driving in his recent past. In this case, the clinician may be able to help the patient understand the link between the assessment score and the dangerous behaviors, and how such a linkage might relate to suicidal thoughts and actions. The patient and the clinician can outline how they could work together using specific strategies in therapy in order to decrease the behavior and thus, lower the score.

Furthermore, the use of objective assessment measures during treatment planning may also help to protect the collaborative working relationship between the clinician and patient. This is especially important when discussing a potentially distressing trait, such as impulsivity. On a basic level, objective measures provide a non-judgmental platform on which to hold a difficult conversation. At a more complex level, patients who are sensitive to receiving feedback may be prone to attributing the psychological threat associated with that feedback to the clinician during the treatment planning process. This could lead to a therapeutic rift that significantly interferes with treatment. Clinicians can protect and strengthen the working relationship by referring to results from objective measures when giving feedback, which transfers potential threats onto the measure and away from the clinician.

Once the patient and clinician have reached the treatment stage, the continued use of assessment data allows for a sustained focus on treatment goals as well as an ongoing tracking of progress towards such goals. The use of assessment data to support the collaborative treatment plan lends itself to maintaining the overall psychotherapy objectives. First, clinicians can redirect patients who become overly tangential during a session by gently asking them to explain how the topic at hand relates to their assessment score(s). Second, in a similar manner, clinicians may be better able to maintain the focus of the treatment by using the data-based goals (i.e., improved problem-solving strategies) as a lens through which to view the patient's story. This method is particularly useful for providing structure to a patient's stories and guiding a clinician's follow-up questions during fast-paced, brief interventions. Third, clinicians may be able to demonstrate to patients how their actions during session can be viewed as manifestations of the problematic traits measured by the assessment.

With respect to measuring progress toward treatment goals, repeated administration of specific assessments allows both the patient and clinician to track movement that the patient has made on key constructs. Psychological assessments used to evaluate progress can be either formal (e.g., Barratt Impulsiveness Scale) or informal (e.g., a daily record of impulsive behaviors). Deciding on what type of assessment to use can be based on a variety of factors including the administration guide recommendations, the preferences of the patient, the length of the treatment, and the patient's motivation and compliance with the assessment plan.

Lastly, assessments can be considered valuable educational tools for clinicians throughout their careers. Analyzing psychological assessments helps clinicians develop expertise in (1) detecting and understanding the characteristics being measured, and (2) recognizing behavior patterns associated with different levels of those characteristics. The long-term clinical advantages to using assessments can be imagined as self-perpetuating, similar to a domino effect, whereby improvements in detecting characteristics and recognizing behaviors lead to increased clarity and relevancy in treatment planning. This, in turn, can lead to breadth and depth of intervention strategies, and sophistication in treatment delivery.

In summary, incorporating assessments into clinical practice with individuals at risk for suicidal self-directed violence helps to identify modifiable maladaptive behavioral styles in an efficient and timely manner. Assessment instruments provide benefits to both clinicians and patients in a variety of ways at each stage of the treatment process and, as such, are strongly recommended for use.

Table 2. Selected Impulsivity & Problem-Solving Measures for Clinical Consideration

Instrument	Construct	Subscales	# of Items	Range of Scores Higher Score Indication	Suicide Specific Information	Citation
The Barratt Impulsiveness Scale (BIS-11)	Personality trait of impulsiveness	Motor Impulsiveness, Nonplanning Impulsiveness, Attentional Impulsiveness	30	Range: 30-120 Higher score = higher level of impulsiveness	Adults with past history of SA score higher on Motor and Attentional subscales	Patton et al. (1995)
The Beck Suicidal Intent Scale (SIS)	Degree of intent to commit suicide among attempters	-	20	Range: 15-45 Higher score = greater intent to die; greater risk of repeat SA	2 items capture impulsivity of SA: (6) active preparation for the attempt; (15) degree of premeditation	Beck et al. (1974)
The Means-Ends Problem-Solving Test (MEPS)	Interpersonal problem-solving, Social means-ends thinking	-	10	Higher score = better problem-solving abilities	Those with history of SA generate significantly fewer alternatives to problems	Platt & Spivack (1975)
The Problem Solving Inventory (PSI – Form B)	Appraisal of own problem-solving abilities and attitudes	Problem-Solving Confidence, Approach-Avoidance Style, Personal Control	32	Range: 32-198 Higher score = perceives self as an ineffective problem-solver	-	Heppner (1988) Heppner & Petersen (1982)
The Social Problem-Solving Inventory (SPSI)	Strengths and weaknesses in problem-solving abilities	Positive Problem Orientation, Negative Problem Orientation, Rational Problem-Solving, Impulsive/Careless Problem-Solving, Avoidance Behavior	Long: 52 Short: 25	Range (Long): 0-208 Range (Short): 0-100 Higher score = more effective social problem- solving abilities	Suicide attempters score higher on Negative Problem Orientation, Impulsive/Careless & Avoidance, lower on Positive Problem Orientation	D’Zurilla et al. (2002)

Instrument	Construct	Subscales	# of Items	Range of Scores Higher Score Indication	Suicide Specific Information	Citation
The Urgency, Premeditation, Perseverance, and Sensation Seeking Impulsive Behavior Scale (UPPS)	Impulsivity across the Five Factor Model of personality	Negative Urgency, Lack of Premeditation, Lack of Perseverance, Sensation Seeking	45	Range: 45-180 Higher score = more impulsive response	3 subscales (Negative Urgency, Lack of Premeditation, and Lack of Perseverance) are predictive of future suicidal behaviors	Whiteside & Lynam (2001)

Selected Psychological Instruments for Measurement of Impulsivity and Problem-Solving

In the sections below, a listing of several commonly used and psychometrically sound instruments for the measurement of impulsivity and problem-solving is provided, in alphabetical order, along with a brief description of each instrument. Table 2 provides a summary of each instrument, the construct measured, subscales, number of items, scoring, as well as publisher information.

Barratt Impulsiveness Scale **(BIS-11)** (Patton, Stanford, & Barratt, 1995) is a 30-item self-report instrument that measures the construct of impulsiveness, which is defined as a predisposition toward rapid, unplanned reactions to internal or external stimuli without regard to the negative consequences of those reactions for oneself or for others. All items are answered on a 4-point Likert scale (Rarely/Never, Occasionally, Often, Almost Always/Always). For example, a participant is asked to rate the frequency to which they feel, "I am restless at the theater or lectures" or "I make up my mind quickly". Items are then scored 1, 2, 3, 4, with 4 indicating the most impulsive response. The higher the summed score for all items (Range: 30-120), the higher the level of impulsiveness. Three second-order impulsiveness factors are identified: Motor Impulsiveness, Nonplanning Impulsiveness, and Attentional Impulsiveness. The first- and second- order factors have been found to be significantly intercorrelated, which suggests that the items are a measure of the general personality trait of impulsiveness (Gibbs et al., 2009). Internal consistency for the BIS-11 was consistent with other methods of assessment of impulsiveness (Carrillo-de-la-Pena, Otero, & Romero, 1993) and within an acceptable range for applied use. The BIS-11 is frequently used to measure impulsivity in clinical (Paul et al., 2002) and non-clinical settings (Spinella, 2007). Specifically, adults with a past history of suicide attempt(s) have been shown to score higher on the motor impulsiveness subscale (Dougherty et al., 2004), or the attentional impulsiveness subscale (Quednow et al., 2006).

Beck Suicidal Intent Scale **(SIS)** (Beck, Schuyler, & Herman, 1974) is a 20-item measure that quantifies the seriousness of the intent to commit suicide among patients who have made at least one suicide attempt. Fifteen items are scored on a 1-3 scale. Thus, the summed total score ranges from 15-45, with higher scores indicative of a greater intent to die and a greater risk of repeated attempts. Scores between 15-19 are classified as 'low intent', scores 20-28 as 'medium intent', and scores 29+ as 'high intent'. Seven SIS items are based on the patient's self-report of the attempt (e.g., "alleged purpose of attempt"), while the remaining items are based upon objective circumstances related to the suicide attempt (e.g., "precautions against discovery/intervention"). The SIS contains two items that capture impulsivity during the suicide attempt: active preparation for the attempt (item 6) and degree of premeditation (item 15). While these two items provide a somewhat limited understanding of a person's level of impulsivity during a suicide attempt, factor analyses of the scale have revealed that the SIS also measures expected lethality and planning for the attempt(s) being examined (Diaz et al., 2003).

Means-Ends Problem-Solving Procedure **(MEPS)** (Platt & Spivack, 1975) is a measure of interpersonal problem-solving that specifically assesses for social means-ends thinking. The procedure is a clinician-administered test of solution generation in which an individual is presented with a series of five to ten incomplete stories focused on achieving goals in interpersonal situations. Individuals are asked to complete the stories by generating the steps that each story's character could take in order to achieve his or her stated goal by the end of the story. Three types of scores are computed from individuals' responses: the number of relevant means generated, the number of obstacles anticipated, and the number of time-based considerations that an individual mentions. Higher scores indicate better problem-solving abilities. The MEPS has shown good internal consistency (r=.80-.84) among adolescents with test-retest reliabilities ranging from .43 to .59 (Ford, 1982). Rotheram-Borus and colleagues (1990) used a modified version of this procedure and reported that individuals with a history of suicide attempts generated significantly fewer alternatives to problems than both psychiatrically disturbed and non-disturbed comparison groups.

Problem-Solving Inventory **(PSI – Form B)** (Heppner & Petersen, 1982; Heppner, 1988) is a 32-item self-report inventory of applied problem-solving. More specifically, the scale assesses an individual's perceived awareness of his/her problem-solving abilities rather than his/her actual problem-solving skills. All items are answered on a 6-point Likert scale between 1 (strongly agree) to 6 (strongly disagree), with the total score range of 32 to 198. A higher score on the PSI would indicate that an individual perceives him- or herself as an ineffective problem-solver. Factor analytic studies reveal three factors: (1) Problem-Solving Confidence (e.g., "Given enough time and effort, I believe I can solve most problems that confront me"), (2) Approach-Avoidance Style (e.g., "When a solution to a problem was unsuccessful, I do not examine why it didn't work"), and (3) Personal Control (e.g., "When confronted with a problem, I tend to do the first thing that I can think of to solve it"). Estimates of reliability indicate that the instrument is internally consistent and stable over a 2-week period, and several estimates of validity have been established (Heppner, 1988). In a clinical sample, problem-solving appraisal (as measured by all three dimensions of the PSI) has been shown to be significantly predictive of depressive symptoms (Nezu, 1986).

Social Problem-Solving Inventory – Revised – Short or Long Version **(SPSI-R)** (D'Zurilla et al., 2002) is a 25- or 52-item measure created to assess an individual's strengths and weaknesses in their problem-solving ability. Both the long and the short versions contain items rated on a 5-point Likert scale between 0 (not at all true of me) to 4 (extremely true of me). Participants are asked to rate how true statements are of their problem-solving styles, for example, "When I have a problem, I usually believe that there is a solution for it" or "After carrying out a solution to a problem, I do not usually take the time to evaluate all of the results carefully." Both versions of the SPSI-R provide total scores, as well as scores for five dimensions of problem-solving appraisal: Positive Problem Orientation (perception of problems has surmountable challenges), Negative Problem Orientation (perception of problems has stressful, insurmountable challenges), Rational Problem-Solving (methodological approach to problem-solving), Impulsive/Careless Problem-Solving (problem-solving based solely on instinct), and Avoidance Behavior (choosing to ignore the existence of the problem altogether) (D'Zurilla, Maydeu-Olivares, & Kant, 1998). The SPSI-R provides for extensive standardized norms, representing both 'normal' adult and adolescent groups, as well as individuals from various clinical groups. Individuals who have attempted suicide have been shown to score higher on the negative problem orientation, impulsive/careless, and avoidance styles, and lower on positive problem orientation in comparison to a normative sample (Ghahramanlou-Holloway et al., 2011).

Urgency, Premeditation, Perseverance, and Sensation Seeking Impulsive Behavior Scale **(UPPS)** (Whiteside & Lynam, 2001) is a 45-item self-report scale that measures impulsivity across dimensions of the Five Factor Model of personality (McCrae & Costa, 1990). Each item is answered using a 4-point Likert scale (Agree Strongly, Agree Some, Disagree Some, Disagree Strongly), with a higher score indicating a more impulsive response (range: 45-180). The participant is asked to rate the degree to which they agree with statements relating to the four facets of personality associated with impulsive behavior: (1) Negative Urgency (e.g., "I often make matters worse because I act without thinking when I am upset"), (2) Lack of Premeditation (e.g., "I usually make up my mind through careful reasoning"), (3) Lack of Perseverance (e.g., "Once I start a project, I almost always finish it"), and (4) Sensation Seeking (e.g., "I quite enjoy taking risks"). Studies using both self-report and interview methodologies (Miller et al., 2003; Smith et al., 2003) provide converging evidence for the UPPS model of impulsivity, and three of the four UPPS facets (negative urgency, lack of premeditation, and lack of perseverance) have been found to be predictive of future suicidal behaviors (Lynam et al., 2011)

Treating Impulsivity and Maladaptive Problem-Solving among Suicidal Individuals

Recommendations for Clinical Practice

As indicated earlier, the relationship among impulsivity, problem-solving, and suicide is complex and multi-faceted. State and trait impulsivity and an impulsive problem-solving style all may play a key role in an individual's suicidal self-directed violence. The following assessment and treatment recommendations are provided for those seeking to measure and/or address impulsive tendencies and problem-solving deficits among suicidal individuals.

Assessment recommendations. The multi-faceted nature of both impulsivity and problem-solving render them difficult constructs to measure. Because formal assessment tools have been developed to measure particular aspects of each construct, such as attentional impulsiveness and rational problem-solving style, each existing psychological tool has unique limitations to its applicability and generalizability across situations. Careful consideration of conceptual and operational definitions of impulsivity and problem-solving are required to correctly interpret an individual's test results. Informed clinicians who are aware of a tool's limitations can supplement the results gleaned from self-report measures with clinical interviews, behavioral assessments, and their own clinical appraisals based on professional knowledge and experience.

Recommendation 1: First, in addition to incorporating as many measures as feasible during an assessment session, clinicians are advised to supplement self-report measures with clinical interviews and behavioral assessments whenever possible because results from self-report measures and other types of appraisals may either conflict with one another or present a limited clinical picture. For instance, although the BIS-11 is highly correlated with other self-report measures of impulsiveness, it is not significantly correlated with behavioral measures of impulsiveness (Stanford et al., 2009). Self-report measures, like the BIS-11, assess personality traits occurring over extended periods of time and reflect an individual's longstanding habits and tendencies while clinical and behavioral appraisals generally identify more of the state-like, context-dependent aspects of impulsivity. Therefore, it is recommended that clinicians use various forms of clinical and behavioral appraisals in addition to both state- and trait-based self-report measures when assessing for impulsivity and problem-solving in relation to suicide risk. Moreover, in particular, assessments of impulsivity may not be equally sensitive to all causes or manifestations of the trait or state and, as a result, may not present equally sensitive or specific results for all patients' impulsive features (Dougherty, Mathias, & Marsh, 2003). When assessing for impulsivity in potentially suicidal individuals, Dougherty and colleagues (2004) make the argument that certain aspects of impulsivity may be differentially related to suicidality.

Recommendation 2: As part of an interview for impulsivity, clinicians are advised to assess for psychiatric diagnoses assigned across one's lifespan, current life stressors, and changes in interpersonal relationships during the past year (at a minimum). A clinical interview can be a valuable tool when assessing for impulsivity with respect to suicidal self-directed violence. Weyrauch and colleagues (2001) found that female gender and a greater number of lifetime psychiatric diagnoses were associated with more impulsive suicide attempts. Additionally in this study, the degree of impulsiveness of a particular suicide attempt was predicted by the number of disrupted interpersonal relationships in the preceding year for the attempter. Counterintuitively, it was found that individuals who had the greatest number of interpersonal losses during the preceding year showed significantly less impulsivity in their suicide attempts. These results seem to indicate that the construct of trait impulsivity may not be expressed in a consistent manner across life situations, including different suicide attempts made by one individual.

Recommendation 3: In order to advance professional knowledge as well as to enhance one's understanding of a patient's reactions when extremely stressed, clinicians are advised to speak with patients about their decisions for suicidal self-directed violence. It may be useful to ask the patient to walk through his or her decision-making process one step at a time so that both the clinician and the patient have a thorough understanding of how the decision to die by suicide was made. Given the emotional gravity associated with a suicide attempt, it is likely that individuals view and undertake the choice to kill themselves very differently from how they consider and commit to other life choices. Consider a man who is very controlled and methodical when deciding how to best invest his money in stocks. Despite his cognitive discipline and even temperament when dealing with financial matters, he impulsively decides to kill himself when the market crashes and he loses most of his life's savings. For this individual, an impulsivity scale may show low levels of both trait and state impulsivity that are highly discrepant from the behavior he engages in when faced with a meaningful crisis. Unfortunately, at present, little is known about the decision-making processes that correspond with acting on and refraining from acting on suicidal impulses.

Treatment recommendations. Suicidal individuals may often view suicide as the *only* option to their life problem(s) and feel an urgency to act. Reducing impulsive decision-making and strengthening problem-solving skills are expected to reduce suicide risk. Treatment of suicidal individuals, therefore, must pay close attention to the constructs of impulsivity and problem-solving such that the patient can be taught skills to more effectively cope with life stressors and to become less reactive. In a sense, the patient is being taught to slow down the story of his or her life such that each decision and its associated consequences can be thoroughly considered before action. The section below provides a series of treatment recommendations, specific to the handling of impulsivity and maladaptive problem-solving.

Recommendation 1. In certain cases (such as in the case of suicidal patients with Bipolar Disorder), it may be beneficial to teach patients about the two-person rule, such that one's decisions must be discussed with two other designated trusted individuals before action is taken. This strategy teaches the patient the potential benefits of patience and the positive role of consultation with others in order to strengthen the efficacy of one's decision-making process.

Recommendation 2. Patients can be asked to simply visualize and subsequently rate the intensity and/or severity of their impulsivity and/or problem-solving deficiencies on a continuum – for instance, on a scale of 0 (lowest) to 100 (highest). This strategy teaches the individual to move away from dichotomous thinking such that a more balanced approach to decision making and problem-solving is taken. This type of continuum can also be used as an assessment strategy to specifically find out what is the "norm" for the individual and then what is the "norm" for the individual during the time of suicide mode activation. Using the thermometer analogy, patients can be taught to visually monitor and control their impulsivity and problem-solving errors.

Recommendation 3. Urge surfing is another technique used in cognitive behavior therapy that can help patients gain a sense of control over one's strong feelings to react immediately. Patients are taught to consider one's own impulsivity as an urge – a strong feeling that must be closely monitored and controlled. At times, patients may erroneously believe that if they don't act right away on their strong feelings (such as the feeling to kill oneself), that the anxiety would become unbearable. In these cases, the impulsivity and the problematic decision making are ironically meant to protect the patient against an aversive "imagined" situation or feeling or thought – or in general psychache. Urge surfing is a technique that teaches the patient to simply accept the pain and to experience it – to observe it without the pressure to change its course. The idea is that eventually the pain subsides, often, much sooner than the patient estimated that it would.

Recommendation 4. For individuals with multiple suicide attempts, impulsivity appears to increase with the most recent attempt, along with certain self-protective behaviors, such as communicating intent (Weyrauch et al., 2001). Therefore, in the case of patients with multiple attempts (which generally in and of itself indicates impulsivity), it is important to acknowledge the patient's disclosure of intent as valid and take the necessary steps towards managing risk. As mentioned previously, Weyrauch and colleagues (2001) found that the number of disrupted interpersonal relationships in the preceding year was a significant predictor of the impulsivity of a suicide attempt. Therefore, they concluded that increasing personal resilience in individuals who have attempted suicide may be more effective at preventing suicide lethality than simply teaching stress-reduction methods. Interventions aimed at building resilience include teaching interpersonal or social skills, development of social support networks, and the refinement of individualized coping strategies. A good example of an intervention that includes these constructs is Dialectical Behavior Therapy (Linehan, 1993) and the modules of Emotion Regulation, Interpersonal Effectiveness, and Distress Tolerance.

Recommendation 5. A change in a suicidal individual's perceptions of their own problem-solving abilities and self-efficacy may play an important role in adaptive coping. Improving positive problem-solving appraisal, or the patient's view that they are able to solve problems effectively, may better equip individuals to cope with life stressors (Sher, 2006). It allows for a more realistic allocation of responsibility or control, through increased confidence that problems can be overcome, and guides individuals to approach, rather than avoid, problems. Research on cognitive-behavior therapy with a focus on problem solving where individuals are taught to prioritize problems and generate and implement alternative solutions shows an overall positive effect. This treatment significantly reduced ratings of hopelessness, depression, and suicidal ideation in suicidal young adults (Salkovskis, Atha, & Storer, 1990). Additionally, cognitive therapy aimed at reducing the cognitive rigidity associated with suicide has also shown efficacious in reducing poor problem-solving appraisal. A study examining the effects of an outpatient cognitive therapy for suicide prevention demonstrated a significantly faster rate of improvement in negative problem orientation and impulsivity/carelessness problem-solving style (as measured by the SPSI) in patient receiving the intervention versus those not receiving the intervention. In addition, this targeted form of cognitive therapy was shown to significantly reduce negative problem orientation and impulsive approaches to problem-solving (Ghahramanlou-Holloway et al., 2011).

CONCLUSION

Individuals who are impulsive and/or demonstrate deficits in problem-solving are at increased risk for suicidal self-directed violence. Yet to date, many clinicians do not closely assess suicidal patients for impulsivity and associated deficits in problem-solving and instead primarily focus on other well-established risk factors such as depression, hopelessness, and suicide ideation. Hence, this chapter has presented a clinical overview of the constructs of impulsivity and problem-solving in relation to suicide risk. A brief review of the scientific literature has been provided to highlight the importance of the relationship among impulsivity, poor problem-solving, and suicide. A number of assessment and treatment recommendations are given to assist clinicians who work with highly vulnerable suicidal patients.

REFERENCES

Baca-Garcia, E., et al. (2001). A prospective study of the paradoxical relationship between impulsivity and lethality of suicide attempts. *J Clin Psychiatry*, *62*(7), 560-564.

Baca-Garcia, E., et al. (2005). Suicide attempts and impulsivity. *Eur Arch Psychiatry Clin Neurosci*, *255*(2), 152-156.

Baechler, J., (1979). *Suicides.* New York: Basic Books.

Baechler, J., (1980). A strategic theory. *Suicide Life Threat Behav*, *10*(2), 70-99.

Baumeister, R. F. (1990). Suicide as escape from self. *Psychol Rev*, *97*(1), 90-113.

Beck, A., Schuyler, D. & Herman, J. (1974). Development of suicidal intent scales. In A. Beck, H. Resnik, & D. J. Lettieri (Eds.), *The Prediction of Suicide* (pp. 45-56). Bowie, MD: Charles.

Beck, A. T. (1976). Cognitive therapy and the emotional disorders. New York: Meridian.

Bender, T. W., et al. (2011). Impulsivity and suicidality: The mediating role of painful and provocative experiences. *J Affect Disord*, *129*(1-3), 301-307.

Brodsky, B. S., et al. (1997). Characteristics of borderline personality disorder associated with suicidal behavior. *Am J Psychiatry*, *154*(12), 1715-1719.

Bryan, C. J. & Rudd, M. D. (2006). Advances in the assessment of suicide risk. *J Clin Psychol*, *62*(2), 185-200.

Carrillo-de-la-Pena, M. T., Otero, J. M. & Romero, E. (1993). Comparison among various methods of assessment of impulsiveness. *Percept Mot Skills*, *77*(2), 567-575.

Center for Disease Control and Prevention. (2011). Learn about the costs of violent deaths. Available from: http://www.cdc.gov/Features/dsWISQARScost/.

Deisenhammer, E. A., et al. (2009). The duration of the suicidal process: How much time is left for intervention between consideration and accomplishment of a suicide attempt? *J Clin Psychiatry*, *70*(1), 19-24.

Diaz, F. J., et al. (2003). Dimensions of suicidal behavior according to patient reports. *Eur Arch Psychiatry Clin Neurosci*, *253*(4), 197-202.

Dixon, W. A., Heppner, P. & Anderson, W. P. (1991). Problem-solving appraisal, stress, hopelessness, and suicide ideation in a college population. *J Couns Psychol*, *38*, 51-56.

Dixon, W. A., Heppner, P. & Rudd, M. D. (1994). Problem-solving appraisal, hopelessness, and suicide ideation : Evidence for a mediational model. *J Couns Psychol*, *41*(1), 91-98.

Dougherty, D. M., Mathias, C. W. & Marsh, D. M. (2003). Laboratory measures of impulsivity. In E. F. Coccaro (Ed.), *Aggression: Psychiatric assessment and treatment* (pp. 247-265). New York: Dekker.

Dougherty, D. M., et al. (2004). Laboratory measured behavioral impulsivity relates to suicide attempt history. *Suicide Life-Threat*, *34*(4), 374-385.

D'Zurilla, T. J., Maydeu-Olivares, A., & Kant, G. L. (1998). Age and gender differences in social problem solving in college students, middle age, and elderly adults. *Pers Indiv Differ*, *25*, 241-252.

D'Zurilla, T. J., Nezu, A. M., & Maydeu-Olivares, A. (2002). Social Problem-Solving Inventory-Revised (SPSI-R). North Tonawanda, NY: Multi-Health Systems, Inc.

Ford, M. (1982). Social cognition and social competence in adolescence. *Dev Psychol*, *18*(3), 323-340.

Ghahramanlou-Holloway, M., et al. (2011). Changes in problem-solving appraisal after cognitive therapy for the prevention of suicide. *Psychol Med*, *42*(6), 1185-1193.

Ghahramanlou-Holloway, M., Cox, D. W. & Greene, F. N. (2012). Post-Admission Cognitive Therapy: A brief intervention for psychiatric inpatients admitted after a suicide attempt. *Cogn Behav Pract*, *19*(2), 233-244.

Gibbs, L. M., et al. (2009). When the solution is part of the problem: Problem solving in elderly suicide attempters. *Int J Geriatr Psychiatry*, *24*(12), 1396-1404.

Gorlyn, M. (2005). Impulsivity in the prediction of suicidal behavior in adolescent populations. *Int J Adolesc Med Health*, *17*(3), 205-209.

Heppner, P. P. & Petersen, C. H. (1982). The development and implications of a personal problem-solving inventory. *J Couns Psychol*, *29*(1), 66-75.

Heppner, P. P. (1988). The Problem Solving Inventory (PSI): Manual. Palo Alto, CA: Consulting Psychologists Press.

Horesh, N. (2001). Self-report vs. computerized measures of impulsivity as a correlate of suicidal behavior. *Crisis*, *22*(1), 27-31.

Joiner, T. E., Jr. Voelz, Z. R. & Rudd, M. D. (2001). For suicidal young adults with comorbid depressive and anxiety disorders, problem-solving treatment may be better than treatment as usual. *Prof Psychol-Res Pr, 32*(3), 278-282.

Joiner, T. E., Jr. (2005). *Why People Die By Suicide*. Cambridge, MA: Harvard University Press.

Kingsbury, S., et al. (1999). Do adolescents who take overdoses have specific psychological characteristics? A comparative study with psychiatric and community controls. *J Am Acad Child Adolesc Psychiatry, 38*(9), 1125-1131.

Linehan, M. M. (1993). *Cognitive Behavior Therapy of Borderline Personality Disorder.* New York, NY: Guildford.

Lynam, D. R., et al. (2011). Testing the relations between impulsivity-related traits, suicidality, and nonsuicidal self-injury: A test of the incremental validity of the UPPS model. *Personal Disord, 2*(2), 151-160.

Mann, J. J., et al. (1999). Toward a clinical model of suicidal behavior in psychiatric patients. *Am J Psychiatry, 156*(2), 181-189.

McCrae, R. R. & Costa, P. T. (1990). *Personality in adulthood.* New York: Guilford.

Miller, J. D., et al. (2003). A test of the four-factor model of impulsivity-related traits. *Pers Indiv Differ, 34*, 1403-1418.

Moeller, F. G., et al. (2001). Psychiatric aspects of impulsivity. *Am J Psychiatry, 158*(11), 1783-1793.

Nezu, A. M. (1986). Efficacy of a social problem-solving therapy approach for unipolar depression. *J Consult Clin Psych, 54*(2), 196-202.

Patton, J. H., Stanford, M. S. & Barratt, E. S. (1995) Factor structure of the Barratt Impulsiveness Scale. *J Clin Psychol, 51*(6), 768-774.

Paul, T., et al., (2002) Self-injurious behavior in women with eating disorders. *Am J Psychiatry, 159*(3), 408-411.

Platt, J. J. & Spivack, G. (1975). *Manual for the means-ends problem solving procedure (MEPS): A measure of cognitive problem solving skill.* Philadelphia: Hahnemann University School of Medicine, Department of Medical Health Sciences.

Quednow, B. B., et al. (2006). Normal prepulse inhibition and habituation of acoustic startle response in suicidal depressive patients without psychotic symptoms. *J Affect Disorders, 92*(2-3), 229-303.

Rotheram-Borus, M. J., et al. (1990). Cognitive style and pleasant activities among female adolescent suicide attempters. *J Consult Clin Psychol, 58*(5), 554-561.

Rudd, M. D., Rajab, M. H. & Dahm, P. F. (1994). Problem-solving appraisal in suicide ideators and attempters. *Am J Orthopsychiat, 64*(1), 136-149.

Rudd, M. D., Joiner, T. & Rajab, M. H. (2001). *Treating suicidal behavior: An effective time limited approach*. New York: Guilford.

Salkovskis, P. M., Atha, C. & Storer, D. (1990). Cognitive-behavioural problem solving in the treatment of patients who repeatedly attempt suicide: A controlled trial. *Brit J Psychiat, 157*, 871-876.

Schotte, D. E. & Clum, G. A. (1982). Suicide ideation in a college population: A test of a model. *J Consult Clin Psychol, 50*(5), 690-696.

Schotte, D. E. & Clum, G. A. (1987). Problem-solving skills in suicidal psychiatric patients. *J Consult Clin Psychol, 55*(1), 49-54.

Sher, L. (2006). Risk & protective factors for suicide in patients with alcoholism. *ScientificWorldJournal*, *6*, 1405-1411.

Simon, T. R., et al. (2002). Characteristics of impulsive suicide attempts and attempters. *Suicide Life-Threat*, *32*(1), 49-59.

Smith, G. T., et al. (2007). On the validity and utility of discriminating among impulsivity-like traits. *Assessment*, *14*(2), 155-170.

Spinella, M., (2007). Normative data and a short form of the Barratt Impulsiveness Scale. *Int J Neurosci*, *117*(3), 359-368.

Stanford, M. S., et al. (2009). Fifty years of the Barratt Impulsiveness Scale: An update and review. *Pers Indiv Differ*, *47*, 385-395.

Van Orden, K.A., et al. (2010). The interpersonal theory of suicide. *Psychol Rev*, *117*(2), 575-600.

Wenzel, A., Brown, G. K. & Beck, A. T. (2008). *Cognitive therapy with suicidal patients: Scientific and clinical applications.* Washington, DC: APA Books.

Weyrauch, K. F., et al. (2001). Stressful life events and impulsiveness in failed suicide. *Suicide Life-Threat*, *31*(3), 311-319.

Whiteside, S. P. & Lynam, D. R. (2001). The Five Factor Model and impulsivity: Using a structural model of personality to understand impulsivity. *Pers Indiv Differ*, *30*(4), 669-689.

Wingate, L. R., et al. (2004). Empirically informed approaches to topics in suicide risk assessment. *Behav Sci Law*, *22*(5), 651-665.

Witte, T. K., et al. (2008). "Impulsive" youth suicide attempters are not necessarily all that impulsive. *J Affect Disord*, *107*(1-3), 107-116.

World Health Organization. (2011). Suicide statistics. Available from: http://www.who.int/mental_health/prevention/suicide/country_reports/en/.

In: Psychology of Impulsivity
Editor: Mary C. Olmstead

ISBN: 978-1-63321-879-6

Chapter 2

HALO EFFECT OF STUDENT MISBEHAVIOR ON TEACHER RATINGS OF IMPULSIVITY AND OTHER EXECUTIVE FUNCTION DEFICITS

David Álvarez-García**, *Trinidad García and Paloma González-Castro
Department of Psychology, University of Oviedo, Spain

ABSTRACT

Introduction. Student problem behaviors at school have a multicausal origin. Among the proposed causes are deficits in impulsivity control and other executive functions. Behavior rating scales are one of the most extensively used techniques to identify such deficits. They provide advantages, but they also have potential drawbacks. The *halo effect* is a possible response bias of these scales. Goals. a) To identify the executive function deficits that best predict student misbehavior, b) to analyze the possible negative halo effect of students´ misbehavior on teacher ratings of executive functioning using behavior rating scales, and c) to identify reasons for the halo effect when it occurs.

Method. Participants. We assessed 179 Primary Education students from 3rd to 6th grade (8-13 years). *Assessment instruments.* The teacher who had more contact with the students completed two behavior rating scales: *Alteración del Comportamiento en la Escuela [Misbehavior at School]* (ACE; Arias, Ayuso, Gil, & González, 2006), reflecting the frequency of students' aggressive and disruptive behavior; and the *Escala de Funcionamiento Ejecutivo para Profesorado [Executive Functioning Scale for Teachers]* (EFE-P; García, Álvarez-García, González-Castro, Álvarez, & Segurola, 2013b), measuring the frequency of children's behaviors indicative of executive function deficits. Specifically, this scale measures students´ behavior related to impulsivity control, activity regulation, emotional control, working memory, planning, organization, flexibility, concentration and attentional focus. High scores in these components are indicative of executive function deficits. The parallel version of the EFE-P *Escala de Funcionamiento Ejecutivo para Familias [Family Executive Functioning Scale for Families]* (EFE-F;

* Corresponding Author address: David Álvarez García. Faculty of Psychology. University of Oviedo. Feijóo, s/n. CP 33003, Oviedo (Spain). Email: alvarezgardavid@uniovi.es.

García, Álvarez-García, González-Castro, Álvarez, & Cueli, 2013a) was administered to the assessed students' parents to compare their responses with those of the teachers.

Results. Stepwise multiple linear regression analysis showed that the executive function deficits that statistically and significantly predicted students´ misbehavior were those based in impulsivity control, activity regulation, and emotional control. The ANOVAs showed that, according to the teachers, students with the worse behavior emitted significantly more behaviors indicative of deficits in impulsivity control. They also seemed to have more problems with the rest of executive functions assessed. In contrast, parents' rating only yielded statistically significant differences in impulsivity control, activity regulation, and organization, with notably lower effect sizes.

Conclusion. Impulsivity and hyperactivity are factors closely related to misbehavior at school. In this sample, we confirmed that misbehavior at school can have a negative halo effect on teacher ratings of executive function deficits. Psychometric, clinical, and educational implications arising from these results are discussed.

Introduction

Behavior rating inventories are one of the most widely used techniques in childhood psychological assessment. They consist of questionnaires in which an informant qualitatively estimates (commonly through Likert-scales) the occurrence or frequency of specific behaviors some time after they have happened (Shaffer, Richters, & Lucas, 1999). The information provided by parents and teachers about children's behavior is usually used to make decisions about diagnosis and psychological and educational treatment, as well as for research in several domains such as executive functioning and impulsivity.

The term "executive functioning" refers to a "complex cognitive construct that encompasses the set of processes that underlie flexible goal-directed behavior (e.g., planning, inhibitory control, attention flexibility, working memory)" (Hughes, 2002, p. 69). Impulsivity, characterized as a tendency towards acting without previous self-reflection, indicates a specific deficit in the process of inhibitory control (Logan, Schachar, & Tannock, 1997).

There are several behavior rating scales which are commonly used in the assessment of executive functioning deficits. Some of the most used scales are the *Behavior Rating Inventory of Executive Function* (BRIEF; Gioia, Isquith, Guy, & Kenworthy, 2000), which evaluates inhibition, shifting, emotional control, initiation, working memory, planning/organizing, organization of materials, and self-monitoring; the *Barkley Deficits in Executive Functioning Scale - Children and Adolescents* (BDEFS-CA; Barkley, 2012), which assesses self-restraint (inhibition), self-management of time, self-organization, self-motivation and self-regulation of emotion; and the *Conners 3* (Conners, 2008), which evaluates, among other aspects, inattention, hyperactivity/impulsivity, and other executive functions. High scores in these components are indicative of deficits.

Behavior rating inventories have been shown to be useful in different settings and offer some advantages in comparison to other assessment methods. Taking the direct observation technique into consideration, behavior rating scales have been shown to be less costly in terms of time and training, as well as the fact that they allow information to be collected about infrequent but highly relevant behaviors, which might not be easily detected during direct observational sessions. In comparison to unstructured interviews, behavior rating inventories provide more reliable information, in the sense that they have been empirically validated. Regarding self-reports, behavior rating scales provide an evaluation of children and adolescents who, given their characteristics, are not able to provide information about themselves. Finally, these questionnaires allow information to be obtained from significant others who are permanently in touch with the children and adolescents, so they offer a higher ecological validity than performance-based measures (Whitcomb & Merrell, 2013).

Nevertheless, behavior rating inventories also present some weaknesses, such as the possible occurrence of the widely known *halo effect*. This refers to a tendency to evaluate people in their entirety on the basis of a prominent trait, positive or negative, and to generalize this evaluation to other specific domains, even unrelated ones, over- or under-valuing them artificially (Forgas, 2011).

Halo effects can affect the quality of the data obtained through behavior rating inventories in many different research settings (Hoyt, 2000). Even within the educational context, this effect has been observed and analyzed in different domains such as parents' evaluations of the school (Moshe, 1995), students' evaluation of their teachers (Keeley, English, Irons, & Henslee, 2013; McNatt, 2010; Royalty, 1997) or of the class (Darby, 2007) and teachers' evaluations of their students. Regarding this last issue, previous research has shown, for instance, the halo effect of oppositional defiant students' behavior on ratings of hyperactivity and impulsivity by teachers (Abikoff, Courtney, Pelham, & Koplewicz, 1993; Hartung et al., 2010; Hartung, Van Pelt, Armendariz, & Knight, 2006; Schachar, Sandberg, & Rutter, 1986; Stevens, Quittner, & Abikoff, 1998). The exclusive use of such scales might therefore lead to identifying students with misbehavior problems, such as students with Attention Deficit Hyperactivity Disorder (ADHD).

However, despite the possible existence of a halo effect, previous studies have shown that some typical hyperactive and impulsive behaviors that may be indicative of inhibitory control deficits are actually exhibited by students with behavior problems (Abikoff et al., 2002). In this sense, there is important empirical evidence, obtained though different methods, suggesting that executive functioning, especially inhibitory control, may be intimately related to externalizing behavior problems as of early childhood (see Schoemaker, Mulder, Deković, & Matthys, 2013, for a revision).

It is therefore pertinent to continue examining the impact of the halo effect on the assessment of students with behavior problems using behavior rating scales in order to establish an accurate diagnosis and its comorbidity. The halo effect can lead to erroneous conclusions, especially when behavior rating scales are the only or primary assessment tool used.

Various reasons have been offered for a possible halo effect in rating scales for teachers. Some of these reasons may be related to the design of the rating scales used. It may thus be possible that the scale contains ambiguous items, referring to too general behaviors that could be interpreted in different ways, or they may include items related to some specific behaviors that are difficult to differentiate subtly (Stevens et al., 1998). Other possible explanations may be related to the informants' degree of expertise or training in the studied phenomenon. More expert and trained informants may be more likely to establish the adequate nuances in their responses to the different questions, or they may simply have a more positive or negative attitude towards students with behavior problems. Some cognitive explanations have also been suggested. Specifically, impression formation processes, which involve automatic and constructive Gestalt mechanisms linking and reinterpreting all available information to form a coherent whole have been proposed (Forgas, 2011). Thus, it is possible for the informant to assess a person's specific behavioral aspects based on general impressions or a prominent feature, even though this feature may not be directly related to the purpose of the evaluation (Murphy, Jako, & Anhalt, 1993).

Taking the above into consideration, the present study has three goals: (a) to identify the executive function deficits that best predict student misbehavior at school, (b) to analyze the possible negative halo effect of students' misbehavior on teacher ratings of executive functioning, using behavior rating scales, and (c) to identify reasons for the halo effect when it occurs.

METHOD

Participants

We assessed 179 Primary Education students from 3rd to 6th grade belonging to 16 Primary schools in Asturias (Spain) and selected through accessibility sampling procedures (Martínez, 1995). Of them, 39.3% were female and 60.7% were male. Age ranged from 8 to 13 years (*M* =10.54, *SD* = 1.11). Of the sample, 7.3% were in 3rd grade, 18.4% in 4th grade, 40.8% on 5th grade, and 33.5% in 6th grade.

Teachers who completed the behavior rating scales were tutors (89.7%), as well as principals or head teachers (10.3%). Of the teachers, 62.7% stated they knew the students they were rating moderately well, whereas the remaining 37.3% knew them well. The rating scales completed by teachers who admitted that they did not know, or knew their students very little, were removed from the analyses.

Regarding behavior rating scales completed by families, the mothers completed 73.5% of the scales, whereas 19.1% of the scales were completed by the fathers and 7.4% by both parents.

Instruments

Alteración del Comportamiento en la Escuela [Misbehavior at School] (ACE; Arias, Ayuso, Gil, & González, 2006). This scale was designed for teachers to indicate the frequency with which the student emits different aggressive and disruptive behaviors at school. It consists of 16 Likert-type items, with 5 response options, ranging from 0 (*never*) to 4 (*frequently and with great intensity*). Scores near to 4 suggest behavioral problems. It was tested with 524 teachers who evaluated a total of 3914 students, from 3rd grade of Infantile Education to 6th grade of Primary Education. Factor analysis suggested a single-factor structure, with high internal consistency (α = 953).

Escala de Funcionamiento Ejecutivo para Profesorado [Executive Functioning Scale for Teachers] (EFE-P; García, Álvarez-García, González-Castro, Álvarez, & Segurola, 2013b). This scale assesses executive functioning deficits in children and adolescents. It was designed for completion by teachers. The informant (the teacher with whom the student has the most contact) was asked to indicate the frequency with which the child shows various behaviors indicative of possible executive functioning deficits. It consists of 27 Likert-type items, with 5 response options, ranging from 1 (*Never)* to 5 (*Always*). High scores in the components of executive function evaluated by this scale are indicative of deficits. It was tested through the information provided by the teachers in a sample of 616 students aged 7-19 years, from 26 schools in Asturias (Spain). Confirmatory factor analysis showed a good fit of the nine-factor model: Impulsivity Control, Activity Regulation, Emotional Control, Concentration, Focus, Planning, Organization, Working Memory, and Flexibility. Reliability was high for the whole scale (α = .966) and its factors (ranging between .772 and .897).

Escala de Funcionamiento Ejecutivo para Familias [Executive Functioning Scale for Families] (EFE-F; García, Álvarez-García, González-Castro, Álvarez, & Cueli, 2013a). This scale is a parallel form of the EFE-P Scale, designed for the same purpose, number and type of items, and assessed behaviors, but referring to the family context. It was tested with the families of 1019 students aged 8-18 years, belonging to 41 schools in Asturias (Spain). Confirmatory factor analysis showed that the same nine-factor model proposed for the EFE-P scale provides the best fit to the data obtained with families. Reliability was high for the whole scale (α = .936) and moderate for its factors (ranging between .608 and .749).

Procedure

Firstly, schools in which the rating scales would be administered were selected through convenience sampling, using ease of access to the sample as a selection criterion. Once the participant schools were selected, appropriate permissions from principals or head teachers were requested. They were also informed about the main goals and the procedure of the study, its voluntary and anonymous character, and the confidential treatment of the results. The questionnaires were delivered to the schools in the second term of the 2011/2012 course and collected at the end of the term. Given the high workload that completing the questionnaires would imply for the teachers, volunteer teachers were asked to complete the questionnaire of five students, the students whose results they were interested in analyzing. Questionnaires for families were handed out by the schools. The main goals of the study, as well as its voluntary, anonymous and confidential character were explained in the questionnaires. Informants did not have a time limit to complete the questionnaires. Instructions about how to complete them were provided on the cover of each questionnaire.

Data Analysis

Only data from those students whose information was obtained in all three questionnaires were analyzed. First, multiple linear stepwise regression analysis was carried out. Subsequently, univariate ANOVAs for independent samples (between-subjects) were conducted, with EFE-F and EFE-P factors as the dependent variables and the presence or absence of severe behavioral disturbance (above percentile 90 in the ACE) as the independent variable. Lastly, repeated measures ANOVAs were performed (within-subjects) to compare the information provided by family and teachers in each factor. To interpret the effect size of the differences, Salkind´s (2010) reference was used, which states that "generally, assuming a moderate sample size, eta-squared values of .09, .14, and .22 or greater could be described in the behavioral sciences as small, medium, and large" (p. 423). Statistical analyzes were conducted using SPSS v18 for Windows.

Results

The multiple linear stepwise regression analysis performed showed that, within the nine factors evaluated with EFE-P, only the scores provided by teachers in three of them—impulsivity control, activity regulation and emotional control—significantly contributed to predicting the overall score of behavior problems in the ACE scale (Table 1). Considering the standardized regression coefficients, impulsivity control was the best predictor variable, followed by activity regulation and emotional control.

The final regression model explained 59% of the variance of teachers' scores on the ACE scale (adjusted R^2= .590). The linear relationship between the dependent variable and the predictor variables was statistically significant, $F_{3,175}$ = 86,238, p = .000.

Table 1. Predictor variables of teachers' ACE scores after multiple linear stepwise regression analysis (*N* = 179)

Predictor variables	B (SE)	β	t	p
Constant	-8.75 (1.50)		-5.819	.000***
Impulsivity Control	3.71 (1.12)	.311	3.305	.001***
Emotional Control	3.22 (1.00)	.252	3.203	.002**
Activity Regulation	3.39 (1.20)	.269	2.818	.005**

B = Nonstandardized regression coefficient; SE = Standard Error; β = Standardized regression coefficient.

$*p \leq .05$. $**p \leq .01$. $***p \leq .001$.

Stepwise method (criterion: probability of F-to-enter ≤.05; probability of F-to-remove ≥.10). Variables excluded from the model: Concentration, Focus, Planning, Organization, Working Memory, and Flexibility.

Predictor variables: scores on each of the nine factors of EFE-P; dependent variable: total ACE score.

Table 2 shows the results from between-subject and within-subject comparisons. Regarding between-subject comparisons, teachers of students with behavior problems at school (above percentile 90 in ACE) reported a higher frequency of behaviors indicative of impulsivity control and activity regulation deficits, as well as in the remaining executive functions evaluated in these students in comparison to their peers. On the other hand, the information provided by the families only revealed statistically significant differences in impulsivity control, activity regulation, and organization, with higher scores (and more deficits) in students with behavior problems. In the case of the information provided by teachers, moderate to high effect sizes were found, in the following order: activity regulation, emotional control, and impulsivity control. Low to moderate effect sizes were found in the remaining variables. With respect to family reports, the three statistically significant variables had low effect sizes.

Table 2. Results from repeated measures ANOVAs (within-subjects) and between-subjects ANOVAs (*N*=179)

		ACE PCTL < 90 (*n* = 159)		ACE PCTL ≥ 90 (*n* = 20)			
		M	*SD*	*M*	*SD*	*p*	η²
Impulsivity Control	Teachers	2.12	0.92	3.57	0.64	.000***	.209
	Families	2.44	0.90	2.87	0.87	.048*	.022
	p	.000***		.006**			
	η²	.081		.334			
Activity Regulation	Teachers	2.02	0.84	3.53	0.67	.000***	.251
	Families	2.01	0.69	2.50	0.76	.003**	.048
	p	-		.000***			
	η²	.000		.517			
Emotional Control	Teachers	1.85	0.82	3.28	0.87	.000***	.231
	Families	2.29	0.95	2.50	0.98	-	.005
	p	.000***		.009**			
	η²	.125		.311			
Working Memory	Teachers	1.79	0.81	2.33	0.84	.005**	.044
	Families	1.86	0.74	1.88	0.90	-	.000
	p	-		-			
	η²	.007		.104			
Planning	Teachers	2.14	0.86	2.87	0.71	.000***	.069
	Families	2.36	0.78	2.40	0.78	-	.000
	p	.004**		.042*			
	η²	.051		.200			
Organization	Teachers	2.04	0.85	3.18	0.78	.000***	.155
	Families	2.05	0.76	2.49	1.05	.020*	.030
	p	-		.015*			
	η²	.000		.272			
Flexibility	Teachers	2.11	0.72	3.22	0.69	.000***	.191
	Families	2.09	0.64	2.27	0.76	-	.008
	p	-		.000***			
	η²	.001		.578			
Concentration	Teachers	2.10	0.92	2.83	0.83	.001***	.062
	Families	2.32	0.77	2.45	0.73	-	.003
	p	.003**		-			
	η²	.056		.126			
Focus	Teachers	2.32	0.86	3.42	0.76	.000***	.144
	Families	2.44	0.79	2.57	0.72	-	.003
	p	-		.004**			
	η²	.014		.362			

$^*p \leq .05$. $^{**}p \leq .01$. $^{***}p \leq .001$.

In the within-subject comparisons (Table 2), with regard to students with a percentile above 90 in the ACE, statistically significant differences between the information provided by teachers and families were found, specifically in impulsivity control, emotional control, planning, and concentration. Families reported greater difficulties than those reported by teachers in these components, with magnitudes ranging from low to moderate (between .051

and .125). Moreover, students with behavior problems were more negatively evaluated by their teachers (with higher scores in the assessed components of executive functioning) than by their families in all the analyzed variables. Two of these variables (working memory and concentration) did not show statistically significant differences, maybe due to the small sample size. Effect sizes for these differences are low for working memory and concentration, moderate for planning, and high for organization, emotional control, impulsivity control, focus, activity regulation, and flexibility.

CONCLUSION

The present study had three goals. First, to identify the executive function deficits that best predict students' behavior problems at school. Second, to analyze the possible negative halo effect of students' misbehavior on teacher ratings of executive functioning, using behavior rating scales. Finally, to identify reasons for the halo effect when it occurs.

Regarding the first goal—to identify the executive function deficits that best predict further misbehavior of students at school—, in the present study, the three variables that statistically and significantly predicted student behavior problems at school (assessed by teacher) were activity regulation, impulsivity control, and emotional control. In this sense, deficit in these variables were a significant and positive predictor of student behavior problems at school. This result supports one of the key findings of the meta-analysis conducted by Schoemaker et al. (2013) for which there is abundant empirical evidence obtained from different methodologies, suggesting that deficits in executive functions, especially in inhibitory control, are related to externalizing behavior problems from early childhood.

Regarding the second goal—to analyze the possible negative halo effect of students' misbehavior on teacher ratings of executive functioning, using behavior rating scales—, the results obtained in the present study suggest the existence of a halo effect in teachers' evaluations. These results are consistent with several previous studies that have shown the halo effect of students' oppositional defiant behavior on ratings of hyperactivity and impulsivity symptoms by teachers (Abikoff et al., 1993; Hartung et al., 2010; Hartung et al., 2006; Schachar et al., 1986; Stevens et al., 1998).

Regarding the third goal—to determine the reasons for the halo effect—, the design of the scales can be ruled out as a reason, because two parallel forms of the scale were used and the halo effect was only found in one of them. The possibility that informants' greater experience or training in this topic may have allowed them to more accurately differentiate the statements or have a more positive attitude towards students' misbehavior can also be excluded. Teachers, commonly with more training and experience about this topic than families, distinguished the nuances of the different behaviors the least and gave students with behavior problems the worst overall rating. These results are consistent with the hypothesis that the evaluation of this type of student involves Gestalt processes, as suggested by Forgas (2011): Behavior problems seem to affect teachers' assessment of the rest of the students' characteristics, even unrelated ones.

Important psychometric, educational, and research implications derive from these results. The main psychometric implication of the results found in the present study arises from the fact that, when validating a rating scale, it is not only important to test its properties with a broad and representative sample and to analyze possible high correlations between factors, but also to determine whether any variable (such as the presence of the halo effect) may affect the interpretation of the results obtained with the tool. In the present study, behavior problems were shown to be an important variable in the assessment of executive functioning made by teachers using the EFE-P scale.

From a clinical point of view, the results of this study stress the need to triangulate information from different contexts, methods, and informants in order to establish a precise diagnosis. According to Sparrow (2010), although a rating scale meets all the required statistical criteria, it should never be the only source of information to establish a diagnosis. Such evaluations must be *multi-modal* (using more than one assessment method), *multi-informant* (collecting data from more than one informant), and *multi-setting* (obtaining information from different contexts). The exclusive or main use of these rating scales for clinical diagnosis may lead—due to a possible halo effect—to an erroneous diagnosis of comorbidity between behavioral disorders. For instance, an ADHD diagnosis might be given to a case of Oppositional Defiant Disorder (ODD) when the patient does not actually have this disorder (Hartung et al., 2010). In fact, some of the core symptoms included in the *Diagnostic and Statistical Manual of Mental Disorders-Text Revision, 4th edition* (American Psychiatric Association, 2000) overlap in many cases, and are especially susceptible to the halo effect. For example, the behavior, "Often deliberately annoys people" (ODD) and "Often interrupts or intrudes on others (e.g., butts into conversations or games)" (ADHD) are only differentiated in their intentionality, an aspect that might not be easily distinguished by the informant. In such cases, it would be necessary to complement the information from rating scales with that obtained with other techniques such as clinical interviews, in which the professional interviewer can warn the interviewee about these nuances and ensure that he or she effectively understands them.

If, as the results suggest, the most plausible reason for the halo effect is related to Gestalt processes, two precautions must be taken, both in clinical and research contexts. The first precaution is to ensure that the teacher who reports children's behavior knows them well. The fewer the gaps in knowledge of the children´s behavior, the less likely it will be for evaluation of certain dimensions of behavior to generalize to other dimensions. Teachers do not always know their students in all the conditions assessed with the rating scale. In fact, in the present study, only 37 % of the teachers stated that they knew the assessed students very well, despite the fact that they were the tutors of almost 90% of the students. They were therefore the teachers who were supposed to have greater contact with these students. In general, increasing the observation time helps informants to be more accurate in their ratings (Pike, 1999). The second precaution is to warn the informants about the possibility of this response bias and the need to rate each statement separately instead of allowing themselves to be influenced by their general impression (Keeley et al., 2013).

An important educational implication derived from the results is that teachers may generalize their evaluation about misbehavior at school to other, not necessarily related, cognitive dimensions. This may affect their teaching methods and even the grades that a student achieves through a process commonly known as the *Pigmalión effect* (Rosenthal & Jacobson, 1968).

The present study thus makes a contribution to the study of impulsivity and other executive function deficits. Nevertheless, some limitations must be considered. The main limitation of this study is related to the sample size and the sampling method used. The sample of assessed students is low, and was obtained by intentional methods, with a very limited age range, and geographically bounded. The study conducted must therefore be considered as an empirical approach to the issue. In order to generalize the conclusions to other contexts and age ranges, it would be necessary to replicate the study in the future, with larger and more representative samples.

References

Abikoff, H. B., Courtney, M., Pelham, W. E., & Koplewicz, H. S. (1993). Teachers' ratings of disruptive behaviors: The influence of halo effects. *Journal of Abnormal Child Psychology, 21*(5), 519-533.

Abikoff, H. B., Jensen, P. S., Arnold, L. L. E., Hoza, B., Hechtman, L., Pollack, S., Martin, D., Alvir, J., March, J. S., Hinshaw, S., Vitiello, B., Newcorn, J., Greiner, A., Cantwell, D. P., Conners, C. K., Elliott, G., Greenhill, L. L., Kraemer, H., Pelham, W. E., Severe, J. B., Swanson, J. M., Wells, K., & Wigal, T. (2002). Observed classroom behavior of children with ADHD: Relationship to gender and comorbidity. *Journal of Abnormal Child Psychology, 30*(4), 349-359.

American Psychiatric Association (2000). *Diagnostic and statistical manual of mental disorders (4th ed., Text Revision).* Washington, DC: American Psychiatric Association.

Arias, A., Ayuso, L. M., Gil, G., & González, I. (2006). *ACE. Alteración del Comportamiento en la Escuela.* Madrid: TEA.

Barkley, R. A. (2012). *Barkley Deficits in Executive Functioning Scale - Children and Adolescents (BDEFS-CA).* New York, NY: Guilford Press.

Conners, C. K. (2008). *Conners 3rd edition.* North Tonawanda, NY: Multi-Heath Systems.

Darby, J. A. (2007). Are course evaluations subject to a 'halo effect'? *Research in Education, 77*, 46-55.

Forgas, J. P. (2011). She just doesn't look like a philosopher...? Affective influences on the halo effect in impression formation. *European Journal of Social Psychology, 41*, 812-817.

García, T., Álvarez-García, D., González-Castro, P., Álvarez, L., & Cueli, M. (2013a). *Propiedades psicométricas de la Escala de Funcionamiento Ejecutivo para Familias (EFE-F)* [Psychometric properties of the Executive Functioning Scale for Families (EFE-F)]. Submitted for publication.

García, T., Álvarez-García, D., González-Castro, P., Álvarez, L., & Segurola, L. A. (2013b). *Propiedades psicométricas de la Escala de Funcionamiento Ejecutivo para Profesorado (EFE-P)* [Psychometric properties of the Executive Functioning Scale for Teachers (EFE-P)]. Submitted for publication.

Gioia, G.A., Isquith, P.K., Guy, S., & Kenworthy, L. (2000). *BRIEF: Behavior Rating Inventory of Executive Function professional manual.* Lutz, FL: Psychological Assessment Resources.

Hartung, C. M., Lefler, E. K., Tempel, A. B., Armendariz, M. L., Sigel, B. A., & Little, C. S. (2010). Halo effects in ratings of ADHD and ODD: Identification of susceptible symptoms. *Journal of Psychopathology and Behavioral Assessment, 32*(1), 128-137.

Hartung, C. M., Van Pelt, J. C., Armendariz, M. L., & Knight, L. A. (2006). Biases in ratings of disruptive behavior in children: Effects of sex and negative halos. *Journal of Attention Disorders, 9*(4), 620-630.

Hoyt, W. T. (2000). Rater bias in psychological research: When is it a problem and what can we do about it? *Psychological Methods*, *5*(1), 64-86.

Hughes, C. (2002). Executive functions and development: Why the interest? *Infant and Child Development*, *11*(2), 69-71.

Keeley, J. W., English, T., Irons, J., & Henslee, A. M. (2013). Investigating halo and ceiling effects in student evaluations of instruction. *Educational and Psychological Measurement, 73*(3), 440-457.

Logan, G. D., Schachar, R. J., & Tannock, R. (1997). Impulsivity and inhibitory control. *Psychological Science*, *8*(1), 60-64.

Martínez, R. (1995). *Psicometría: teoría de los tests psicológicos y educativos* [Psychometry: theory of the psychological and educational tests]. Madrid: Síntesis.

McNatt, D. B. (2010). Negative reputation and biased student evaluations of teaching: Longitudinal results from a naturally occurring experiment. *Academy of Management Learning & Education*, *9*(2), 225-242.

Moshe, T. (1995). The prestige of the High School as viewed by parents. *British Journal of Sociology of Education*, *16*(1), 93-108.

Murphy, K. R., Jako, R. A., & Anhalt, R. L. (1993). Nature and consequences of halo error: A critical analysis. *Journal of Applied Psychology*, *78*(2), 218-225.

Pike, G. R. (1999). The constant error of the halo in educational outcomes research. *Research in Higher Education*, *40*(1), 61-86.

Rosenthal, R., & Jacobson, L. (1968). *Pygmalion in the classroom.* New York, NY: Holt, Rinehart & Winston.

Royalty, J. (1997). The halo effect and student evaluations of instructors. *Perceptual & Motor Skills*, *84*(1), 345.

Salkind, N. J. (2010). *Encyclopedia of research design. Volume 1.* Thousand Oaks, CA: SAGE Publications.

Schachar, R., Sandberg, S., & Rutter, M. (1986). Agreement between teachers' ratings and observations of hyperactivity, inattentiveness, and defiance. *Journal of Abnormal Child Psychology*, *14*(2), 331-345.

Schoemaker, K., Mulder, H., Deković, M., & Matthys, W. (2013). Executive functions in preschool children with externalizing behavior problems: A meta-analysis. *Journal of Abnormal Child Psychology*, *41*(3), 457-471.

Shaffer, D., Richters, J., & Lucas, C. P. (1999). *Diagnostic assessment in child and adolescent psychopathology*. New York, NY: Guilford Press.

Sparrow, E. P. (2010). *Essentials of Conners' Behavior Assessments*. Hoboken, NJ: John Wiley & Sons.

Stevens, J., Quittner, A. L., & Abikoff, H. (1998). Factors influencing Elementary School teachers' ratings of ADHD and ODD behaviors. *Journal of Clinical Child Psychology*, *27*(4), 406-414.

Whitcomb, S. A., & Merrell, K. W. (2013). *Behavioral, social, and emotional assessment of children and adolescents*. New York, NY: Routledge.

In: Psychology of Impulsivity
Editor: Mary C. Olmstead

ISBN: 978-1-63321-879-6

Chapter 3

DAPP-BQ PERSONALITY PROTOTYPES IN A GENERAL PSYCHIATRIC INPATIENT POPULATION: ASSOCIATIONS WITH SYMPTOM EXPRESSION AND TREATMENT INDICATORS

Tim Bastiaens[1,*], Laurence Claes[2], Eva Ceulemans[2], Dominique Vanwalleghem[1] and Marc De Hert[1,3]

[1]UPC KU Leuven Campus Kortenberg, Kortenberg, Belgium
[2]KU Leuven, Faculty of Psychology and Educational Sciences, Leuven, Belgium
[3]KU Leuven, Faculty of Medicine, Leuven, Belgium

ABSTRACT

The present chapter contributes to the study of Impulsivity as it sets out to demonstrate evidence for an impulsive cluster of personality functioning (labelled Undercontrolled) overarching a heterogeneous clinical population. Conceptualizing Impulsivity as a combination of high Neuroticism, low Agreeableness and low Conscientiousness, our study makes use of a clustering approach as opposed to a dimensional one. We investigated personality prototypes using the personality dimensions of the Dimensional Assessment of Personality Pathology Basic Questionnaire (DAPP-BQ; Livesley & Jackson, 2009). One hundred and ten psychiatric inpatients filled out the DAPP-BQ and the MMPI-2. The number of personality prototypes was determined by means of a model-based cluster analysis, which yielded three distinct personality clusters. Patients in cluster 1 (labelled Overcontrollers) were identified by higher scores on emotional dysregulation and compulsiveness. Patients in cluster 2 (labelled Resilients) were characterized by lower scores on the emotional dysregulation and the dissocial dimensions. Patients in cluster 3 (the impulsive cluster, labelled Undercontrollers) were identified by higher scores on the dissocial dimension and lower scores on the compulsiveness dimension. The clusters were validated by means of the MMPI-2 scales. Resilients reported being less overwhelmed by problems (MMPI-2 K scale), presented themselves more well-adjusted (MMPI-2 S scale), showed no MMPI-2

* Corresponding author: Tim Bastiaens, MSc. Clinical Psychologist UPC KULeuven Campus Kortenberg, Leuvensesteenweg 517, 3070 Kortenberg, Belgium (+32) (0)2758 0669, tim.bastiaens@uc-kortenberg.be.

Content scale elevations, and presented themselves with significantly more tolerance for confrontation, self-confidence, responsibility and good reality testing (MMPI-2 Es, Do and Re scales) compared to Overcontrollers and Undercontrollers. Overcontrollers showed significantly more hypochondriac concerns (MMPI-2 Hs scale), depression related problems (MMPI-2 D scale) and social introversion (MMPI-2 Si scale) than Resilients, but did not differ from Undercontrollers on these dimensions. Undercontrollers displayed distinctively higher levels of Antisocial Practices (MMPI-2 ASP) and acting-out (MMPI-2 Pd and Ma scales) than Overcontrollers as well as Resilients, differences which were not attributable to state-dependent demoralization (MMPI-2 DEM) but represented valid trait-like features (MMPI-2 RC4 and RC9 scales). While Undercontrollers specifically reported the highest levels of psychopathology and expressed need for help (MMPI-2 F and Fb scales), they nevertheless displayed the least positive attitude towards treatment (MMPI-2 TRT scale). In conclusion, current results demonstrate evidence for the existence and clinical relevance of an Impulsive cluster of personality functioning (labelled Undercontrolled) overarching a heterogeneous clinical population. With the Undercontrolled cluster representing the opposite of the Overcontrolled cluster in terms of Compulsivity, two of the three personality prototypes center around (the inverse of) Impulsivity. Implications for further research and clinical practice are discussed.

1. INTRODUCTION

As early as 1980, Block and Block described three personality types: Overcontrollers, Undercontrollers and Resilients. The Overcontrolled type is characterized by high scores on the Big Five Neuroticism and Conscientiousness dimensions, and low scores on the Agreeableness dimension. The Undercontrolled (Impulsive) type is conceptualized by high scores on Neuroticism and low scores on Conscientiousness and Agreeableness. The Resilient type is defined by average to low scores on Neuroticism and average to high scores on Conscientiousness, Agreeableness and Extraversion. By use of the NEO-Personality Inventory (NEO-PI) or NEO-Five Factor Inventory (NEO-FFI) measures (Costa & McCrae, 1985, 1992), these three personality prototypes have been identified in non-clinical samples (e.g. Asendorpf, Borkenau, Ostendorf, & Van Aken, 2001; Grumm & von Collani, 2009; Mertz & Roesch, 2012) as well as clinical samples such as patients with eating disorders (Claes, Vandereycken, Vandeputte, & Braet, 2013; Claes, Vandereycken, Luyten, Soenens, Pieters, & Vertommen, 2006; Steiger et al., 2009) and addiction disorders (Graña, Muñoz, & Navas, 2009). Claes, Tavernier, Roose, Bijttebier, Smith, and Lilienfeld (2012) also identified the same personality prototypes in their sample of male prisoners. The three personality types are associated with differences in co-occurring psychopathology (Akse, Hale, Engels, Raaijmakers, & Meeus, 2007; Grumm & von Collani, 2009) and have led to different treatment suggestions (Grumm & von Collani, 2009; Fowler & Westen, 2011; Wildes & Marcus, 2013; Gazzillo, Lingiardi, Peloso, Giordani, Vesco, Zanna, Filippucci & Vicari, 2013). In eating disorders specifically, they have been associated with different therapeutic interventions and treatment outcome (Thompson-Brenner & Westen, 2005).

The present chapter contributes to this line of research by replicating these Personality Prototypes in a general clinical population (as opposed to pathology-specific groups) based on the domain scores of the Dimensional Assessment of Personality Pathology Basic Questionnaire (DAPP-BQ; Livesley & Jackson, 2009; in contrast to the NEO-PI or NEO-FFI measures). Indeed, in clinical populations, measures of maladaptive Five Factor Model (FFM) variants (like the DAPP-BQ) are acknowledged to have advantages over their classic counterparts (NEO-PI or NEO-FFI) (Krueger et al., 2011; Lynam, 2012). The DAPP-BQ excellently captures clinical variance (Livesley & Jackson, 2009; Livesley, 2001; Livesley, Jang, & Vernon, 1998), shows a solid factor structure (Livesley et al., 1998; Kushner, Quilty, Tackett, & Bagby, 2011; Livesley & Jackson, 2009; van Kampen, 2002, 2006) and maps on general personality dimensions (van Kampen, 2002, 2006; Verheul & Widiger, 2009; Krueger et al., 2011; see also Appendix A). Also, its potential for personality prototyping has already been demonstrated in eating disorders (Goldner et al., 1999; Wonderlich et al., 2005, 2007). In addition to replication of the previously described Personality Prototypes in a general clinical population (as opposed to pathology-specific groups) by means of a maladaptive FFM variant measure (in contrast to the NEO-PI or NEO-FFI measures), the present study tries to relate these prototypes to co-occurring psychopathology and attitude towards treatment.

Our undertaking is very relevant to the study of Impulsivity as it sets out to demonstrate evidence for the existence and clinical relevance of an impulsive cluster of personality functioning (labelled Undercontrolled) being present not just in pathology-specific groups, but overarching a heterogeneous clinical population. Conceptualizing Impulsivity as a combination of high Neuroticism, low Agreeableness and low Conscientiousness, our study makes use of a clustering approach as opposed to a dimensional one. With the Undercontrolled cluster representing the opposite of the Overcontrolled cluster in terms of Compulsivity, replication of the three Personality Prototypes in a heterogeneous clinical population would put forth Impulsivity as a central notion in the personality prototype model. That is, two of the three personality prototypes would center around (the inverse of) Impulsivity.

2. METHOD

2.1. Participants and Procedure

All consecutive admitted inpatients of different sections of the University Psychiatric Centre KU Leuven Campus Kortenberg (Belgium) were invited to participate in this study by the psychologist who conducted the general assessment for clinical purposes upon intake. A total number of one hundred and ten inpatients were included. Fifty two participants (47%) were females and 58 (53%) were males. The mean age of the total group was 31.66 (SD = 11.86). No mean difference in age was found between females and males ($F(1, 109) = 0.19$, $p = 0.89$). With respect to marital status, 66.4% of the total group were single, 13.6% married, 9.1% divorced and 10.9% living together. We did not find a significant relationship between gender and marital status ($\chi^2(3) = 2.59$, $p = .459$). All patients filled in the questionnaires after written informed consent was obtained. The study was approved by the medical ethical committee of the University Psychiatric Centre Campus Kortenberg.

2.2. Measures

To assess the maladaptive variants of the FFM dimensions, we used the Dimensional Assessment of Personality Pathology Basic Questionnaire (DAPP-BQ; Livesley & Jackson, 2009; Dutch translation: van Kampen & de Beurs, 2009). The DAPP-BQ consists of 290 items to be scored on a 5-point Likert scale. Its domain scores relate to the Big Five dimensions in the following way: Emotional Dysregulation relates to Neuroticism, Inhibition (inversely) to Extraversion, Dissocial (inversely) to Agreeableness, and Compulsivity to Conscientiousness (Verheul & Widiger, 2009; see also appendix A).

To validate the personality types, we used the Minnesota Multiphasic Personality Inventory (MMPI-2; Butcher et al., 2001). The MMPI-2 is a well-known 567-item inventory measuring symptoms, beliefs, and attitudes in a true-false format. To assess (1) the reported severity of pathology, we used the F, Fb and Fp scales. To asses (2) the displayed variety of pathology, we used the classic clinical scales, the restructured scales, the content scales and the supplementary scales. To assess (3) the attitudes towards treatment, we used the Negative Treatment Indicators scale. The Negative Treatment Indicators (TRT) scale represents a negative attitude towards treatment, associated with feelings of helplessness and pessimism about working out one's problems, combined with an inability and/or unwillingness to reveal personal information, a lack of taking responsibility for one's own actions, and a belief that mental illness is a sign of weakness (Graham, 2006).

Patients' age at admission, gender and marital status were based on the electronic patient files of the hospital.

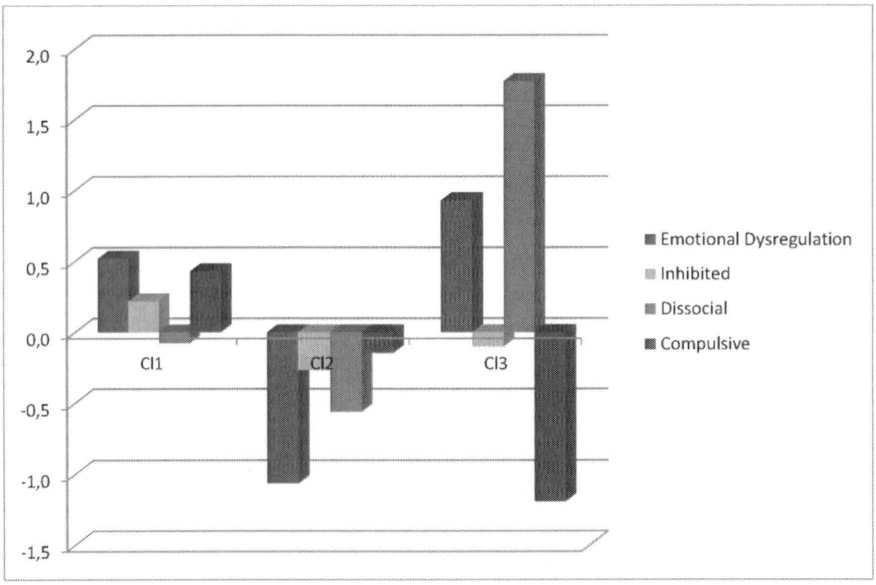

Figure 1. Three distinct personality clusters characterized by their standardized DAPP-BQ patterns in the total sample (N=110). Cluster 1 (*n*=55, Overcontrolled) = high Emotional Dysregulation and high Compulsiveness. Cluster 2 (*n*=40, Resilient) = low Emotional Dysregulation and low Dissocial. Cluster 3 (n=15, Undercontrolled) = high Emotional Dysregulation, high Dissocial, low Compulsiveness.

2.3. Analyses

To obtain three personality clusters, we applied model based cluster analysis on the DAPP-BQ scale scores, using the MCLUST package of Fraley and Raftery (2007). Additionally, to compare mean level differences between the three personality clusters we performed Multivariate Analyses of Variance (MANOVA) by means of SPSS version 22. Scheffé's/Bonferroni post-hoc comparisons were used to investigate which clusters statically differed from each other.

3. Results

3.1. Cluster Analysis

Model-based cluster analysis revealed three distinct personality clusters (Figure 1). Compared to clusters 2 and 3, patients in cluster 1 (*n*=55, labelled Overcontrolled) were identified by a pattern of high Emotional Dysregulation and Compulsiveness. Patients in cluster 2 (*n*=40, labelled Resilient) represented a more resilient group identified by low scores on the Emotional Dysregulation and the Dissocial dimension relative to cluster 1 and cluster 3. Patients in cluster 3 (*n*=15, labelled Undercontrolled), were characterized by high Emotional Dysregulation like cluster 1, but significantly less Compulsiveness compared to cluster 2 and cluster 1, while exhibiting higher scores on the Dissocial dimension (Figure 1). Table 1 shows the mean differences in DAPP-BQ domain scores between the different personality subtypes.

Table 2 shows means and standard deviations of the DAPP-BQ personality variables compared to normative European data provided by Pukrop et al. (2009). Resilients scored within non-clinical average range on Emotional Dysregulation and Compulsivity, and showed more Inhibitedness and less Dissocial Behavior compared to non-clinical norms. Overcontrollers scored within non-clinical average range on Dissocial Behavior and showed more Compulsivity, Emotional Dysregulation and Inhibitedness compared to non-clinical norms. Undercontrollers showed less Compulsivity and much more Emotional Dysregulation, Inhibitedness and Dissocial Behavior compared to non-clinical norms.

3.2. Relationship between Clusters and Socio-Demographic Variables

We did not find a significant relationship between cluster membership and relational/marital status ($\chi^2(6) = 6.90$, $p = .33$). The relationship between cluster membership and gender was borderline significant ($\chi^2(2) = 6.03$, $p = .049$), with a tendency towards more males than females in the Undercontrolled cluster and more females than males in the Overcontrolled and the Resilient cluster. The three clusters significantly differed with respect to age [$F(2, 107) = 5.54$, $p<0.01$]: patients of the Undercontrolled cluster ($M = 23.4$, $SD = 6.4$) were significantly younger than patients of the Overcontrolled ($M = 31.6$, $SD = 11.9$) and the Resilient cluster ($M = 34.9$, $SD = 12.1$).

Table 1. Means (Standard Deviations) of the DAPP-BQ and MMPI-2 personality variables for the three personality clusters

	cluster1 Overcontrolled n=55		cluster2 resilient n=40		cluster3 undercontrolled n=15		F		Post-hoc Comparisons
	M	SD	M	SD	M	SD			
DAPP-BQ									
Emotional Dysregulation	3.14	0.36	2.14	0.36	3.39	0.41	109.27	***	3>2; 1>2
Inhibitedness	2.80	0.65	2.50	0.58	2.60	0.41	2.94	n.s.	
Dissocial Behavior	2.17	0.38	1.89	0.41	3.25	0.40	65.82	***	3>1>2
Compulsivity	3.47	0.70	3.02	0.65	2.19	0.61	22.57	***	1>2>3
MMPI-2 variables									
Validity Scales									
L (Lie)	43.75	10.25	48.45	8.90	37.80	7.02	7.23	***	2>3
F (Infrequency)	76.84	18.67	57.52	11.80	95.29	28.55	26.24	***	3>1>2
K (Correction)	38.55	9.51	52.33	9.50	38.00	9.22	27.23	***	2>1; 2>3
TRIN (True Response Inconsistency)	58.22	5.66	57.13	11.36	52.86	16.28	1.67	n.s.	
VRIN (Variable Response Inconsistency)	52.58	10.14	50.35	8.34	60.36	14.04	5.10	**	3>1; 3>2
Fb (Back Infrequency)	88.16	23.70	58.25	11.36	111.29	33.21	38.69	***	3>1>2
Fp (Infrequency Psychopathology)	59.45	13.26	51.77	12.47	71.86	30.93	8.24	***	3>1; 3>2
S (Superlative Self-presentation)	34.75	11.52	50.40	9.56	30.07	8.72	32.67	***	2>1; 2>3
Clinical Scales									
Hs (Hypochondriasis)	65.58	14.97	57.22	11.72	63.93	10.38	4.66	*	1>2
D (Depression)	79.42	11.87	65.42	13.73	78.43	12.48	15.07	***	1>2
Hy (Hysteria)	67.96	14.99	63.30	15.27	69.79	10.77	1.58	n.s.	
Pd (Psychopathic Deviate)	74.44	12.81	67.60	11.37	85.00	10.74	11.31	***	3>1>2
Mf (Masculinity – Femininity)	51.71	13.89	50.07	10.82	53.21	6.22	0.413	n.s.	
Pa (Paranoia)	76.11	12.53	61.68	11.46	80.43	18.46	18.06	***	3>2; 1>2

	cluster1 Overcontrolled n=55		cluster2 resilient n=40		cluster3 undercontrolled n=15		F		Post-hoc Comparisons
	M	SD	M	SD	M	SD			
Pt (Psychasthenia)	79.75	12.05	63.82	12.63	85.50	9.53	27.00	***	3>2; 1>2
Sc (Schizophrenia)	77.02	15.85	61.57	10.65	86.00	15.03	21.40	***	3>2; 1>2
Ma (Hypomania)	54.65	13.45	49.80	10.63	69.00	16.18	11.52	***	3>1; 3>2
Si (Social Introversion)	65.73	10.84	53.18	10.56	61.43	13.01	15.04	***	1>2
Restructured Scales									
RC (Demoralization)	77.44	8.37	60.65	9.96	80.93	5.92	51.53	***	3>2; 1>2
RC1 (Somatic Complaints)	68.09	15.59	52.78	11.40	67.00	13.49	14.92	***	3>2; 1>2
RC2 (Low Positive Emotions)	70.85	13.37	58.95	10.97	71.64	15.16	11.29	***	3>2; 1>2
RC3 (Cynicism)	55.53	12.22	45.30	9.04	57.00	10.94	11.72	***	3>2; 1>2
RC4 (Antisocial Behavior)	63.51	15.23	55.50	9.98	87.57	19.76	26.32	***	3>1>2
RC6 (Ideas of Persecution)	62.69	20.27	44.88	13.25	71.93	23.54	15.75	***	3>2; 1>2
RC7 (Dysfunctional Negative Emotions)	71.80	13.86	50.98	8.87	75.50	11.76	41.53	***	3>2; 1>2
RC8 (Abberant Experiences)	62.00	14.00	51.40	9.54	71.21	16.85	14.52	***	3>2; 1>2
RC9 (Hypomanic Activation)	53.24	13.63	44.93	10.69	66.07	16.58	14.25	***	3>1>2

Table 2. Means (Standard Deviations) of the DAPP-BQ personality variables compared to normative data for the three personality clusters

	normative data Pukrop et al., 2009 n=165		cluster1 controlled n=55				cluster2 resilient n=40				cluster3 undercontrolled n=15			
	M	**SD**	**M**	**SD**	***F***	**sign**	**M**	**SD**	***F***	**sign**	**M**	**SD**	***F***	**sign**
DAPP-BQ														
Emotional Dysregulation	2.25	0.37	3.14	0.36	241.87	***	2.14	0.36	3.69		3.39	0.41	370.66	***
Inhibitedness	2.34	0.46	2.80	0.65	33.08	***	2.50	0.58	4.35	*	2.60	0.41	13.89	***
Dissocial Behavior	2.13	0.34	2.17	0.38	0.54		1.89	0.41	18.48	***	3.25	0.40	408.73	***
Compulsivity	3.01	0.54	3.47	0.70	25.62	***	3.02	0.65	0.01		2.19	0.61	89.03	***

*p<0.05; **p<0.01; ***p<0.001.

3.3. Mean Differences between Clusters in Symptom Expression

3.3.1. Mean differences between clusters in reported severity of psychopathology

Table 1 displays the mean MMPI-2 T-scores of the Validity scales per cluster (also allowing comparisons of scale scores per cluster to non-clinical norms). Patients of the Undercontrolled cluster reported the highest level of psychopathology (high F) and manifest symptoms (high Fb), sequentially followed by patients of the Controlled cluster and the Resilient cluster. Patients of the Undercontrolled cluster reported more infrequent inpatient psychopathology (high Fp) and more response inconsistency (high VRIN) compared to patients of the Controlled and Resilient clusters, while normatively still presenting valid protocols [T(Fp) < 100 and T(VRIN) < 80]. Finally, patients of the Undercontrolled and Overcontrolled cluster reported feeling more overwhelmed by problems (low K) and presented themselves less well-adjusted (low S) compared to Resilients.

3.3.2. Mean differences between clusters in displayed variety of psychopathology

Clinical Scales & Restructured Scales

Table 1 also displays the mean MMPI-2 T-scores of the Clinical and Restructured Scales per cluster. Patients of the Undercontrolled cluster scored significantly higher than patients of the Overcontrolled and Resilient cluster on the MMPI-2 Psychopathic Deviation (scale 4) and Hypomania (scale 9) scales. Additionally, patients of the Undercontrolled and Overcontrolled group showed significantly more suspiciousness (scale 6), proneness to worry (scale 7) and aberrant experiences (scale 8) than patients of the Resilient group, but did not differ from each other. Finally, patients of the Overcontrolled cluster showed significantly more hypochondriac concerns (scale 1), depression related problems (scale 2), and social introversion (scale 0) than patients of the Resilient group, whereas patients of the Undercontrolled cluster took an intermediate position. Both patients of the Undercontrolled and the Overcontrolled group reported significantly more state-dependent exacerbation of symptoms than patients in the Resilient group (RC Demoralization). The patterns of the Restructured scale scores, which represent a purer representation of the trait-like features of the Clinical scale scores by controlling for the effects of state-dependent exacerbation, replicated the patterns of the Clinical Scale scores.

Content scales & Supplementary Scales

Table 3 displays the Mean MMPI-2 T-scores of the Content and Supplementary Scales per cluster. Patients of the Undercontrolled group scored significantly higher than patients of the Overcontrolled group and the Resilient group on the Content Scale Antisocial Practices (ASP). Looking at ASP subscales, patients of the Undercontrolled group did not differ from patients of the Overcontrolled group on Antisocial Attitudes (ASP1), but scored higher on Antisocial Behavior (ASP2) specifically. On all other Content Scales (except TRT, see 3.4), patients of the Undercontrolled cluster and of the Overcontrolled cluster scored significantly higher than patients of the Resilient group. Conversely, patients of the Resilient group scored significantly higher than the two other groups on the Supplementary scales Ego-Strength (Es; measuring tolerance for confrontation, persistency, self-confidence, resourcefulness, reality testing, interpersonal coping skills, developed interests and competitiveness), Dominance (Do; measuring assertiveness, responsibility, leadership, realism, task-orientedness, perseverance and optimism) and Social Responsibility (Re; measuring sense of duty, strong standards, confidence in self and others, and ethical concerns), and significantly lower on the Supplementary Scales Anxiety (A), Hostility (Ho), College Maladjustment (Mt), Masculine sex role (GM) and Post-Traumatic Stress Disorder – K (PK).

3.4. Mean Differences between Clusters in Attitude towards Treatment

Patients in the Undercontrolled group showed the most negative attitude towards treatment, i.e. a distrustful, indecisive attitude, lack of responsibility for one's own actions, and a belief that mental illness is a sign of weakness (TRT). They scored significantly higher than patients of the Overcontrolled group, followed by the patients of the Resilient group (Table 3). Looking at TRT subscales, the same pattern emerged concerning Low Motivation (TRT1), while regarding Inability to Disclose (TRT2), patients of the Undercontrolled cluster as well as of the Overcontrolled cluster reported significantly higher levels compared to patients of the Resilient cluster.

Table 3. Means (Standard Deviations) of the MMPI-2 Content and Supplementary Scales for the three personality clusters

	cluster1 Overcontrolled n=55		cluster2 resilient n=40		cluster3 undercontrolled n=15				Post-hoc Comparisons
	M	SD	M	SD	M	SD	F		
Content scales									
ANX	78.76	9.28	60.63	10.83	77.86	11.21	39.89	***	3>2; 1>2
FRS	60.02	13.05	47.65	7.99	64.07	15.11	16.60	***	3>2; 1>2
OBS	68.93	10.92	52.15	10.84	73.14	8.62	35.69	***	3>2; 1>2
DEP	79.91	11.51	62.62	10.99	85.43	8.11	37.17	***	3>2; 1>2
HEA	68.15	15.32	52.78	10.80	68.00	12.05	16.52	***	3>2; 1>2
BIZ	62.53	14.82	49.35	8.31	69.43	19.36	16.13	***	3>2; 1>2
ANG	63.85	12.14	49.78	9.61	70.50	14.71	24.05	***	3>2; 1>2
CYN	55.02	11.19	44.35	8.22	56.79	11.24	14.94	***	3>2; 1>2
ASP	53.49	10.57	46.13	10.64	70.64	18.11	22.56	***	3>1>2
TPA	58.78	13.11	46.30	10.24	63.43	14.12	15.95	***	3>2; 1>2
LSE	73.58	12.72	53.12	9.92	76.93	13.83	40.24	***	3>2; 1>2
SOD	60.82	13.00	51.90	11.72	58.50	14.52	5.75	**	1>2
FAM	70.07	13.72	57.20	13.26	78.50	14.47	16.58	***	3>2; 1>2
WRK	76.98	11.45	56.75	11.22	81.86	10.13	46.45	***	3>2; 1>2
TRT	72.45	11.94	54.10	8.96	80.79	10.62	47.21	***	3>1>2
Supplementary Scales									
A	76.15	9.23	57.75	10.12	80.36	8.81	52.90	***	3>2; 1>2
R	51.36	11.37	51.83	10.20	46.43	12.48	1.32		n.s.
Es	28.71	13.19	43.63	10.76	25.79	10.98	21.18	***	2>1; 2>3
MAC-R	49.71	12.94	46.62	12.02	64.86	14.02	10.83	***	3>2; 3>1
Ho	60.25	11.90	46.75	9.86	66.07	10.62	23.98	***	3>2; 1>2

	cluster1 Overcontrolled n=55		cluster2 resilient n=40		cluster3 undercontrolled n=15				Post-hoc Comparisons
	M	SD	M	SD	M	SD	F		
O-H	43.64	9.62	51.35	9.99	36.93	9.64	13.58	***	2>1; 2>3
Do	34.69	9.01	47.10	8.97	32.14	15.54	21.40	***	2>1; 2>3
Re	44.82	12.43	53.18	8.35	28.43	12.49	26.12	***	2>1>3
Mt	79.38	10.14	61.60	12.86	83.86	8.48	37.15	***	3>2; 1>2
GM	33.51	9.67	46.57	9.11	35.79	11.38	21.70	***	2>1; 2>3
GF	46.29	11.08	49.92	12.69	29.64	16.12	14.12	***	2>3; 1>3
PK	84.45	13.57	60.87	11.76	90.86	11.97	49.68	***	3>2; 1>2
MDS	77.11	13.86	61.55	11.39	85.57	12.94	25.14	***	3>2; 1>2
AAS	70.44	23.91	57.05	11.28	95.71	30.98	17.35	***	3>1>2
APS	59.73	10.52	55.55	10.04	65.86	12.14	32.67	***	3>2

*p<0.05; **p<0.01; ***p<0.001. ANX=Anxiety; FRS=Fears; OBS=Obsessiveness; DEP=Depression; HEA=Health Concerns; BIZ=Bizarre Mentation; ANG=Anger; CYN=Cynicism; ASP=Antisocial Practices; TPA=Type A Behavior; LSE=Low Self-Esteem; SOD=Social Discomfort; FAM=Family Problems; WRK=Work Interference; TRT=Negative Treatment Indicators; A=Anxiety; R=Repression; Es=Ego Strength; MAC-R=MacAndrew Alcoholism Scale; Ho=Hostility; O-H=Overcontrolled Hostility; Do=Dominance; Re=Social Responsibility; Mt=College Maladjustment; GM=Masculine Gender Role; GF=Feminine Gender Role; PK=Posttraumatic Stress Disorder; MDS=Marital Distress Scale; AAS=Addiction Acknowledgement Scale; APS=Addiction Potential Scale.

CONCLUSION

In this chapter, we demonstrated evidence for the existence and clinical relevance of an impulsive cluster of personality functioning (labeled Undercontrolled) in a heterogeneous inpatient population, using a clustering approach as opposed to a dimensional one. Starting from a personality prototype perspective, we conceptualized Impulsivity as a combination of high Neuroticism, low Agreeableness and low Conscientiousness, and were able to replicate the well-known Personality Prototypes (Overcontrollers, Undercontrollers and Resilients) in a heterogeneous inpatient population. This by means of the DAPP-BQ as a measure of maladaptive variants of the FFM dimensions, as opposed to the classic FFM measures. Additionally, we demonstrated that these personality prototypes reflected significant clinical differences.

Patients of the Impulsive, Undercontrolled cluster reported being maladjusted and overwhelmed by problems just like Overcontrollers, but exhibited even higher (the highest, in fact) levels of psychopathology (MMPI-2 F) and manifest symptoms (MMPI-2 Fb). Next to experiencing more serious problems than the other two groups, they also displayed the strongest appeal for help by overreporting the problems experienced (Fp). At the same time, Undercontrollers showed the most negative attitude towards treatment, not so much because of a reluctance or even perceived inability to disclose personal information (TRT 1; which they shared with Overcontrollers) but because of low motivation (TRT 2). This seemingly contradictory configuration represents a well-known, but challenging paradox for the psychotherapist, who has to walk a tightrope between taking over all responsibility and eliciting experienced rejection by identifying the patient as being merely manipulative. Indeed, with their highest F-score Undercontrollers are also associated with more chronic pathology classification as reported by Cukrowicz, Reardon, Donohue, and Joiner (2004).

Patients in the Overcontrolled cluster differed from Undercontrollers in their significantly lower scores on the externalizing/acting-out scales (Pd, Ma). These differences were not attributable to state-dependent effects of Demoralization (DEM), but represented valid trait-like features (RC4, RC9). Interestingly, Overcontrollers showed Antisocial Attitudes (ASP1) just as well as Undercontrollers (both differing from Resilients), but appeared to be far less inclined to act upon them (ASP2). In fact, Overcontrollers did not differ from Resilients on the latter. Importantly, we did not find Overcontrollers to exhibit more internalizing pathology than Undercontrollers, just less externalizing.

Resilients (who showed no normative elevations) differed from both Overcontrollers as well as Undercontrollers in two ways. Firstly, by their lower scores on virtually all clinical scales mapping psychopathology. Secondly, by their higher scores on the positive personality scales Ego-Strength, Dominance and Social Responsibility. As the concept of Resilience embodies personality traits that can serve as a buffer in times of adversity, rather than merely the absence of psychopathology, this last finding is of specific interest regarding the validation of the cluster.

In general, scale patterns showed elevations on internalizing scales in both Overcontrollers and Undercontrollers, additional elevations on the acting-out, externalizing pathology in the Undercontrolled group, and the overall absence of pathology and the presence of positive personality traits in the Resilient group. Conceptually, one might associate the foregoing with the historic, but still present-day (Eurelings-Bontekoe, Luyten, Ijssennagger, van Vreeswijk, & Koelen, 2010; Eurelings-Bontekoe, Peen, Noteboom, Alkema, & Dekker, 2012) idea of acting-out of aggression in impulsive borderline pathology, the overcontrol of aggression in neurotic pathology and the absence of both problems and presence of good reality testing, confidence in self and others and good interpersonal skills in more high-functioning personalities. Or, in a more contemporary paradigm, the idea of a severe level of impairment (representing little remaining possibilities for mentalization and thus acting upon momentarily experienced emotions), a moderate to mild level of impairment (relating to constraint in expression of strong emotions because of their distressing nature), and a healthy level of personality functioning (tolerating and self-regulating a full range of emotions and showing adequate self-direction), as advocated in Section III of the Diagnostic and Statistical manual of Mental disorders, fifth edition (DSM-5; APA, 2013).

An additional demographic finding of interest is the significantly lower mean age of the Undercontrolled group compared to the Overcontrolled and the Resilient group, for which several possible post-hoc explanations are conceivable. One might be that Undercontrollers run a greater risk of hospital admission earlier in life, due to the specifically dysfunctional nature of their pathology. Indeed, at least in eating disorders Thompson-Brenner and Westen (2005) found that patients belonging to the Dysregulated/Undercontrolled personality subtype show the highest rate of prior psychiatric hospitalizations, followed by Constricted/Overcontrolled and High-functioning patients respectively. Prior to this, also in eating disorders, Westen and Harnden-Fischer (2001) found that, unlike axis I categorization, classification by personality cluster (high-functioning/perfectionistic versus constricted/overcontrolled versus emotionally dysregulated/undercontrolled) strongly predicted history of psychiatric hospitalization. However, as data on possible previous hospital admissions per patient were not available in current study, it might just as well be that we caught the patients belonging to the Overcontrolled and the Resilient cluster at their second or third time of hospitalization. Yet another explanation might be that the mean age difference reflects a cohort effect representing an increase of Undercontrolled, impulsive borderline-like pathology over Overcontrolled, so-called neurotic pathology, as advocated by some authors (Verhaeghe, 2009).

There are important limitations to the current study. First, the current sample is to be regarded as limited. Further research in larger general psychiatric samples is warranted in order to investigate replication. Second, in analyzing the results, DSM-diagnoses were not taken into account. Further research in larger samples including descriptive diagnosis can clarify to what degree personality prototyping coincides with descriptive DSM-diagnoses. Notwithstanding the former, Impulsivity could be thought of as a notion central to the personality prototype model, contrasting Undercontrollers with Overcontrollers in their respective abundance versus problematic shortage of it.

REFERENCES

Akse, J., Hale, B., Engels, R., Raaijmakers, Q. & Meeus, W. (2007). Co-occurrence of depression and delinquency in personality types. *European Journal of Personality*, *21*, 235–256.

American Psychiatric Association. (2013). *Diagnostic and statistical manual of mental disorders* (5th ed.). Arlington, VA: Author.

Arbisi, P. A. & Ben-Porath, Y. S. (1995). An MMPI–2 infrequent response scale for use with psychopathological populations: The Infrequency-Psychopathology scale, F(p). *Psychological Assessment*, *7*, 424–431.

Archer, R. P., Handel, R. W., Greene, R. L., Baer, R. A. & Elkins, D. E. (2001). An evaluation of the effectiveness of the MMPI-2 F(p) scale. *Journal of Personality Assessment*, *76*, 282-293.

Asendorpf, J. B., Borkenau, P., Ostendorf, F. & Van Aken, M. A. G. (2001). Carving personality description at its joints: Confirmation of three replicable personality prototypes for both children and adults. *European Journal of Personality*, *15*, 169–198.

Berry, J. W., Elliott, T. R. & Rivera, P. (2007). Resilient, Undercontrolled, and Overcontrolled Personality Prototypes Among Persons With Spinal Cord Injury. *Journal of Personality Assessment*, *87*, 292-302.

Block, J. H. & Block, J. (1980). The role of ego-control and ego-resiliency in the organization of behavior. In W.A. Collins (Ed.), *Minnesota Symposium on Child Psychology* (pp. 39-101). Hillsdale, NJ: Erlbaum.

Butcher, J. N., Graham, J. R., Ben-Porath, Y. S. Tellegen, A. , Dahlstrom, W. G. & Kaemmer, B. (2001). *Minnesota Multiphasic Personality Inventory-2 (MMPI-2): Manual for administration and scoring*. Minneapolis: University of Minnesota Press.

Butcher, J. N., Dahlstrom, W. G., Graham, J. R., Tellegen, A. & Kaemmer, B. (1989). *MMPI–2: Manual for administering and scoring*. Minneapolis: University of Minnesota Press.

Butcher, J. N., Graham, J. R., Williams, C. L. & Ben-Porath, Y. S. (1990). *Development and use of the MMPI—2 content scales.* Minneapolis: University of Minnesota Press.

Claes, L., Tavernier, G., Roose, A., Bijttebier, P., Smith, S., Lilienfeld, S. (2013). Identifying personality subtypes based on the Five Factor Model dimensions in male prisoners: Implications for psychopathy and criminal offending. *International Journal of Offender Therapy and Comparative Criminology*, in press.

Claes, L., Vandereycken, W., Luyten, P., Soenens, B., Pieters,G. & Vertommen, H. (2006). Personality Prototypes in Eating Disorders Based on the Big Five Model. *Journal of Personality Disorders*, *20*, 401-416.

Claes, L, Vandereycken, W., Vandeputte, A. & Braet, C. (2013). Personality Subtypes in Female Pre-Bariatric Obese Patients: Do They Differ in Eating Disorder Symptoms, Psychological Complaints and Coping Behaviour? *European Eating Disorders Review*, *21*, 72-77.

Costa, P. T., Jr. & McCrae, R. R. (1985). *The NEO personality inventory manual.* Odessa, FL: Psychological Assessment Resources.

Costa, P. T. & McCrae, R. R. (1992). The Five-Factor Model of Personality and its relevance to personality disorders. *Journal of Personality Disorders*, *6*, 343-359.

Cukrowicz, K. C., Reardon, M. L., Donohue, K. F. & Joiner, T. E. (2004). MMPI-2 F scale as a predictor of acute versus chronic disorder classification. *Assessment*, *11*, 145-51.

Eurelings-Bontekoe, E. H. M., Luyten, P., Ijssennagger, M., van Vreeswijk, M. & Koelen, J. (2010). Relationship between personality organization and Young's cognitive model of personality pathology. *Personality and Individual Differences*, *49*, 198-203.

Eurelings-Bontekoe, E. H. M, Peen, J., Noteboom, A., Alkema, M. & Dekker, J. (2012). Differential Treatment Response of Subtypes of Patients With Borderline Personality Organization, as Assessed With Theory-Driven Profiles of the Dutch Short Form of the MMPI: A Naturalistic Follow-Up Study. *Journal of Personality Assessment*, *94*, 380–392.

Fowler, K. A. & Westen, D. (2011). Subtyping Male Perpetrators of Intimate Partner Violence. Journal of Interpersonal Violence, *26*, 607-639.

Gazzillo, F., Lingiardi, V., Peloso, A., Giordani, S., Vesco, S., Zanna, V., Filippucci, L. & Vicari, S. (2013). Personality subtypes in adolescents with anorexia nervosa. *Comprehensive Psychiatry*, *54*, 702–712.

Goldner, E. M., Srikameswaran S., Schroeder, M. L., Livesley, W. J. & Birmingham, C. L. (1999). Dimensional assessment of personality pathology in patients with eating disorders. *Psychiatry Research*, *85*, 151-159.

Graham, J. R. (2006). *MMPI-2: assessing personality an psychopathology. Fourth edition.* New York: Oxford University Press.

Graña, J. L., Muñoz, J. J. & Navas, E. (2009). Normal and pathological personality characteristics in subtypes of drug addicts undergoing treatment. *Personality and Individual Differences*, *46*, 418–423.

Grumm, M. & von Collani, G. (2009). Personality types and self-reported aggressiveness. *Personality and Individual Differences*, *47*, 845-850.

Hathaway, S. R. & McKinley, J. C. (1951). *Minnesota multiphasic personality inventory: manual revised.* New York: Psychological corporation.

Krueger, R. F., Eaton, N. R., Clark, L. A., Watson, D., Markon, K. E., Derringer, J. Skodol, A. & Livesley, W. J. (2011). Deriving an empirical structure of personality pathology for DSM-5. *Journal of Personality Disorders, 25*, 170-191.

Kushner, S. C., Quilty, L. C., Tackett, J. L. & Bagby, R. M. (2011). The hierarchical structure of the Dimensional Assessment of Personality Pathology (DAPP-BQ). *Journal of Personality Disorders, 25*, 504-516.

Livesley, W. J. & Jackson, D. N. (2009). *Manual for the Dimensional Assessment of Personality Pathology – Basic Questionnaire (DAPP-BQ)*. Port Huron, MI: Sigma Press.

Livesley, W. J. (2001). Conceptual and taxonomic issues. In W. J. Livesley (Ed.), *Hanbook of personality disorders. Theory, research, and treatment* (pp. 3-38). New York: Guilford.

Livesley, W. J., Jang, K. L. & Vernon, P. A. (1998). Phenotypic and genetic structure of traits delineating personality disorder. *Archives of General Psychiatry, 55*, 941-948.

Lynam, D. R. (2012). Assessment of Maladaptive Variants of Five-Factor Model Traits. *Journal of Personality, 80*, 1593–1613.

Mertz, E. L. & Roesch, S. C. (2012). A latent profile analysis of the Five Factor Model of personality: Modelling trait interactions. *Personality and Individual Differences, 51, 915-919.*

Pukrop, R., Steinbring, I., Gentil, I., Schulte, C., Larstone, R. & Livesley, J. W. (2009). Clinical validity of the dimensional assessment of personality pathology (DAPP) for psychiatric patients with and without a personality disorder diagnosis. *Journal of Personality Disorders, 23*, 572-586.

Sellbaum, M. & Ben-Porath, Y. S. (2005). Mapping the MMPI-2 Restuctured Clinical Scales onto normal personality traits: evidence of construct validity. *Journal of Personality Assessment, 85*, 179-187.

Steiger, H., Richardson, J., Schmitz, N., Joober, R., Israel, M., Bruce, K. R., Gauvin, L., Dandurand, C., Anestin, A. (2009). Association of trait-defined, eating-disorder subphenotypes with (biallelic and triallelic) 5HTTLPR variations. *Journal of Psychiatric Research, 43*, 1086-1094.

Tellegen, A., Ben-Porath, Y. S., McNulty, J., Arbisi, P., Graham, J. R. & Kaemmer, B. (2003). *MMPI-2:Restructured clinical (RC) scales.* Minneapolis: University of Minnesota Press.

Thompson-Brenner, H. & Westen, D. (2005). Personality subtypes in eating disorders: validation of a classification in a naturalistic sample. *the British Journal of Psychiatry, 186*, 516-524.

van Kampen, D. (2002). The DAPP-BQ in the Netherlands: Factor structure and relationship with basic personality dimensions. *Journal of Personality Disorders, 16*, 235-254.

van Kampen, D. (2006). The Dutch DAPP-BQ: Improvements, lower- and higher-order dimensions, and relatiionship with the 5DPT. *Journal of Personality Disorders, 20*, 81-101.

van Kampen, D. & de Beurs, E. (2009). *DAPP-BQ Handleiding.* Amsterdam: Hogrefe.

Verhaeghe, P. (2009). *Het einde van de psychotherapie*. Amsterdam: De Bezig Bij.

Verheul, R. & Widiger T. (2009). Dimensionale modellen van persoonlijkheidspathologie. In E.H.M. Eurelings-Bontekoe, R. Verheul, & W. M. Snellen (Eds.), *Handboek persoonlijkheidspathologie* (pp. 181-200). Houten: Bohn Stafleu van Loghum.

Westen, D. & Harnden-Fischer, J. (2001). Personality Profiles in Eating Disorders: Rethinking the Distinction Between Axis I and Axis II. *American Journal of Psychiatry, 158*, 547–562.

Wildes, J. E. & Marcus, M. D. (2013). Alternative methods of classifying eating disorders: Models incorporating comorbid psychopathology and associated features. *Clinical Psychology Review, 33*, 383–394.

Wonderlich, S. A., Crosby, R. D., Engel, S. G., Mitchell, J. E., Smyth, J. & Miltenberger R. (2007). Personality-Based Clusters in Bulimia Nervosa: Differences in Clinical Variables and Ecological Momentary Assessment. *Journal of Personality Disorders, 21*, 340-357.

Wonderlich, S. A., Crosby, R. D., Joiner, T., Peterson, C. B., Bardone-Cone, A., Klein, M., Crow, S., Mitchell, J. E., Le Grange, D., Steiger, H., Kolden, G., Johnson, F. & Vrshek, S. (2005). Personality subtyping and bulimia nervosa: psychopathological and genetic correlates. *Psychological Medicine, 5*, 649-657.

APPENDIX A

Higher order factors of DAPP-BQ and NEO-PI

instrument	factor I	factor II	factor III	factor IV	factor V
DAPP-BQ	Emotional Dysregulation	Inhibition	Dissocial	Compulsivity	/
NEO-PI	Neuroticism	Extraversion	Agreeableness	Conscientiousness	Openness

In: Psychology of Impulsivity
Editor: Mary C. Olmstead

ISBN: 978-1-63321-879-6

Chapter 4

DIFFERENTIAL ROLE OF IMPULSIVITY IN ADOLESCENTS' SUICIDAL BEHAVIOR WITH BORDERLINE PERSONALITY DISORDER AND MAJOR DEPRESSION

Daniel Serrani Azcurra*
Faculty of Psychology, National University of Rosario, Argentina

ABSTRACT

The objective of the study was to examine the differential role of impulsivity in suicidal behavior attempts among adolescents with borderline personality disorder (BPD) and major depressive disorder (MDD).

Seventy eight adolescents were recruited for the research, of whom thirty-nine had BPD and the rest had MDD. Among participants who had exhibited a recent suicidal attempt, 18 belonged to the BPD group and 16 to the MDD.

Assessments were made with the Barratt Impulsiveness Scale, the Diagnostic Interview Schedule for Children, the Deliberate Self-harm Inventory, the Beck Depression Inventory, the Beck Hopelessness Scale, the Beck Hopelessness Scale, the Multidimensional Anger Inventory and the Lifetime History of Aggression

Results showed that the adolescents with BPD had more anger, aggression, and impulsiveness than those with MDD, but similar levels of depression and hopelessness. Suicidal versus non-suicidal adolescents were more depressed, hopeless, and aggressive, but not more angry or impulsive. There were no significant differences in impulsiveness for the MDD suicidal group versus the MDD non-suicidal group, but the suicidal BPD adolescents were significantly more impulsive than the non-suicidal BPD adolescents.

In the participants with BPD, impulsiveness and aggression correlated significantly and positively with suicidal behavior, but no such associations were found in the participants with MDD. In both diagnostic groups, depression and hopelessness, but not anger, had a positive association with suicidal behavior. The suicidal participants with MDD had significantly higher suicidal intent scores than the suicidal adolescents with BPD.

* Corresponding author: danielserrani@argentina.com, Address: Estanislao Zeballos 1625 (S2000BQG). Argentina.

As a conclusion it seems that suicidal behavior in adolescents with BPD and MDD shares a common basis related to hopelessness but impulsivity trait plays a differential role in those participants with BPD, apart from those with MDD. These features may help to differentiate suicidal risk behavior in adolescents with BPD and MDD, and implement predictive and protective measures.

INTRODUCTION

Affective disorders are usually associated with high rates of suicide attempts (SA) and related behaviors, which in turn raise important public health concerns, particularly in adolescent populations. Recent data show that suicide is the third leading cause of death for youth between the ages of 10 and 24 (CDC, 2008). Given the costs, both in terms of lost productivity (Corso et al., 2007) and the emotional trauma suffered by surviving family, friends, and communities (Cerel et al., 2008), the identification of markers of impending suicide attempts and related behaviors which could aid in prevention and intervention efforts is important to undertake.

However, the same suicide risks may threaten adolescents suffering from major depressive disorders (MDD) (Rohde et al., 2013). For instance, it has been estimated that the rate of suicide attempts in MDD patients is two times higher than in the general population (Lamers et al., 2012). Not all patients suffering from MDD actually attempt suicide. Additional factors must therefore play a role in increasing the suicide risk in these clinical populations. Impulsivity has been strongly suggested as a risk or predisposing factor for suicide attempts, acting either independently or in conjunction with aggressive and/or anxious traits (Hawton et al., 2012).

Accordingly, impulsivity should be more pronounced in mood disorder patients who have made one or more suicide attempts than in those other patients who never displayed such behavior (Carpiniello et al., 2011). This relationship must also be somehow independent of the nature of the underlying disorder, as it has been observed that impulsive behavior is commonly associated with borderline personality disorder (BPD), a condition characterized by recurrent depressive episodes and repeated suicide attempts (Leichsenring et al., 2011). In some research studies (Yen et al., 2013), BPD washes out the effects of MDD for both suicidal behavior and suicide attempts.

Despite such findings, few studies of suicide-related behaviors in adolescents have explicitly examined or controlled for BPD (Derbidge et al., 2014). This is somewhat surprising as the suicide rate for BPD patients (8-10%) is as high as many of the other major mental disorders (Sharp et al., 2012). The risk factors for suicidal behavior in young patients with BPD are previous suicide attempts, impulsiveness, antisocial personality, higher education, and depressive mood (Hankin & Abela, 2011). People with BPD are classically characterized by both aggressive and suicidal behavior. This suicidal behavior seems to be related to emotional dysregulation and problems with aggression and impulse control (Crowell et al., 2012).

From this perspective, the present study aims to compare impulsivity and aggressive traits in controls and in patients with either BPD or MDD, according to their previous history of suicide attempts. We expected that patients suffering from affective liability such as BPD would display higher impulsivity than controls. It was also hypothesized that participants with a history of suicide attempts would have higher impulsivity levels, compared to those who never attempted suicide.

We also examined if impulsivity would be as pronounced in MDD as in BPD suicide attempters. In other words, do BPD patients, particularly with a history of suicide attempts, show higher impulsivity scores than MDD patients? We finally investigated the possibility that the correlation between impulsive and aggressive traits could be a better marker for suicide risk than either trait alone.

METHODS

Participants

The sample included 78 adolescents admitted to an Adolescent Treatment Program of an outpatient community care facility specializing in the evaluation and stabilization of adolescents who had failed to respond to previous usual interventions. Adolescents were between the ages of 17 and 21 years (*M* age = 19.47; *SD* = 1.45). All patients received a comprehensive psychiatric evaluation at intake. There were 50 girls and 28 boys. All the patients came from middle-class backgrounds, most of them Hispanics and Caucasians.

Of the sample, 39 participants were diagnosed as suffering from BPD (26 girls and 13 boys). Eighteen of these participants had made a recent (first ever) suicide attempt and the rest had never attempted suicide during their lifetime. *Recent* was defined as being within 30 days of the assessment. Nine of the participants with BPD also met criteria for MDD, 11 had dysthymic disorder, 3 met criteria for conduct disorder and 11 received a concomitant diagnosis of anxiety disorder.

There were no differences in the distribution of co-morbid diagnoses between the suicidal and non-suicidal participants with BPD. Thirty-nine participants (34 girls and 5 boys) met DSM-IV criteria for MDD. Sixteen had made a recent (first ever) suicide attempt and 23 had never made a suicide attempt during their lifetime. None of the patients with MDD had BPD or any other significant co-morbidity except anxiety disorder, generalized sub-type.

There were no significant statistical differences among BPD and MDD patients in gender (p=.76), age (p=.32), thoughts of death or dying (p=.54), suicidal ideation in the past month (p=.63), suicide plan (p=.52) or lifetime suicide attempt (p=.33). Exclusion criteria were as follows: co-morbid diagnosis of substance abuse, schizophrenia or any psychotic disorder; an IQ < 70 or mental retardation; lack of comprehension of instructions; or an inability to provide informed consent either by the patient or their parents.

Patients were selected based on date of admission (consecutive admissions from May 2012 to May 2013) and their ability to consent to participate. Three participants who refused to participate in the study were not included. Attempted suicide was defined according to the criteria of the International Classification of Diseases 10th Edition (ICD-10) as "an act with nonfatal outcome, in which an individual deliberately initiates non-habitual behavior that, without intervention from others, will cause self harm, or deliberately ingests a substance in excess of the prescribed or generally recognized therapeutic dosage, and which is aimed at realizing changes which the subject desired via the actual or expected physical consequences" (Schmidtke A, Bille-Brahe et al., 1996). The study protocol was approved by the Local ethics committee of the University and participants were recruited after informed written consent was obtained.

Assessment

Barratt Impulsiveness Scale

The Barratt Impulsiveness Scale (BIS-10) is a psychometric measure of impulsivity with a multidimensional structure, generally separated into three components: motor (behavior), attentional (cognitive), and non-planning (Patton, 1995).

Diagnostic Interview Schedule for Children

The Diagnostic Interview Schedule for Children (DISC) (Shaffer et al., 2000) includes an assessment of suicidal behaviors, used to form the following binary variables: (a) thoughts of death or dying (without specific thoughts of suicide) during the past year, (b) suicidal ideation during the past year, (c) suicidal ideation and a plan (e.g., method, place, time) to commit suicide during the past year, (d) recent suicide ideation in the past four weeks, (e) suicide attempt in the past year, and (f) lifetime suicide attempt. The DISC was administered to adolescents, since research has demonstrated stronger validity for adolescent report of suicidal behaviors compared with parent report (Prinstein et al., 2001). Patients with values of 4 or 5, *i.e.*, who had made a definite recent suicide attempt, were classified as suicidal. Those with scores lower than 4 and who reported having never made a suicide attempt in their lifetime were classified as non-suicidal.

Self-Harm Behavior

The Deliberate Self-harm Inventory (DSHI) is a 17-item self-report measure that assesses the frequency, severity, duration, and type of self-harm behavior. The DSHI has high internal consistency ($\alpha = .82$); adequate construct, convergent, and discriminate validity; and adequate test-retest reliability over a 2–4 week period. Internal consistency in this sample was good with a Cronbach's alpha of .76 (Gratz, 2001).

Beck Depression Inventory

The well known Beck Depression Inventory (BDI) consists of 21 items related to symptoms of depression. The scoring is based on a Likert scale, with 12 items with 4 points, eight with 5 points, and one with 6 points. Scoring is based on the average score of each item times the number of items. The range of scores is thus 21 to 94 (Beck & Steer, 1987).

Beck Hopelessness Scale

The well known Beck Hopelessness Scale (BHS) measures hopelessness and has 20 items. The range is 0 to 20. Internal consistency in the present study was .90 (Beck et al., 1974).

Multidimensional Anger Inventory

The original form of the Multidimensional Anger Inventory (MAI) questionnaire was 38 items. We used a short form with 24 items. The internal consistency of the scale is reported to be .84. In this study, it was .87. Answers are given on a 5-point Likert scale. The scale describes anger as a trait that usually characterizes the person. The scale consists of four factors: those related to intensity, duration, and frequency of angry feelings; those related to a range of situations that may elicit anger; a factor called *hostile outlook*, and a factor related to how anger is expressed. Two subscales from this instrument were also calculated: anger in and anger out. Anger in (6 items) is related to anger that remains contained. The scale measures fear of expressing anger and the tendency to block or delay expressions of anger. Anger out (6 items), measures ways in which anger is directly expressed toward others. The Chronbach's alpha of both scales is higher than 0.8. The scale gives a range of 24 to 120 (Siegal, 1986).

Lifetime History of Aggression (LHA)

It is a nine-item interview assessing lifetime aggressive behaviors in adolescence and adulthood. In this study, internal consistency was .85 (Brown et al., 1979).

PROCEDURE

All participants were interviewed within 1 month of admission, confirming that all suicide attempts had been made during the month before the assessment.

Borderline Personality Disorder

To determine a diagnosis of BPD in adolescents, the child interview for DSM-IV borderline personality disorder (CI-BPD) (Zanarini, 2003) was used. The CI-BPD is a semi-structured interview that assesses DSM-IV BPD in children age six and older, as well as adolescents. It was adapted for use in children and adolescents from the Diagnostic Interview for DSM-IV Personality Disorders. After asking a series of corresponding questions, the interviewer rates each DSM-based criterion with a score of 0 (absent), 1 (probably present), or 2 (definitely present). The patient meets criteria for BPD if five or more criteria are met at the 2-level. The CI-BPD demonstrated adequate inter-rater reliability in the original validation study.

In the current sample, inter-rater reliability was performed on 15% of the sample, with two independent raters trained by the principal investigator of the study. The results of the inter-rater analyses and the original diagnosis varied from Kappa = .78 ($p < .001$) to Kappa = 1.00 ($p < .001$), with the average Kappa = .89. Internal consistency was good with a Cronbach's alpha of .83. To avoid a potential confound between the independent (BPD) and dependent variables (suicide-related behaviors), we excluded the self-harm/suicide item/criterion of the CI-BPD in our analyses.

We used the Borderline Features of the Personality Assessment Inventory for Adolescents (Morey, 2007) To assess borderline symptoms dimensionally, The PAI is a self-report measure of personality traits for use with adolescents ages 12 to 18. It contains 264 items rated on a four-point scale ranging from false to very true. The Borderline Features subscale produces a standardized continuous measure of personality traits typically characterizing BPD. Of importance to the current study is the fact that the subscale does not contain any suicide-related items, thereby avoiding confounding the independent (BPD) and dependent (suicide-related) variables.

Major Depressive Disorder

For a categorical diagnosis of MDD, the clinician- administered computerized NIMH-Diagnostic Interview Schedule for Children-IV (Shaffer et al., 2000) was used. The CDISC is one of the most widely used diagnostic instruments for children and adolescents. It covers DSM-IV, DSMIII-R, and ICD-10, for over 30 diagnoses. The interview is organized into six diagnostic sections: anxiety disorders, mood disorders, disruptive disorders, substance-use disorders, schizophrenia, and miscellaneous disorders (eating, elimination, and so on).

Within each section, each disorder is assessed for presence within the past year and currently (last four weeks). For the purposes of the current study, we used the current definition of depression. Depressive symptoms were assessed continuously using the Youth Self Report (Achenbach & Rescorla, 2001). The YSR is a self-report questionnaire for use with adolescents between the ages of 12 and 18. The measure contains 112 problem items, each scored on a three-point scale (0 = not true, 1 = somewhat or sometimes true, or 2 = very or often true). The measure yields a number of scales, some empirically derived (the Syndrome Scales) and some theoretically based (the DSM-Oriented Scales).

Table 1. Demographic and clinical characteristic of MDD and BPD participants

	BPD (n=39)	**MDD (n=39)**	**MDD vs. BPD**
	Mean (SEM)	**Mean (SEM)**	***F*(2,74) *p*<.001**
Age	19.02(1.43)	19.67 (1.21)	0.32
Gender F/m)	26/13	34/5	0.76
%thoughts of death / dying	47	41	0.54
%suicidal ideation, past month	45	44	0.63
%suicide plan	32	35	0.52
%lifetime suicide attempt	39	38	0.33
DSHI	6.32(1.21)	3.32(1.11)	0.003
YSR Affective Problems	71.43(9.56)	76.12 (9.84)	0.04
PAI-A	76.34 (10.32)	64.23(10.01)	0.08
BIS-10			
Total	64.12(9.86)	52.89(12.19)	0.002
Non-planning	27.12(4.87)	21.73(9.23)	0.002
Motor	23.43(7.21)	19.32(5.98)	0.001
Attentional	27.98(9.91)	21.76(10.52)	0.009
LHA	29.98(9.66)	18.82(6.98)	0.001
MAI	49.90(21.10)	40.53(11.35)	0.003
BDI	12.43(5.76)	14.23(11.32)	0.032
BHS	10.63(6.34)	11.32(5.32)	0.051

Note. BIS-10 = Barratt Impulsiveness scale; DSHI = Deliberate Self-Harm Inventory; YSR = Youth Self-Report; PAI-A = Personality Assessment Inventory for Adolescents, MAI = multidimensional anger inventory; BSI = Beck depression inventory; BHS = Beck Hopelessness scale.

The DSM Oriented Affective Problems scale was used in this study as a continuous measure of self-reported depressive symptoms. In previous studies (Van Lang et al., 2005). There is a strong correlation with the YSR Affective Problems scale and the MDD scale of the Revised Child Anxiety and Depression Scale (Chorpita et al., 2000). In a similar way, other authors have found support for convergent validity with positive, significant correlations of the Affective Problems subscale with several well-established dimensional measures of youth depression (Nakamura et al., 2009).

An experienced clinician administered the questionnaires in random order during the first 2 weeks of outpatient treatment.

Statistical Analysis

Data were analyzed with 2 x 2 multivariate analysis of variance (MANOVA), to compare diagnostic (BPD vs MDD) and suicidal versus non-suicidal groups. Simple Main Effect analysis was used to assess interactions, and Pearson coefficients were used for correlational analysis.

Results

Table 1 presents the comparison of adolescents diagnosed with BPD and MDD on all measures of depression (BDI), hopelessness (BHS), aggression (LHA), anger (MAI), and impulsivity (BIS).

A 2 x 2 MANOVA analysis showed a significant difference between the two diagnostic groups (Wilks' Lambda = .73, $F[3,75] = 8.31$, $p = .001$). When the comparisons were made for each of the variables separately, the differences occurred mainly in the aggression related variables, that is, anger, aggression, and impulsiveness. There were no significant differences between the two groups on levels of depression and hopelessness (Table 1).

The comparison of the suicidal versus non-suicidal adolescents on the same variables using MANOVA also showed significant differences (Wilks' Lambda = 50, $F[3,75] = 18.76$, $p = .001$). When comparing each variable, depression and hopelessness were higher in the suicidal than in the non-suicidal group. Suicidal adolescents were more aggressive, but not more angry or impulsive, than the non-suicidal adolescents.

When interactions were analyzed, a significant interaction was found for impulsiveness (BIS-10) and suicide and diagnosis ($F[3,75] = 5.57$, $p = .004$). Thus, there were no significant differences in impulsiveness for the depressed suicidal group versus the depressed non-suicidal group ($F[2,27] = 2.11$, $p = 0.14$), but the suicidal BPD adolescents were significantly more impulsive than the non-suicidal BPD adolescents ($F[2,24] = 3.58$, $p = .005$). None of the other variables measured (anger, aggression, depression, and hopelessness) showed significant interactions between suicidal behavior and diagnosis. Only the on anger sub-scale reliably separated suicidal from non-suicidal adolescents ($F[1,23] = 3.57$, $p = .05$). While the anger out sub-scale was higher (mean, 25.26; SD, 8.46) in the non-suicidal group compared with the suicidal one (mean, 17.01; SD, 3.91), the anger in sub-scale was higher in the suicidal, compared with non-suicidal participants. However, no interaction with diagnostic group was found. Outward anger sub-scale had higher scores for BPD group (mean, 16.49; SD, 5.22; versus mean, 11.21; SD, 3.86 for MDD; $F[1,24] = 11.57$, $p = .001$). Pearson correlations between scores on the DISC and the other measures showed that in BPD participants, impulsiveness (BIS-10) and aggression (LHA) correlated significantly and positively with suicidal behavior, but not in MDD participants. Both diagnostic groups exhibited a robust correlation between depression (BDI) and hopelessness (BHS), but not anger (MAI) and suicidal behavior (Table 3).

A Fisher z-score analysis showed the difference in correlation to be significant for impulsiveness ($z = 3.21$, $p = .001$) and for aggression ($z = 2.71$, $p = .05$). When considering lifetime suicide attempt, suicidal MDD had significantly higher scores than the suicidal BPD (MDD: mean, 19.2; SD, 3.25; versus BPD: mean, 11.7; SD, 5.16; $t(28) = 3.57$; $p = .01$).

Table 2. Comparison between suicidal and non-suicidal adolescents in impulsivity, self harm, anger, depression and hopelessness traits

	Suicidal adolescents (n=34)	Non-suicidal adolescents(n=44)	$F(2,77)$ $p<.001$
	Mean (SEM)	Mean (SEM)	
DSHI	6.21(1.31)	3.26(1.00)	.003
BIS-10			
Total	56.31(8.74)	53.31(11.27)	.62
Non-planning	26.21(4.74)	24.65(9.41)	.56
Motor	21.35(7.15)	19.51(5.58)	.98
Attentional	26.47(9.28)	24.48(11.43)	.19
LHA	31.21(9.47)	17.28(4.71)	.001
MAI	49.90(21.10)	43.53(11.35)	.34
BDI	14.56(6.86)	7.15(12.31)	.002
BHS	11.76(2.17)	8.21(3.91)	.001

Note. BIS-10 = Barratt Impulsiveness scale; DSHI = Deliberate Self-Harm Inventory; YSR = Youth Self-Report; PAI-A = Personality Assessment Inventory for Adolescents, MAI = multidimensional anger inventory; BSI = Beck depression inventory; BHS = Beck Hopelessness scale.

Table 3. Pearson correlation between variables and diagnostic groups

	MDD non-suicidal	MDD suicidal	BPD non-suicidal	BPD suicidal
DSHI	.33	.35	.36	.47
BIS-10	.27	.32	.45	.76***
LHA	.35	.47	.56*	.71**
MAI	-.32	-.22	-.37	-.18
BDI	.67*	.69*	.72*	.77***
BHS	.24	.56	.32	.68**

Note. BIS-10 = Barratt Impulsiveness scale; DSHI = Deliberate Self-Harm Inventory; YSR = Youth Self-Report; PAI-A = Personality Assessment Inventory for Adolescents, MAI = multidimensional anger inventory; BSI = Beck depression inventory; BHS = Beck Hopelessness scale.

***p<.001, ** p<.01, *p<.05 (two-tailed test)

Conclusion

According to our hypothesis, suicidal behavior and concomitant impulsivity traits exhibited some subtle differences between suicidal BPD and MDD participants. In fact, aggressive and impulsive drives tended to become more overt in BPD whereas depression and hopelessness where more common in MDD, even without suicide attempts. Trait impulsivity was elevated in BPD participants whether they had suicide attempts or not. MDD participants only scored high on BIS-10 if they had suicide attempts. Severe lifetime aggressive behaviors were displayed by suicide attempters and non-attempters in both diagnostic groups.

BPD participants were high in outward aggression and the opposite proved true for MDD. Finally, suicide attempters, whether suffering from a BPD or MDD, showed a strong correlation between impulsive and aggressive traits. Trait impulsivity has already been associated with BPD and MDD. In fact, impulsivity/aggression have been associated with impaired decision making, which in turn lowers barriers and defenses against suicide attempts (Bridge, et al., 2012).

Impulsivity and aggressive traits have been associated, not only with vulnerability to suicidal behavior across diagnoses, but also with structural and functional abnormalities in brain networks involved in the regulation of mood and executive function, including impulsivity (Soloff et al., 2014).

Moreover, lethality of suicide attempts was highly positively correlated with impulsivity (assessed by the BIS-10), aggression (evaluated with the LHA), and negatively correlated with gray matter volume across multiple fronto-temporal–limbic regions. Recently, elevated BIS scores were also reported in depressed BD and MDD patients compared to controls, but impulsivity appeared to be less independent of mood state in MDD than in BD participants (Perroud et al., 2011).

Recent work on impulsivity and self-injurious behaviors, including non-suicidal self-injury and suicide attempts, has showed that in depressed patients, suicide is more related to guilt and self-punishment, while in patients with BPD, the meaning of suicide has more of a communication of fear to loneliness and abandonment, or demands for help (Derbidge & Beauchaine, 2014). This model helps to explain the findings of the present study regarding the association between outward impulsivity found in BPD and inward directed impulsivity in MDD, suggesting that mood dysregulation (hopelessness, depression, anger, self-harm), being unable to restrain impulsive drives, pave the way for its overt expression resulting in self-injury or suicide attempts.

There were no significant differences in impulsiveness for the MDD suicidal group versus the MDD non-suicidal group, but the suicidal BPD adolescents were significantly more impulsive than the non-suicidal BPD adolescents. In the latter group, impulsiveness and aggression correlated significantly and positively with suicidal behavior, but no such associations were found in participants with MDD. The suicidal participants with MDD had significantly higher suicidal intent scores than the suicidal adolescents with BPD. Given those differences, other factors besides impulsivity and mood dysregulation may be considered to explain those differences.

In fact, it seems that links between impulsivity and suicide behaviors appear to be anything but simple, rendering that association dependent not only on individual factors such as the underlying psychiatric disorder, with its associated mood dysregulation and impulsivity traits, but also on the social environment including family strengths and frailties (family coercion, invalidation, peer group contagion), all of which increase the likelihood of self-injury (Stepp et al., 2012).

In all, these findings suggest that aggressive and increased impulsivity traits seen in suicidal behavior plays a differential role in adolescents with MDD or BPD. The latter had more anger, aggression, and impulsiveness than those with MDD, but similar levels of depression and hopelessness. Suicidal versus non-suicidal adolescents were more depressed, hopeless, and aggressive, but not more angry or impulsive. As long as outward impulsivity plays a key role as one of the basic traits underlying BPD, and inward impulsivity is seen more frequently in MDD participants, the presence and quality of impulsivity may help to differentiate suicidal risk behavior in adolescents with BPD and MDD, and implement predictive and protective measures.

References

Achenbach, T. M. & Rescorla, L. A. (2001). *Manual for ASEBA school-age forms and profiles*. Burlington, Vermont: University of Vermont, Research Center for Children, Youth and Families.

Beck, A. T. & Steer, R. A. (1987). *Manual for the revised Beck Depression Inventory*. San Antonio, TX: Psychological Corp.

Beck, A. T., Weissman, A., Lester, D. & Trexler, L. (1974) The measurement of pessimism: The Hopelessness Scale. *J Consult Clin Psychol.*, *42*, 861–865.

Bridge, J. A., McBee-Strayer, S. M., Cannon, E. A., Sheftall, A. H., Reynolds, B., Campo, J. V. & Brent, D. A. (2012). Impaired decision making in adolescent suicide attempters. *Journal of the American Academy of Child & Adolescent Psychiatry*, *51*(4), 394-403.

Brown, G. L., Goodwin, F. K., Ballenger, J. C., Goyer, P. F. & Major, L. F. (1979). Aggression in humans correlates with cerebrospinal fluid amine metabolites. *Psychiatry Res.*, *1*, 131–139.

Carpiniello, B., Lai, L., Pirarba, S., Sardu, C. & Pinna, F., 2011. Impulsivity and aggressiveness in bipolar disorder with co-morbid borderline personality disorder. *Psychiatry Res.*, *188*, 40–44.

Centers for Disease Control and Prevention. (2008). Youth Suicide. Accessed at: http://www.cdc.gov/ncipc/dvp/suicide/youthsuicide.htm. Retrieved on: 20 June 2013).

Cerel, J., Jordan, J. R. & Duberstein, P. R. (2008). The impact of suicide on the family. *Crisis: The Journal of Crisis Intervention and Suicide Prevention*, *29*(1), 38-44.

Chorpita, B. F., Yim, L., Moffitt, C., Umemoto, L. A. & Francis, S. E. (2000). Assessment of symptoms of DSM-IV anxiety and depression in children: A revised child anxiety and depression scale, *Behaviour Research and Therapy*, *38*, 835–855.

Corso, P. S., Mercy, J. A., Simon, T. R., Finkelstein, E. A. & Miller, T. R. (2007). Medical costs and productivity losses due to interpersonal and self-directed violence in the United States. *American journal of preventive medicine*, *32*(6), 474-482.

Crowell, S. E., Beauchaine, T. P., Hsiao, R. C., Vasilev, C. A., Yaptangco, M., Linehan, M. M. & McCauley, E. (2012). Differentiating adolescent self-injury from adolescent depression: possible implications for borderline personality development. *Journal of abnormal child psychology*, *40*(1), 45-57.

Derbidge, C. M. & Beauchaine, T. P. (2014). A developmental model of self-inflicted injury, borderline personality, and suicide risk. In *Handbook of developmental psychopathology* (pp. 521-542). Springer US.

Derbidge, C. M. & Beauchaine, T. P. (2014). A developmental model of self-inflicted injury, borderline personality, and suicide risk. In *Handbook of developmental psychopathology* (pp. 521-542). Springer US

Gratz, K. L. (2001). Measurement of deliberate self-harm: Preliminary data on the deliberate self-harm inventory. *Journal of Psychopathology and Behavioral Assessment*, *23*, 253–263.

Hankin, B. L. & Abela, J. R. (2011). Nonsuicidal self-injury in adolescence: Prospective rates and risk factors in a 2 ½year longitudinal study. *Psychiatry research*, *186*(1), 65-70.

Hawton, K., Saunders, K. E. & O'Connor, R. C. (2012). Self-harm and suicide in adolescents. *The Lancet*, *379*(9834), 2373-2382.

Lamers, F., Burstein, M., He, J. P., Avenevoli, S., Angst, J. & Merikangas, K. R. (2012). Structure of major depressive disorder in adolescents and adults in the US general population. *The British Journal of Psychiatry*, *201*(2), 143-150.

Leichsenring, F., Leibing, E., Kruse, J., New, A.S. & Leweke, F. (2011) Borderline personality disorder. *Lancet*, *377*, 74–84.

Morey, L. C. (2007). *The personality assessment inventory professional manual* (2nd ed.). Lutz, FL: Psychological Assessment Resources.

Nakamura, B. J., Ebesutani, C., Bernstein, A. & Chorpita, B. F. (2009). A psychometric analysis of the child behavior checklist DSM-oriented scales. *Journal of Psychopathology and Behavioral Assessment*, *31*, 178–189.

Patton, J. H., Stanford, M. S. & Barratt, E. S. (1995) Factor structure of the Barratt impulsiveness scale. *J. Clin. Psychol.*, *51*, 768–774.

Perroud, N., Baud, P., Mouthon, D., Courtet, P. & Malafosse, A. (2011). Impulsivity, aggression and suicidal behavior in unipolar and bipolar disorders. *Journal of affective disorders*, *134*(1), 112-118.

Prinstein, M. J., Nock, M. K., Spirito, A. & Grapentine, W. L. (2001). Multimethod assessment of suicidality in adolescent psychiatric inpatients: Preliminary results. *Journal of the American Academy of Child & Adolescent Psychiatry*, *40*, 1053–1061.

Rohde, P., Lewinsohn, P. M., Klein, D. N., Seeley, J. R. & Gau, J. M. (2013). Key characteristics of major depressive disorder occurring in childhood, adolescence, emerging adulthood, and adulthood. *Clinical Psychological Science*, *1*(1), 41-53.

Schmidtke, A., Bille-Brahe, U., DeLeo, D., Kerkhof, A., Bjerke, T., Crepet, P., Haring, C., et al.. (1996). Attempted suicide in Europe: Rates, trends and sociodemographic characteristics of suicide attempters during the period 1989–1992. Results of the WHO/EURO Multicentre Study on Parasuicide. *Acta Psychiatr Scand.*, *93*, 327–338.

Shaffer, D., Fisher, P., Lucas, C. P., Dulcan, M. K. & Schwab-Stone, M. E. (2000). NIMH Diagnostic Interview Schedule for Children version IV (NIMH DISC-IV): Description, differences from previous versions, and reliability of some common diagnoses. *Journal of the American Academy of Child & Adolescent Psychiatry*, *39*, 28–38.

Sharp, C., Green, K. L., Yaroslavsky, I., Venta, A., Zanarini, M. C. & Pettit, J. (2012). The incremental validity of borderline personality disorder relative to major depressive disorder for suicidal ideation and deliberate self-harm in adolescents. *Journal of personality disorders*, *26*(6), 927.

Siegal, J. M. (1986). The Multidimensional Anger Inventory. *J Pers Soc Psychol.*, *51*, 191–200.

Soloff, P., White, R. & Diwadkar, V. Impulsivity, aggression and brain structure in high and low lethality suicide attempters with borderline personality disorder, Psychiatry Research: Neuroimaging, Available at: http://dx.doi.org/10.1016/j.pscychresns.2014.02.006, accessed on 18 February 2014)

Stepp, S. D., Whalen, D. J., Pilkonis, P. A., Hipwell, A. E. & Levine, M. D. (2012). Children of mothers with borderline personality disorder: Identifying parenting behaviors as potential targets for intervention. *Personality Disorders: Theory, Research, and Treatment*, *3*(1), 76.

Van Lang, N. D., Ferdinand, R. F., Oldehinkel, A. J., Ormel, J. & Verhulst, F. C. (2005). Concurrent validity of the DSM-IV scales affective problems and anxiety problems of the youth self-report. *Behavior Research and Therapy*, *43*, 1485–1494.

Yen, S., Gagnon, K. & Spirito, A. (2013). Borderline personality disorder in suicidal adolescents. *Personality and mental health*, *7*(2), 89-101.

Zanarini, M. C. (2003). *The child interview for DSM-IV borderline personality disorder.* Belmont, MA: McLean Hospital.

In: Psychology of Impulsivity
Editor: Mary C. Olmstead

ISBN: 978-1-63321-879-6

Chapter 5

IMPULSIVE BEHAVIORS THAT DISTRACT FROM DISTRESS: NON-SUICIDAL SELF-INJURY

Elizabeth N. Riley[1,*], Jessica L. Combs[2], Heather A. Davis[1] and Gregory T. Smith[1]

[1]University of Kentucky, Department of Psychology, KY, US
[2]Michael E. DeBakey Veterans Affairs Medical Center, Psychology Service, TX, US

ABSTRACT

There appear to be a set of behaviors that belong to a common response class, which are characterized by rash, impulsive actions that provide immediate relief from intense negative affect. First, we will review evidence identifying several behaviors as members of this "impulsive behavior for negative reinforcement" response class, including heavy drinking, smoking, and binge eating/purging. Second, we will review emerging evidence that identifies non-suicidal self-injury (NSSI) as an additional member of this response class. NSSI refers to the direct, deliberate destruction of bodily tissue without suicidal intent (American Psychiatric Association, 2013). Third, we highlight the role of negative urgency, the personality disposition to act rashly when distressed, as a personality trait precursor to all behaviors in the response class, including NSSI. Fourth, we review a model designed to help understand why an individual would choose to engage in one behavior in the response class over another. This model emphasizes psychosocial learning, measured as expectancies for reinforcement from a given behavior. Expectancies are understood to reflect summaries of an individual's psychosocial learning history concerning anticipated reinforcement from behaviors. Individuals tend to choose behaviors that are likely to provide reinforcement. Prediction from expectancies is disorder-specific: for example, alcohol expectancies predict drinking problems and eating and thinness expectancies predict bulimia nervosa. The use of measures that assess individuals' expectancies for reinforcement from NSSI will (a) test the basic model of NSSI (American Psychiatric Association, 2013); (b) clarify further the risk process for behaviors in this response class; and (c) test the hypothesis that risk for NSSI is a function of both personality traits and psychosocial learning.

---

* Corresponding author: Elizabeth Riley, 111K Kastle Hall, Department of Psychology, University of Kentucky, Lexington, KY 40506; email: enriley1231@gmail.com.

INTRODUCTION

Recent research advances suggest there is a set of behaviors that belong to a common response class characterized by rash, impulsive acts designed to alleviate intense negative affect. Several behaviors, such as heavy drinking, smoking, and disordered eating, have been shown to function along a negative reinforcement pathway, such that these rash, immediate acts are reinforced because they help to avoid or alleviate distress (Baker, Piper, McCarthy, Majeskie, & Fiore, 2004; Haedt-Matt & Keel, 2011; Smyth et al., 2007; Swendson et al., 2000). We propose, based on emerging research, that non-suicidal self-injury (NSSI), defined as the direct, deliberate destruction of bodily tissue without suicidal intent (American Psychiatric Association, 2013) is an additional member of this response class.

We emphasize the role of negative urgency, the personality disposition to act rashly when distressed (Cyders & Smith, 2008a; Whiteside & Lynam, 2001), as a trait-based predictor of all behaviors in the proposed response class, including NSSI. Individuals high in the trait of negative urgency are more likely than others to respond to intense negative affect by acting impulsively to distract from or alleviate their distress (Doran, Khoddam, Sanders, Schweizer, Trim, & Myers, 2013; Pearson, Combs, Zapolski, & Smith, 2012; Settles, Cyders, & Smith, 2010). In longitudinal research, negative urgency has been shown to predict disordered eating, problem drinking, smoking, and, more recently, self-harm (Adams, Kaiser, Lynam, Charnigo, & Milich, 2012; Fischer, Peterson, & McCarthy, 2013; Martens, Pedersen, Smith, Stewart, & O'Brien, 2011; Doran et al. 2013; Pearson et al., 2012; Pearson, Riley, Davis, & Smith, 2014; Riley, Combs, Jordan, & Smith, 2014; Settles et al., 2010). We see this common risk factor as substantial support for the theory that all of these behaviors belong to the same response class. In addition, there is a great deal of evidence that negative urgency operates through a negative reinforcement process (Adams et al., 2012; Coskunpinar & Cyders, 2012; Martens et al., 2011; Settles et al., 2010), which is further consistent with the theory that the behaviors all serve a similar function.

As all of the behaviors in a response class serve to produce a similar outcome in response to a precipitating event, it is crucial to understand why an individual would choose to engage in one behavior over another. There are many possible reasons why individuals would choose one behavior over another, including ease of access to a certain behavior, cultural norms that might lead more men or women to choose a behavior, and, in the case of NSSI, the capacity to tolerate physically harming oneself (Joiner, 2005). In this chapter, we review a model designed to help understand one set of contributors to this choice process. This model emphasizes individual differences in psychosocial learning histories, which can be measured as expectancies for reinforcement from a given behavior.

Expectancy Theory proposes that individuals will engage in one behavior over another, depending on the anticipated consequences of the behavior (Tolman, 1932). For example, some people learn to associate drinking with relief from distress, others learn to associate smoking with such relief, others binge eating, and others self-harm. Expectancies are understood to reflect summaries of an individual's psychosocial learning history concerning anticipated reinforcement from behaviors. These anticipated consequences result from both observational and experiential learning and, most importantly, they guide future behavior (Goldman, Brown, Christiansen, & Smith, 1991; Hohlstein, Smith, & Atlas, 1998). Individuals tend to choose behaviors that are likely to provide reinforcement, and prediction from expectancies is disorder-specific: alcohol expectancies predict drinking problems and eating and thinness expectancies predict bulimia nervosa (Fischer, Settles, Collins, Gunn, & Smith 2012; Fischer & Smith, 2008).

Although we have emphasized the negative reinforcement function of NSSI, because it is based on the most developed theory and has the strongest empirical support (Armey, Crowther, & Miller, 2011; Bresin, Gordon, Bender, Gordon & Joiner, 2010; Chapman et al., 2006), there may be other reinforcing functions of NSSI as well (Bentley, Nock, & Barlow, 2013; Nock, 2010). Identification and prediction of different functional aspects and reinforcing properties of non-suicidal self-injury using assessment measures such as the Inventory of Statements About Self-Injury (ISAS, Klonsky & Glenn, 2009) or the Functional Assessment of Self-Mutilation (FASM, Lloyd, Kelley, & Hope, 1997) that attempt to capture the expected consequences of NSSI may eventually inform individualized prevention and treatment of this maladaptive behavior.

Behavioral Response Class

A behavioral response class refers to a collection of behaviors, all of which are precipitated by the same event and serve a similar function in response to that event (Haynes, 1990). The definition of behavioral responses classes, and identification of behaviors that belong to a common class, are useful because doing so results in a clearer understanding of the functional role of problem behaviors and can thus lead to effective prevention and intervention methods. It has been well documented that behaviors such as problem drinking, disordered eating, and smoking (a) are often precipitated by subjective distress and (b) function to provide relief from that distress (Baker et al., 2004; Doran et al., 2013; Haedt-Matt & Keel, 2011; Smyth et al., 2007; Swendson et al., 2000). These behaviors are often described as rash or impulsive because engagement in them often undermines an individual's health, interests, or long-term goals (Birkley & Smith, 2011; Cyders & Smith, 2008a). Thus, because this set of maladaptive behaviors share similar antecedent and consequent events, they should be considered members of a behavioral response class of rash, immediate acts that function to alleviate or avoid intense negative affect through similar processes of negative reinforcement.

A fundamental requirement for inclusion in the response class is that all behaviors share similar antecedent and consequent events. Individuals who engage in behaviors such as problem drinking, disordered eating, and smoking appear to do so when they are highly distressed. Indeed, several studies have employed ecological momentary assessment (EMA) and experience sampling methods to show that distress immediately precedes and predicts engagement in behaviors such as alcohol consumption and binge eating (Haedt-Matt & Keel, 2011; Smyth et al., 2007; Swendson et al., 2000). For some of these behaviors, such as binge eating, there is evidence that mood is improved following the behavior: negative affect increases leading up to a binge, but drops immediately following the binge episode (Smyth et al., 2007). Binge eating and alcohol consumption have been tied very closely in time to the experience of distress and, longitudinally, to depression and negative affect, data which support the theory that these behaviors all function as a response to distress (Hussong et al., 2001; Swendson et al., 2000; Pearson et al., 2014; Stice, Burton, & Shaw, 2004).

Despite a strong body of evidence on the immediate predictive properties of intense negative affect on problem drinking and disordered eating behaviors, this same connection is less well understood for smoking behavior. There is somewhat conflicting evidence on the immediacy of the predictive relationship between negative affect and smoking behavior: while several EMA studies show little or no effect of antecedent mood on smoking (Shapiro et al., 2002; Shiffman et al., 2002, 2004), this is largely in contrast to smokers' self-reports of the triggering effects of negative mood on smoking behavior (Baker et al., 2004; Shiffman, 1993). While the exact nature of the relationship between smoking and distress is unclear, it is possible that individuals' perception of the reinforcing properties of smoking to alleviate negative affect is what principally serves to reinforce this behavior. It is also possible that individuals engage in smoking behavior in order to alleviate the distress associated with withdrawal symptoms (Baker et al., 2004), which may represent another pathway of negative reinforcement from this behavior. Another possibility is that relief from distress motivates smoking only in a subset of smokers. Others may smoke for positive reinforcement, be it social or psychopharmacological.

Thus, there is extensive (though not unanimous) evidence to support the theory that problem drinking, disordered eating behaviors, and smoking are all negatively reinforced behaviors that belong to a response class of rash, immediate acts that serve to distract from or alleviate distress. Recent work suggests the possible inclusion of other behaviors such as gambling, risky sexual behavior, and NSSI into this same response class (Chapman, Gratz, & Brown, 2006; Cooper, Agocha, & Sheldon, 2000; Cooper, Shapiro, & Powers, 1998). More research into the reinforcing properties of these particular behaviors is needed to fully understand the functions of the rash, immediate acts that constitute this response class.

Negative Urgency as a Risk Factor

To the degree that problem drinking, disordered eating and smoking belong to response class of rash, immediate acts, they should be predicted by personality traits that predispose an individual to act in impulsive ways in response to distress. One useful model of impulsivity traits was developed by Whiteside and Lynam (2001) and added to by Cyders and Smith (2007); they identified five personality traits that can lead to impulsive action. The traits are (1) negative urgency: the tendency to act rashly when distressed; (2) positive urgency: the tendency to act rashly when in an unusually positive mood; (3) lack of planning: the tendency to act without forethought; (4) lack of perseverance: the inability to maintain focus on tasks; and (5) sensation-seeking: the need to seek out novel, thrilling, risky stimulation.

Of all the identified personality traits included in the model, negative urgency has been shown to be the strongest predictor of engagement in maladaptive behaviors in response to intense negative affect. Indeed, elevations in the trait of negative urgency longitudinally predict risk for and engagement in alcohol consumption (Settles et al., 2010), disordered eating behavior (Pearson et al., 2012, 2014) and smoking (Doran et al., 2013). There is evidence to suggest that the impulsivity related traits also predict engagement in other behaviors such as risky sex and gambling (Cyders & Smith, 2007, 2008b; Zapolski, Cyders, & Smith, 2009) but, more research is needed in this area to clarify the specific role of negative urgency in this process. Negative urgency represents a general risk factor for engagement in behaviors in this response class. No doubt there are other such general risk factors as well, and integration of negative urgency with such other factors is an important step toward the development of comprehensive models of risk. The focus of this chapter is on negative urgency as one common risk factor for behaviors in this response class, and on behavior-specific risk factors that we discuss below.

An Introduction to NSSI

NSSI refers to the direct, deliberate destruction of bodily tissue without any suicidal intent (American Psychiatric Association, 2013). NSSI is differentiated from other harmful behaviors that are indirect (e.g. smoking, the intentions of which are not to cause harm) and from behaviors for which there is an intent to die or an ambivalence about the potential consequence of dying (APA, 2013; Nock, 2010). It is also distinguished from personality disorders, including borderline personality disorder (BPD): Although it shares some features with BPD, the two disorders often occur separately from each other and they are associated with similar levels of functional impairment (Selby, Bender, Gordon, Nock, & Joiner, 2012).

Lifetime prevalence rates of NSSI are estimated to be between 4 and 35% among adults (Muehlenkamp, 2006; Nock, 2010) and between 13 and 45% among adolescents (Ross and Heath, 2002; Fischer et al., 2013). In a study of 439 US adults, the lifetime prevalence of NSSI was 5.9% (3.2% had self-injured between one and four times, 1.4 % between five and nine times and 1.3% >10 times); the 12-month prevalence rate was 0.9% (Klonsky, 2011). Unfortunately, the exact prevalence rates of NSSI are unknown, largely due to the lack of large, epidemiological studies of the behavior. The age-of-onset of self-harm is consistently reported to be between 12-14 years, and, as noted above, lifetime prevalence rates are consistently higher among adolescents than among adults.

The most common method of NSSI is cutting or carving oneself with a sharp implement, such as a knife, but most people report using multiple methods; most injury occurs on the arms, legs and stomach. Of those endorsing any form of NSSI, 35% reported cutting, 35% scraping or scratching skin, 31% burning, 31% hitting, 31% biting, 23% interfering with wound healing and 19% skin picking (Klonsky, 2011). NSSI frequently co-occurs with other psychiatric disorders such as BPD, post-traumatic stress disorder, eating disorders, substance use disorders, major depression, and anxiety disorders (Nock, 2010). A number of variables have been implicated as risk factors for NSSI, including childhood abuse and loss (Gratz, 2003), biological vulnerabilities to emotional dysregulation (Linehan, 1993; Nock, 2010), BPD features (Glenn and Klonsky, 2011; Lynam, Miller, Miller, Bornovalova, & Lejuez, 2011), negative urgency (Glenn and Klonsky, 2010; Bresin et al., 2012) as well as alcohol use, drug use and smoking (Deliberto & Nock, 2008; Serras, Saules, Cranford, & Eisenberg, 2010).

NSSI and the Negative Reinforcement Process

The functions and consequences of NSSI are not fully understood. Many researchers consider it to be a negatively reinforced coping or emotion-regulation strategy that temporarily relieves or helps avoid unwanted emotional arousal or feelings of guilt, sadness, or distress (Chapman, Gratz & Brown, 2006; Favazza, 1998; Gordon et al., 2010; Klonsky &

Glenn, 2009; Nock, 2010; Nock & Prinstein, 2004). Indeed, proposed diagnostic criteria for NSSI (the disorder is currently listed in Section 3 of the DSM-5 as a condition that requires further research) identify precipitants such as (a) negative affect, (b) the urge to act, and (c) the expectation that engaging in NSSI will relieve a negative feeling (American Psychiatric Association, 2013).

A useful way to understand the role of negative affect in NSSI can be taken from emotional cascade theory (Selby, Anestis, & Joiner, 2008). According to this theory, one experiences an upsetting event and becomes distressed, then ruminates on that distress, which results in steadily increasing negative affect (Selby et al., 2008; Selby, Connell, & Joiner, 2010). This heightened negative affect may serve as the precipitating event for the self-harm event. It is thought that the self-harming act provides quick, temporary relief or distraction from the negative affect, and is thus negatively reinforced. Of course, the self-harm does not address or resolve the original source of the negative affect, so the distress returns. Because self-harm was previously reinforced, it becomes an even more likely response to distress the next time. The result is a cycle that perpetuates engagement in self-injurious behavior. In the Chapman et al. (2006) Experiential Avoidance Model of deliberate self-harm, the authors suggest that NSSI is perpetuated by a negative reinforcement cycle based on the avoidance of unwanted emotional experience, which is relieved through the act of deliberate self-harm. That is, one's focus shifts to, or narrows to, the self-harm act, to the exclusion of prior sources of distress.

There have been a number of self-report studies in which participants specifically cite the reduction or avoidance of aversive emotional states as a primary motivator for engaging in self-injurious behavior (e.g., Briere & Gil, 1998; Favazza & Conterio, 1989; Gratz, 2000; Rodham, Hawton, & Evans, 2004). More recently, Bresin, Gordon, Bender, Gordon & Joiner (2010) conducted a study in which participants were asked to provide momentary affect ratings immediately preceding and following the experience of pain. Results of this study indicated that the participants experienced decreases in negative affect after the experience of pain. This relationship, however, was moderated by the typical level of emotional reactivity endorsed by the individuals, which may indicate an additional individual difference in the reinforcing properties of NSSI (Bresin et al., 2010). In a study of 36 college students with a history of NSSI, researchers used EMA to assess changes in affect before and after engagement in self-harm behavior. Results indicated that individuals experienced increases in distress immediately preceding an episode of NSSI and a slower decrease in that negative affect following engagement in the behavior (Armey, Crowther, & Miller, 2011). Furthermore, some researchers have suggested that in addition to individuals feeling less distressed after an episode of engagement in self-injurious behavior, NSSI may also become more reinforcing over time. This may occur because later episodes can result in more intense feelings of physical pain, and thus more complete distraction from other sources of distress (Gordon et al., 2010).

As noted above, a behavioral response class is a collection of behaviors, all of which are precipitated by the same type of event and serve a similar function. There is a great deal of evidence demonstrating that NSSI shares similar antecedent and consequent events with other maladaptive behaviors such as disordered eating, drinking, and smoking (i.e., the experience of increasing negative affect leading up to engagement in the behavior and the subsequent decrease in distress following the episode). Given the substantial body of evidence to suggest that NSSI functions along a similar process of negative reinforcement, there is good reason to include NSSI in the behavioral class that includes disordered eating, drinking, and smoking. Thus, we propose that all of these behaviors together comprise a response class of rash, immediate acts that serve to temporarily relieve or help avoid distress.

Negative Urgency as a Predictor of NSSI

It has been well documented that elevations in negative urgency predict engagement in many other behaviors in this putative response class (Doran et al., 2013; Pearson et al., 2012; Settles et al., 2010). To the degree that NSSI does fit into this response class, it should similarly be predicted by elevations in negative urgency. Various personality traits related to impulsive behavior have been identified as potentially important correlates of NSSI. However, the findings on these relationships have been inconsistent, possibly because of the use of multiple different constructs under the common label of impulsivity (Glenn & Klonsky, 2010). As noted above in this chapter, we find it useful to conceptualize impulsivity using the Whiteside and Lynam (2001) and Cyders and Smith (2007) model of five personality traits that lead to impulsive action, the most relevant of which is negative urgency, the tendency to act rashly when distressed.

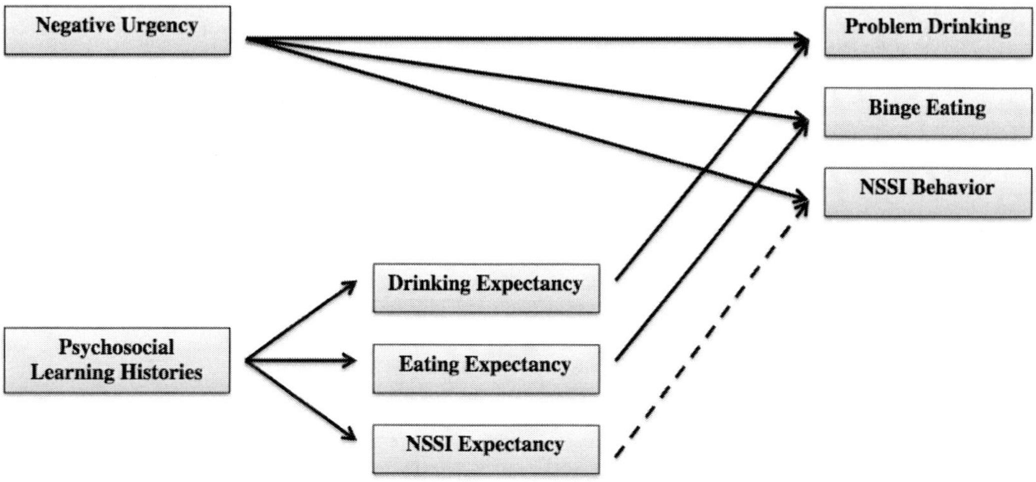

Note. The solid lines represent empirically demonstrated associations between the risk factors and behaviors in the response class. The dotted lines represent a new, hypothesized pathway of risk for NSSI behavior.

Figure 1. Model depicting the general risk factor of negative urgency and behavior-specific expectancies that predict engagement in behaviors in the response class.

Riley, Combs, Jordan, & Smith (2014) analyzed the predictive effects of all five impulsivity-related traits (negative urgency, lack of planning, lack of perseverance, sensation seeking, and positive urgency) in the longitudinal prediction of NSSI. Negative urgency was the only impulsivity-related trait measured at Time 1 that significantly predicted self-harming behavior at Time 2, and predicted engagement in that behavior above and beyond prior NSSI behavior. Furthermore, negative urgency has been shown to reliably distinguish between individuals who did and those who did not engage in self-harm, predict the urge to engage in NSSI, and provide incremental validity in the statistical prediction of NSSI behavior (Bresin et al., 2013; Glenn & Klonsky, 2010; Riley et al., 2014). In a college sample of NSSI-active individuals and matched controls, negative urgency was significantly associated with self-harming frequency, variety of self-harm methods, and number of years self-harming (Dir, Karyadi, & Cyders, 2013).

Thus, all of the behaviors in the proposed response class (disordered eating, drinking, smoking and NSSI) appear to be predicted, longitudinally, from the trait of negative urgency (Adams et al., 2012; Martens et al., 2011; Doran et al., 2013; Pearson et al., 2012; Riley et al., 2014; Settles et al., 2010). In addition, recent work has shown that negative urgency was the only impulsivity-related trait serving as a common risk factor for increased self-harm, alcohol use and problematic eating, all of which are typically associated with negative reinforcement (Dir, Karyadi, & Cyders, 2013; Fischer, Settles, Collins, Gunn, & Smith, 2012).

In addition, there is consistent evidence that negative urgency operates through negative reinforcement (Adams et al., 2012; Coskunpinar & Cyders, 2012; Martens et al., 2011; Settles et al., 2010). This finding is of course consistent with the conceptualization of the behaviors in the proposed response class as immediate tools used to respond to intense negative affect. The evidence that disordered eating, drinking, smoking, and NSSI are all predicted by negative urgency as substantial support for the idea that they belong to a negatively-reinforced behavioral response class of rash, immediate acts that serve to temporarily relieve or help avoid distress.

Expectancy Theory

As all of the behaviors in the response class serve a similar function or produce a similar outcome in response to a precipitating event, it is crucial to understand why an individual would choose to engage in one behavior over another. For example, why might one individual engage in alcohol consumption to relieve distress and another choose to engage in NSSI? There are, no doubt, many factors, including cultural and gender-based factors that may bias men to heavy drinking and women to disordered eating (American Psychiatric Association, 2013; Keel & Klump, 2003; Miller & Pumariega, 2001; Smith, Spillane, & Annus, 2006), and, in the case of NSSI, the capacity to tolerate physically harming oneself (Joiner, 2005). In this chapter, we focus on individual differences in psychosocial learning history. That is, some individuals learn to associate drinking with relief from distress, others learn to associate smoking with such relief, others binge eating, and others NSSI. Learned associations like these can be measured as behavior-specific expectancies (Goldman et al., 1991).

Expectancy Theory holds that an individual will engage in a certain behavior over other behaviors because he or she expects reinforcement from the behavior (Tolman, 1932). Individuals come to anticipate consequences of behavior through processes of observational learning and experiential reward and punishment; anticipated consequences of behavior then influence future behavior choices (Goldman et al., 1991; Hohlstein, Smith, & Atlas, 1998). Psychosocial learning histories, which are in part comprised of these learned associations between behaviors and consequences, can be operationalized by measures of individuals' expectancies for given behaviors. Expectancies for reinforcement from a given behavior make engagement in that behavior more likely. Of course, reinforcement can be positive (creating or enhancing a positive state) or negative (removing or reducing a negative state).

Once at risk for the general response class of rash behaviors that provide relief from distress, in part due to elevations in the trait of negative urgency, endorsed expectancies, or anticipated consequences, for specific behaviors are likely to predict engagement in that particular behavior. The work of Fischer et al. (2012) suggests that elevations in negative urgency may represent a global, general risk factor for engagement in behaviors in this response class, and that specific behavioral choices within that response class are best predicted by endorsement of behavior-specific expectancies (Figure 1 depicts such a model). For example, individuals who engage in binge eating and dieting endorse eating/dieting expectancies but not drinking expectancies, and vice versa (Fischer et al., 2012).

Several longitudinal studies have documented prediction of behaviors in the target response class from behavior-specific expectancies. Specifically, the expectancy that eating helps alleviate negative affect predicts subsequent binge eating behavior (Pearson et al., 2012; Smith, Simmons, Flory, Annus, & Hill, 2007). The motive to drink to cope with distress (presumably based in part on expectancies that drinking helps alleviate distress) predicts subsequent drinking behavior (Armeli et al., 2014; Settles et al., 2010). Expectancies for negative affect reduction from smoking predict subsequent smoking behavior (Doran et al., 2013; Guller, Zapolski, & Smith, in press; Heinz, Kassel, Berbaum, & Mermelstein, 2010). Thus, expectancies for negative reinforcement from several behaviors, along with associated elevations in negative urgency, longitudinally predict engagement in those behaviors. We propose that the same is true for NSSI.

Existing theory and the provisional definition of NSSI in DSM-5 (American Psychiatric Association, 2013) are consistent with this perspective. Nock (2010) proposes a multi-level risk model that may lead an individual to engage in self-harm behavior. Although there has been surprisingly little research on what brings people to the point of NSSI, he suggests that people possess both intrapersonal and interpersonal vulnerabilities that limit their ability to respond to stressful events in an adaptive way, which increases the odds of responding in a maladaptive way. These general, predisposed vulnerabilities to respond to aversive events in a maladaptive way will, in his theory, interact with NSSI-specific risk factors to produce engagement in this behavior (Nock, 2010). Just as we believe negative urgency is one general vulnerability factor, we propose that one such NSSI-specific risk factor could be the endorsement of expectations for reinforcement from self-harm.

CONCLUSION

Expectancies for Reinforcement from NSSI

We have so far emphasized the negative reinforcement function of NSSI, in which someone engages in the behavior in order to alleviate or avoid intense negative affect, because it is based on the most developed theory and has the strongest empirical support. However, there has been some recent theoretical work that suggests the possibility of other reinforcing functions of NSSI. Nock & Prinstein (2004) proposed a four-function model of self-harm that highlights the negative reinforcement function of relief from distress along with three other proposed functions.

This model yields four possible reinforcement processes for NSSI: automatic negative reinforcement (reduction of aversive affective or cognitive state), automatic positive reinforcement (generation of positive feelings or stimulation, such as a feelings of invincibility or resilience), social negative reinforcement (escape from social situations or removal of interpersonal demands, such as the reduced parental pressure to achieve high grades due to attention on the NSSI behavior), and social positive reinforcement (increasing attention or access to resources, such as increased therapist check-ins in order to ensure safety). These additional putative functions of NSSI have not yet received the empirical scrutiny that has been applied to the negative reinforcement hypothesis. Thus, more research is needed in this area to explore these other reinforcement hypotheses.

In addition to the Four Fold Model proposed by Nock & Prinstein (2004) and elaborated upon by Bentley et al. (2013), a number of NSSI-specific risk factors and possible functional aspects of self-injury have been proposed (e.g., Briere & Gil, 1998; Favazza & Conterio, 1989; Gratz, 2000; Klonsky & Glenn, 2009; Nock, 2010). Three of the most prominent hypotheses for the functions of self-harm include the self-punishment hypothesis, in which an individual might self-harm in order to punish himself or herself for a failure, the dissociation hypothesis, in which someone who struggles with dissociative tendencies may use NSSI as a grounding tool or to feel more connected to his/her body, and the pragmatic hypothesis, which states that some people, especially young adolescents, might engage in NSSI because it is merely the most accessible mechanism of coping with distress.

The recent inclusion of NSSI into Section 3 of the DSM-5 as a condition needing future research highlights the increased attention being put on the functional aspects of self-harm. Indeed, one of the APA criteria for NSSI is engagement in the behavior in order to relieve a negative affective or cognitive state (APA, 2013). It is clear that much more research is needed in this area in order to explore the functional aspects of NSSI, and it would be useful for this research to extend beyond just the negative reinforcement properties of NSSI to include other proposed functions such as positive and social reinforcement.

Functional Assessment

There are a great many assessment measures to choose from when determining the level or degree to which an individual is engaging in self-injurious behavior. Most self-harm inventories assess the frequency, duration, and severity of the self-harm behavior. Particularly in light of the recent inclusion of NSSI into the DSM, the assessment of NSSI must move beyond a purely descriptive nature and rather employ assessment measures such as the ISAS or FSAM to capture the functions of self-injurious behavior.

The functional uses of self-injurious behavior likely stem, in part, from an individual's expected consequences of the behavior, expectancies formed both prior to engagement in the behavior and expectancies developed and refined throughout the behavior engagement period. Expectancies of behavior reinforcement are understood to be formulated based on lifelong psychosocial learning histories and are maintained through positive and negative reinforcement processes based on reward and punishment.

The consistent use of measures of expectancies of reinforcement from self-harm would facilitate a number of tests related to the theories surrounding NSSI: (1) Does NSSI indeed fit into the behavioral response class of rash, immediate acts that are negatively reinforced and serve to alleviate or avoid intense negative affect? (2) What other functions does engagement in NSSI behavior serve for the individual? Do proposed functions such as positive and social reinforcement processes, self-punishment, and providing a grounding tool during periods of dissociation actually operate? If so, for which different populations are each of the NSSI functions most salient? (3) Is engagement in the behavior associated with elevations in both negative urgency and NSSI-specific expectancies? These tests, and others, will further clarify the process by which NSSI is begun and maintained.

By using a functional assessment measure of the reinforcing properties of NSSI, it may be possible to identify the different functional aspects of NSSI, which may eventually inform individualized prevention and treatment of this maladaptive behavior. Several evidence-based interventions such as dialectical behavior therapy (Kerr et al., 2010; Linehan, 1993; Muehlenkamp, 2006) and manual-based cognitive behavioral therapy have been shown to lessen the frequency and/or severity of self-injurious behaviors in clients with varying degrees of success. However, there remain no evidence-based interventions that have been developed to directly target this maladaptive behavior (Kerr et al., 2010; Bentley et al., 2013). A treatment modality specifically designed to address NSSI is sorely needed; with the recent addition of NSSI into DSM-5, this may be on the horizon. This development is particularly exciting because using a theoretical framework for conceptualizing and assessing NSSI may lay the foundation for individualized, function-based interventions for non-suicidal self-injury.

REFERENCES

Adams, Z. W., Kaiser, A. J., Lynam, D. R., Charnigo, R. J. & Milich, R. (2012). Drinking motives as mediators of the impulsivity-substance use relation: Pathways for negative urgency, lack of premeditation, and sensation seeking. *Addictive Behaviors*, *37*(7), 848-855.

American Psychiatric Association. (2013). *Diagnostic and Statistical Manual of Mental Disorders* (5th ed.). Arlington, VA: American Psychiatric Publishing.

Armeli, S., Dranoff, E., Tennen, H., Austad, C. S., Fallahi, C. R., Raskin, S. & Pearlson, G. (2014). A longitudinal study of the effects of coping motives, negative affect and drinking level on drinking problems among college students. *Anxiety, Stress, & Coping*, Advance online publication. doi: 10.1080/10615806.2014.895821

Armey, M. F., Crowther, J. H. & Miller, I. W. (2011). Changes in ecological momentary assessment reported affect associated with episodes of nonsuicidal self-injury. *Behavior therapy*, *42*(4), 579-588.

Baker, T. B., Piper, M. E., McCarthy, D. E., Majeskie, M. R. & Fiore, M. C. (2004). Addiction motivation reformulated: an affective processing model of negative reinforcement. *Psychological Review*, *111*(1), 33.

Bentley, K. H., Nock, M. K. & Barlow, D. H. (2014). The Four-Function Model of Nonsuicidal Self-Injury Key Directions for Future Research. *Clinical Psychological Science*, 2167702613514563.

Bresin, K., Carter, D. L. & Gordon, K. H. (2013). The relationship between trait impulsivity, negative affective states, and urge for nonsuicidal self-injury: A daily diary study. *Psychiatry Research, 205*(3), 227-231.

Bresin, K., Gordon, K. H., Bender, T. W., Gordon, L. J. & Joiner Jr, T. E. (2010). No pain, no change: Reductions in prior negative affect following physical pain. *Motivation and Emotion, 34*(3), 280-287.

Briere, J. & Gil, E. (1998). Self-mutilation in clinical and general population samples: Prevalence, correlates, and functions. *American Journal of Orthopsychiatry, 68*(4), 609-620.

Chapman, A. L., Gratz, K. L. & Brown, M. Z. (2006). Solving the puzzle of deliberate self-harm: The experiential avoidance model. *Behaviour Research and Therapy, 44*(3), 371-394.

Cooper, M. L., Agocha, V. B. & Sheldon, M. S. (2000). A motivational perspective on risky behaviors: The role of personality and affect regulatory processes. *Journal of Personality, 68*(6), 1059-1088.

Cooper, M. L., Shapiro, C. M. & Powers, A. M. (1998). Motivations for sex and risky sexual behavior among adolescents and young adults: a functional perspective. *Journal of Personality and Social Psychology, 75*(6), 1528.

Coskunpinar, A. & Cyders, M. A. (2012). Mediation–moderation analysis of problematic alcohol use: The roles of urgency, drinking motives, and risk/benefit perception. *Addictive Behaviors, 37*(7), 880-883.

Cyders, M. A. & Smith, G. T. (2007). Mood-based rash action and its components: Positive and negative urgency. *Personality and Individual Differences, 43*(4), 839-850.

Cyders, M. A. & Smith, G. T. (2008a). Emotion-based dispositions to rash action: positive and negative urgency. *Psychological Bulletin, 134*(6), 807.

Cyders, M. A. & Smith, G. T. (2008b). Clarifying the role of personality dispositions in risk for increased gambling behavior. *Personality and Individual Differences, 45*(6), 503-508.

Deliberto, T. L. & Nock, M. K. (2008). An exploratory study of correlates, onset, and offset of non-suicidal self-injury. *Archives of Suicide Research, 12*(3), 219-231.

Dir, A. L., Karyadi, K. & Cyders, M. A. (2013). The uniqueness of negative urgency as a common risk factor for self-harm behaviors, alcohol consumption, and eating problems. *Addictive Behaviors, 38*(5), 2158-2162.

Doran, N., Khoddam, R., Sanders, P. E., Schweizer, C. A., Trim, R. S. & Myers, M. G. (2013). A prospective study of the acquired preparedness model: The effects of impulsivity and expectancies on smoking initiation in college students. *Psychology of Addictive Behaviors, 27*(3), 714.

Favazza, A. R. (1998). The coming of age of self-mutilation. *The Journal of Nervous and Mental Disease, 186*(5), 259-268.

Favazza, A. R. & Conterio, K. (1989). Female habitual self- mutilators. *Acta Psychiatrica Scandinavica, 79*(3), 283-289.

Fischer, S., Peterson, C. M. & McCarthy, D. (2013). A prospective test of the influence of negative urgency and expectancies on binge eating and purging. *Psychology of Addictive Behaviors, 27*(1), 294.

Fischer, S., Settles, R., Collins, B., Gunn, R. & Smith, G. T. (2012). The role of negative urgency and expectancies in problem drinking and disordered eating: Testing a model of comorbidity in pathological and at-risk samples. *Psychology of Addictive Behaviors, 26*(1), 112.

Fischer, S. & Smith, G. T. (2008). Binge eating, problem drinking, and pathological gambling: Linking behavior to shared traits and social learning. *Personality and Individual Differences, 44*(4), 789-800.

Glenn, C. R. & Klonsky, E. D. (2010). A multimethod analysis of impulsivity in nonsuicidal self-injury. *Personality Disorders: Theory, Research, and Treatment, 1*(1), 67.

Glenn, C. R. & Klonsky, E. D. (2011). Prospective prediction of nonsuicidal self-injury: a 1-year longitudinal study in young adults. *Behavior Therapy, 42*(4), 751-762.

Goldman, M. S., Brown, S. A., Christiansen, B. A. & Smith, G. T. (1991). Alcoholism and memory: broadening the scope of alcohol-expectancy research. *Psychological Bulletin, 110*(1), 137.

Gordon, K. H., Selby, E. A., Anestis, M. D., Bender, T. W., Witte, T. K., Braithwaite, S., ... & Joiner Jr, T. E. (2010). The reinforcing properties of repeated deliberate self-harm. *Archives of Suicide Research, 14*(4), 329-341.

Gratz, K. L. (2001). Measurement of deliberate self-harm: Preliminary data on the Deliberate Self-Harm Inventory. *Journal of Psychopathology and Behavioral Assessment, 23*(4), 253-263.

Gratz, K. L. (2003). Risk factors for and functions of deliberate Self-Harm: An empirical and conceptual review. *Clinical Psychology: Science and Practice, 10*(2), 192-205.

Guller, L., Zapolski, T.C., Smith, G.T. (in press) Longitudinal test of a transactional model of smoking expectancies and smoking experience in youth. *Psychology of Addictive Behaviors.*

Haedt-Matt, A. A. & Keel, P. K. (2011). Revisiting the affect regulation model of binge eating: A meta-analysis of studies using ecological momentary assessment. *Psychological Bulletin, 137*(4), 660.

Haynes, S. N. (1990). Behavioral assessment of adults. *Handbook of Psychological Assessment*, 423-463.

Heinz, A. J., Kassel, J. D., Berbaum, M. & Mermelstein, R. (2010). Adolescents' expectancies for smoking to regulate affect predict smoking behavior and nicotine dependence over time. *Drug and Alcohol Dependence, 111*(1), 128-135.

Hohlstein, L. A., Smith, G. T. & Atlas, J. G. (1998). An application of expectancy theory to eating disorders: Development and validation of measures of eating and dieting expectancies. *Psychological Assessment, 10*(1), 49.

Hussong, A. M., Hicks, R. E., Levy, S. A. & Curran, P. J. (2001). Specifying the relations between affect and heavy alcohol use among young adults. *Journal of Abnormal Psychology, 110*(3), 449.

Joiner Jr., T. E. (2005). *Why people die by suicide*. Cambridge: Harvard University Press.

Kerr, P. L., Muehlenkamp, J. J. & Turner, J. M. (2010). Nonsuicidal self-injury: a review of current research for family medicine and primary care physicians. *The Journal of the American Board of Family Medicine, 23*(2), 240-259.

Keel, P.K. & Klump, K.L. (2003). Are eating disorders culture-bound syndromes? Implications for conceptualizing their etiology. *Psychological Bulletin, 129*, 747–769.

Klonsky, E. D. (2011). Non-suicidal self-injury in United States adults: prevalence, sociodemographics, topography and functions. *Psychological Medicine*, *41*(9), 1981-6.

Klonsky, E. D., & Glenn, C. R. (2009). Assessing the functions of non-suicidal self-injury: Psychometric properties of the Inventory of Statements About Self-injury (ISAS). *Journal of Psychopathology and Behavioral Assessment*, *31*(3), 215-219.

Linehan, M. (1993). Cognitive-Behavioral Treatment of Borderline Personality Disorder. Guilford Press.

Lloyd, E. E., Kelley, M. L., & Hope, T. (1997, April). Self-mutilation in a community sample of adolescents: Descriptive characteristics and provisional prevalence rates. In *annual meeting of the Society for Behavioral Medicine, New Orleans, LA*.

Lynam, D. R., Miller, J. D., Miller, D. J., Bornovalova, M. A. & Lejuez, C. W. (2011). Testing the relations between impulsivity-related traits, suicidality, and nonsuicidal self-injury: A test of the incremental validity of the UPPS model. *Personality Disorders: Theory, Research, and Treatment*, *2*(2), 151.

Lynam, D., Smith G.T., Cyders, M. A., Fischer, S., Whiteside, S. A. The UPPS-P: A multidimensional measure of risk for impulsive behavior. 2007 Unpublished technical report.

Martens, M. P., Pedersen, E. R., Smith, A. E., Stewart, S. H. & O'Brien, K. (2011). Predictors of alcohol-related outcomes in college athletes: The roles of trait urgency and drinking motives. *Addictive Behaviors*, *36*(5), 456-464.

Miller, M. N. & Pumariega, A. J. (2001). Culture and eating disorders: A historical and cross-cultural review. *Psychiatry: Interpersonal and Biological Processes, 64*, 93–110.

Muehlenkamp, J. J. (2006). Empirically supported treatments and general therapy guidelines for non-suicidal self-injury. *Journal of Mental Health Counseling*, *28*(2), 166-185.

Nock, M. K. (2010). Self-injury. *Annual Review of Clinical Psychology*, *6*, 339-363.

Nock, M. K., & Prinstein, M. J. (2004). A functional approach to the assessment of self-mutilative behavior. *Journal of consulting and clinical psychology*, *72*(5), 885.

Pearson, C. M., Combs, J. L., Zapolski, T. C. & Smith, G. T. (2012). A longitudinal transactional risk model for early eating disorder onset. *Journal of Abnormal Psychology*, *121*(3), 707.

Pearson, C. M., Riley, E. N., Davis, H. A. & Smith, G. T. (2014). Research Review: Two pathways toward impulsive action: an integrative risk model for bulimic behavior in youth. *Journal of Child Psychology and Psychiatry*. Advance online publication. doi: 10.1111/jcpp.12214

Rodham, K., Hawton, K. & Evans, E. (2004). Reasons for deliberate self-harm: Comparison of self-poisoners and self-cutters in a community sample of adolescents. *Journal of the American Academy of Child & Adolescent Psychiatry*, *43*(1), 80-87.

Ross, S. & Heath, N. (2002). A study of the frequency of self-mutilation in a community sample of adolescents. *Journal of Youth and Adolescence*, *31*(1), 67-77.

Riley, E. N., Combs, J. L., Jordan, C. E. & Smith, G. T. (*under review)* Negative urgency and depression: Trait-based predictors of self-injury over time.

Selby, E. A., Anestis, M. D. & Joiner, T. E. (2008). Understanding the relationship between emotional and behavioral dysregulation: Emotional cascades. *Behaviour Research and Therapy*, *46*(5), 593-611.

Selby, E. A., Bender, T. W., Gordon, K. H., Nock, M. K. & Joiner, Jr. T. E. (2012). Non-suicidal self-injury (NSSI) disorder: A preliminary study. *Personality Disorders: Theory, Research, and Treatment*, *3*(2), 167.

Selby, E. A., Connell, L. D. & Joiner, Jr. T. E. (2010). The pernicious blend of rumination and fearlessness in non-suicidal self-injury. *Cognitive Therapy and Research*, *34*(5), 421-428.

Serras, A., Saules, K. K., Cranford, J. A. & Eisenberg, D. (2010). Self-injury, substance use, and associated risk factors in a multi-campus probability sample of college students. *Psychology of Addictive Behaviors*, *24*(1), 119.

Settles, R. F., Cyders, M. & Smith, G. T. (2010). Longitudinal validation of the acquired preparedness model of drinking risk. *Psychology of Addictive Behaviors*, *24*(2), 198.

Shapiro, D., Jamner, L. D., Davydov, D. M. & James, P. (2002). Situations and moods associated with smoking in everyday life. *Psychology of Addictive Behaviors*, *16*(4), 342.

Shiffman, S. (1993). Assessing smoking patterns and motives. *Journal of Consulting and Clinical Psychology*, *61*(5), 732.

Shiffman, S., Gwaltney, C. J., Balabanis, M. H., Liu, K. S., Paty, J. A., Kassel, J. D., ... & Gnys, M. (2002). Immediate antecedents of cigarette smoking: an analysis from ecological momentary assessment. *Journal of Abnormal Psychology*, *111*(4), 531.

Shiffman, S. & Waters, A. J. (2004). Negative affect and smoking lapses: a prospective analysis. *Journal of Consulting and Clinical Psychology*, *72*(2), 192.

Smith, G. T., Fischer, S. & Fister, S. M. (2003). Incremental validity principles in test construction. *Psychological Assessment*, *15*(4), 467.

Smith, G. T., Simmons, J. R., Flory, K., Annus, A. M. & Hill, K. K. (2007). Thinness and eating expectancies predict subsequent binge-eating and purging behavior among adolescent girls. *Journal of Abnormal Psychology*, *116*(1), 188.

Smith, G. T., Spillane, N. S. & Annus, A. M. (2006). Implications of an emerging integration of universal and culturally specific psychologies. *Perspectives on Psychological Science*, *1*(3), 211-233.

Smyth, J. M., Wonderlich, S. A., Heron, K. E., Sliwinski, M. J., Crosby, R. D., Mitchell, J. E. & Engel, S. G. (2007). Daily and momentary mood and stress are associated with binge eating and vomiting in bulimia nervosa patients in the natural environment. *Journal of Consulting and Clinical Psychology*, *75*(4), 629.

Swendson, J. D., Tennen, H., Carney, M. A., Affleck, G., Willard, A. & Hromi, A. (2000). Mood and alcohol consumption: An experience sampling test of the self-medication hypothesis. Journal of Abnormal Psychology, *109*, 198-204.

Tolman, E. C. (1932). *Purposive behavior in animals and men*. University of California Press.

Whiteside, S. P. & Lynam, D. R. (2001). The five factor model and impulsivity: Using a structural model of personality to understand impulsivity. *Personality and Individual Differences*, *30*(4), 669-689.

Zapolski, T. C., Cyders, M. A. & Smith, G. T. (2009). Positive urgency predicts illegal drug use and risky sexual behavior. *Psychology of Addictive Behaviors*, *23*(2), 348.

In: Psychology of Impulsivity
Editor: Mary C. Olmstead

ISBN: 978-1-63321-879-6

Chapter 6

IMPULSIVE ACTION AND IMPULSIVE INACTION: TOWARD AN INTEGRATIVE THEORY OF IMPULSIVITY

Leila Guller[1,*], Lauren Boyle[1], Nichea S. Spillane[2] and Gregory T. Smith[1]

[1]University of Kentucky, Department of Psychology, KY, US
[2]Brown University, Department of Behavioral and Social Sciences, RI, US

ABSTRACT

Historically, the construct of impulsivity, also referred to as disinhibition or behavioral undercontrol, has been understood to reflect the tendency to act in rash, ill-advised ways. In recent years, theory and research have moved toward a different and broader understanding of impulsivity. Carver, Johnson, and Joorman (2008) defined a construct called reflexive responsivity to emotion (RRE), which refers to the tendency to respond to intense negative emotions in an immediate way, with the goal of distracting oneself from, reducing, or avoiding subjective distress. From their perspective, the traditional conceptualization of impulsive action is only one form of RRE. The impulsive actions of heavy drinking, disordered eating, smoking, and gambling (as well as other behaviors) often serve the function of distracting one from the distress one was in prior to the impulsive act. The second form of RRE is referred to as impulsive inaction. Impulsive inaction refers to a tendency not to act, when acting would better serve one's interests. At times, inaction helps one avoid intense subjective distress. Examples include not asking one's boss for a raise or not asking a date to the prom. Those two forms of inaction are impulsive in the sense that they are often not chosen because, after careful consideration, one believes they meet one's ongoing needs and goals. Rather, they are chosen without reflection because they provide immediate relief from distress, even though they are inconsistent with one's needs and goals. This chapter reviews these recent advances in the context of the traditional conceptualization of externalizing and internalizing psychopathology, and addresses several questions: (1) Is there empirical evidence that there are common risk factors for impulsive action and impulsive inaction? (2) What are the neurobiological underpinnings of RRE? To what degree do the same brain systems

* Corresponding author: Address: Leila Guller, 111K Kastle Hall, Department of Psychology, University of Kentucky, Lexington, Kentucky 40506; Email: leila.guller@uky.edu.

underlie impulsive action and impulsive inaction? (3) What factors influence whether a given person is more disposed toward impulsive action or impulsive inaction? (4) How can we understand RRE in the context of development?

1. INTRODUCTION

Externalizing dysfunction, such as substance abuse and aggression, and internalizing dysfunction, such as depression and anxiety, are understood to reflect two central dimensions of psychopathology (Krueger & Markon, 2006). The use of these two terms reflects the ideas that the pathology of externalizing disorders is manifest external to the self, in that it tends to disrupt the lives of others, whereas internalizing disorders are thought primarily to disrupt the sufferer's own life. Traditionally, externalizing and internalizing behaviors have been conceptualized as existing on opposite sides of the psychopathology spectrum. Efforts to develop more comprehensive understanding of psychopathology have focused on viewing externalizing and internalizing dysfunction as transdiagnostic terms that reflect liability for, in the case of externalizing dysfunction, a spectrum of disorders reflecting a propensity toward behavioral disinhibition, and, in the case of internalizing dysfunction, a spectrum of disorders characterized by high negative affect, low positive affect, and anxiety (Iacono, Malone, & McGue, 2008; Krueger & Markon, 2006; Krueger et al., 2002).

However, the two types of dysfunction do not operate independently, and their co-occurrence within both children and adults is very common (Krueger & Markon, 2006; Lilienfeld, 2003). Indeed, some recent research has argued for a single, general dimension of psychopathology that includes both externalizing and internalizing (Caspi et al., 2013). The correlation between higher-order factors representing externalizing and internalizing dysfunction has been estimated to be as high as $r = .50$ (Krueger & Markon, 2006). These findings highlight several important questions for psychopathology research. Is there a shared liability for externalizing and internalizing dysfunction? If so, what is its nature? Just as the two types of dysfunction often co-occur, they also often occur separately. What factors contribute to solely externalizing expressions of dysfunction and what factors contribute to solely internalizing expressions of dysfunction?

One possible model of common liability for externalizing and internalizing dysfunction has emerged from recent advances in the theory of impulsivity, particularly work by Carver, Johnson, and Joormann (2008). To understand this advance and place it in context, a very brief review of the recent history of theory and research concerning the personality underpinnings of impulsive behavior is warranted. Until very recently, impulsivity has been thought to contribute to liability for externalizing dysfunction in particular (Birkley & Smith, 2011; Smith & Guller, in press; Settles et al., 2012; Whiteside & Lynam, 2001). A great deal of research has shown that impulsivity-related personality traits prospectively predicted the onset of, or increases in, several externalizing behaviors (Corbin, Iwamoto, & Fromme, 2011; Cyders & Smith, 2008a; Doran, Schweizer, & Myers, 2011; Fischer, Peterson, & McCarthy, 2013; Pearson, Combs, Zapolski, & Smith, 2012; R. F. Settles, Cyders, & Smith, 2010).

As research clarified the specific nature of personality underpinnings to impulsive behavior, the identification of a disposition toward emotion-based rash or impulsive action was made. The trait of urgency refers to the tendency to act rashly or impulsively when experiencing intense emotion, and it has the two facets of negative urgency (rash action when extremely upset) and positive urgency (rash action when in an unusually positive mood: Cyders & Smith, 2007, 2008b; Whiteside & Lynam, 2001). Recognition of a disposition toward emotion-based impulsive behavior was important, because when multiple impulsivity-related traits are considered together, the urgency traits, in particular negative urgency, most effectively predict numerous behaviors that are described as impulsive and considered part of the externalizing domain (Coskunpinar, Dir, & Cyders, 2013; Fischer, Smith, & Cyders, 2008; Stautz & Cooper, 2013; Zapolski, Cyders, & Smith, 2009).

The mechanism by which negative urgency increases risk for externalizing behaviors is understood to be as follows. Rash acts when distressed, such as heavy drinking or binge eating, provide the immediate reinforcement of distraction from the source of one's distress. In that way, the acts are reinforced (Cyders & Smith, 2008b; Pearson, Riley, Davis, & Smith, 2014). In addition to this negative reinforcement, behaviors such as drinking and binge eating also provide the positive reinforcement associated with engagement in desired acts (Cyders & Smith, 2008b). On each occasion in which a person high in negative urgency acts rashly, (a) the rash behavior is reinforced and (b) the individual does not learn other, more adaptive responses to distress). Over time, the person comes to rely more heavily on the reinforced rash acts, thus increasing risk for problems such as problem drinking or disordered eating (Smith & Guller, in press).

Turning back to externalizing and internalizing dysfunction, the strong theoretical emphasis on the distinction between the two (Krueger & Markon, 2006) led to theory concerning the differential liabilities for the two domains. Markers of behavioral disinhibition or impulsivity were identified as important risk factors for externalizing dysfunction, and high negative affect, low positive affect, and anxiety were identified as risk factors for internalizing dysfunction (Iacono et al., 2008; Settles et al., 2012). In a series of three studies on children, emerging adults, and adults, Settles et al. (2012) showed that negative urgency consistently predicted several markers of externalizing dysfunction. In that same series of studies, a different liability for internalizing dysfunction was identified: high levels of negative affectivity predicted markers of internalizing dysfunction. Based on the above findings, Smith and Guller (in press) argued that urgency constitutes a transdiagnostic liability for impulsive behavior and thus externalizing dysfunction. From this perspective, risk is increased for externalizing behaviors such as excessive drinking, drug use, risky sex, and problem gambling by elevations in the traits of negative and positive urgency. Risk for internalizing dysfunction, in contrast, is based on high levels of trait depression and negative affect (Settles et al., 2012).

2. Common Underpinnings of Externalizing and Internalizing Dysfunction

Interestingly, Carver et al. (2008) offered a broader conceptualization of the role of urgency, resulting in a very different understanding of the liability provided by elevations in the trait. They identified urgency as part of a larger overall construct: reflexive responsivity to emotion (RRE). In their model, individuals may respond reflexively to emotions either with rash action (which can lead to externalizing dysfunction) or with ill-advised inaction (which can lead to internalizing dysfunction). Similar to the Cyders and Smith (2008b) theory, rash action such as heavy drinking can be a response to intense emotion that provides either the negative reinforcement of relief by providing a distraction from the source of the distress or positive reinforcement by enhancing a celebratory mood (Cyders & Smith, 2008b). However, in contrast to our theory, in Carver and colleagues (2008) model, ill-advised inaction can also be a response to intense emotion, with the similar goal of relief from distress. For example, choosing not to ask a date to the prom or failing to ask one's boss for a raise or promotion, can provide immediate relief from distress, even though these forms of inaction work against one's ongoing interests. Failure to act to pursue one's interests or to obtain potential reinforcement is associated with depressive symptomatology (Jacobson, Martell, & Dimidjian, 2001; Lewinsohn, 1975; Skinner, 1953). Thus, counter to our theory, Carver et al. (2008) identify urgency as a marker of RRE; thus, it should be predictive of both rash action and ill-advised inaction. From this alternative conceptualization, urgency should predict dysfunction reflecting rash action (such as heavy drinking or binge eating) as well as dysfunction reflecting ill-advised inaction (such as depressive symptomology). That is, it should increase liability for impulsive action and impulsive inaction. If that is the case, urgency may increase risk for both externalizing and internalizing dysfunction and thus be of even broader transdiagnostic importance.

To test these two models of rash action, we conducted a comparative test of our model of urgency versus the Carver model of urgency, using a prospective design in a developmental context (Smith, Guller, & Zapolski, 2013). This study specifically focused on urgency, externalizing behaviors (alcohol consumption, cigarette smoking, and binge eating), and internalizing symptomology (depression) during the important developmental period of early adolescence to answer the following questions: (1) Does urgency predict a range of externalizing behaviors, such as alcohol consumption, smoking, and binge eating across early adolescent development, as implied by its prediction of specific behaviors (Pearson et al., 2012; Settles & Smith, 2011)? (2) Does urgency predict depression across early adolescent development? If so, does urgency predict depression, controlling for prior depression and for addictive behavior involvement? Both the Cyders and Smith (2008b) and the Carver et al. (2008) models hold that urgency should predict externalizing behaviors, but only the Carver model also predicts that urgency will predict the internalizing dysfunction of depression as well. Support for the Carver et al. (2008) framework would suggest that responding reflexively to intense emotion, as indexed by urgency, increases risk for both externalizing and internalizing dysfunction. A failure to support Carver et al. (2008) would suggest the possibility that urgency is important primarily for externalizing dysfunction, and other, different traits contribute more heavily to internalizing dysfunction, consistent with Settles et al. (2012).

The study did, indeed, yield positive findings for *both* outcomes (i.e. urgency predicted later risky behaviors and depression), thus providing support for Carver and colleagues' (2008) model of impulsive action and impulsive inaction, with the implication that urgency increases liability for both externalizing and internalizing dysfunction. Its support for the Carver et al. (2008) model is noteworthy for several reasons. First, urgency's prediction of subsequent depression was robust to several other important predictors of depression. Second, the prediction was in young children, vastly reducing the possibility that the urgency – depression relationship reflects scars of ongoing psychopathology and life disruption. Third, early adolescence is a potential turning point in development for many youth (Graber & Brooks-Gunn, 1996), so prediction of depressive symptom endorsement by urgency across that transition may increase understanding of risk for a maladaptive transition and, potentially, progression along a more negative developmental trajectory.

A fourth reason that the findings in support of the Carver et al. (2008) model are striking concerns the content of the urgency items. Examples include "When I feel bad, I often do things I later regret in order to make myself feel better now," "When I am upset I often act without thinking," "I tend to act without thinking when I am very, very happy," and "When I am really happy, I tend to get out of control." The items consistently refer to tendencies toward action and include both very negative and very positive moods. There appears to be no measurement bias toward overlap with depressive symptomatology, nor is there a measurement bias toward overlap with inaction. In addition, urgency predicted depressive symptoms after controlling not just for prior depression but also for involvement in addictive behaviors, thus reducing the likelihood that urgency's predictive influence on depression was actually an artifact of its relationship with addictive behavior involvement (such as might have been the case if depressive symptom endorsement stemmed from negative consequences of addictive behavior involvement). Given that items with this content predicted depressive symptomology, over time and with stringent controls, suggests that the intended construct, urgency, can be viewed as a marker of RRE. Because of the item focus on action, we do not view urgency as isomorphic with RRE; in their work, Carver and colleagues supplement urgency with measures of emotion-based inaction to get a broader array of indicators of RRE. Our use of only urgency to predict depression makes the test we conducted a particularly stringent one.

Thus, the findings of Smith et al. (2013) provide clear support for a conceptualization of urgency as a marker of a tendency to respond reflexively to emotion, whether with rash action or ill-advised inaction, and as important for both externalizing and internalizing dysfunction. Adults sometimes engage in rash actions, such as heavy alcohol consumption, risky sexual behavior, problem gambling, binge eating, self-harm, and other behaviors, with the apparent goal of relief from, or distraction from, subjective distress (Cyders & Smith, 2008; Fischer et al., 2008; Riley et al. 2014; Settles et al., 2010; Smyth et al., 2007; Swendsen et al., 2000). Similarly, inaction can serve the same purpose, even when action would be beneficial (Carver et al., 2008; Carver, Johnson, Joormann, Kim, & Nam, 2011). In both children and adults, individual differences in the trait of urgency should perhaps be understood to reflect this general disposition toward RRE, and hence to increase risk for both the internalizing and externalizing spectra of behaviors, rather than simply a disposition toward impulsive action.

This support for the Carver et al. (2008) framework is consistent with cognitive neuroscience literature that identifies some of the same brain process as underlying both externalizing dysfunction and the classic internalizing dysfunction of depression. As discussed in greater detail in the following section, low levels of serotonin in a functional brain system relating the orbitofrontal and ventromedial prefrontal cortex to the amygdala and striatum are implicated in both (Carver et al., 2008; Cyders & Smith, 2008b). Davidson (2003) makes a similar observation. From his perspective, low levels of serotonin in this brain system are associated with deficits in what he calls affect-guided planning, which is the capacity to stay affectively connected to one's long-term goals, and choose behaviors that further those goals, even when one is experiencing intense emotion in the moment. There thus appears to be convergence between the Carver et al. (2008) and the Davidson (2003) perspectives: high levels of RRE appear analogous to low levels of affect-guided planning; both are associated with specific functional deficits in the same identified brain system.

Urgency may thus be viewed as a marker of high RRE, and thus presumably of low affect-guided planning. Perhaps urgency is the tendency to respond to intense emotion with actions or with inactions that reduce distress but that are ill-advised, in that they are not chosen with an eye toward one's ongoing interests.

3. Neurobiological Underpinnings of RRE

Evidence from the neuroscience literature offers further support for common etiologic underpinnings of externalizing and internalizing dysfunction. There are many relevant domains of inquiry in neuroscience; we focus on a subset of domains that we consider particularly important for understanding the neurobiological underpinnings of externalizing and internalizing dysfunction. Specifically, research on neuroanatomical, neuromodulatory, and genetic influences have clarified the common rapture nature of risk across the two domains. Carver et al. (2008) offer such evidence from the neuroscience literature to support their framework, in particular noting that both impulsive behavior and depressive symptomology are related to low levels of serotonin in the same brain system, which can be influenced by genetic polymorphisms due to the regulatory role they play in relation to serotonergic functioning. Cyders and Smith (2008b) focus on similar neurocircuitry in their review of urgency theory.

3.1. Neuroanatomical Structures

Neuronal connections between the amygdala, which is subcortical, and parts of the prefrontal cortex (PFC), notably the orbitofrontal cortex (OFC) and its medial sector (the ventromedial prefrontal cortex [VMPFC]; Bechara, 2005; Lewis & Todd, 2007) play a crucial role in RRE. The amygdala appears to provide information about the emotional significance of sensory input, thereby influencing activity in the OFC and VMPFC. Thus, the emotional significance of events influences subsequent cortical activity. In turn, the OFC and VMPFC appear to exhibit a regulating effect on the amygdala and the brain stem (Bechara, 2005; Ghashghaei & Barbas, 2002; Lewis & Todd, 2007). The OFC can interrupt the direct connection between emotion and response: OFC activity overrides emotional responses, apparently by providing information and a bias toward long-term, goal directed behavior (Lewis & Todd, 2007). The result is the capacity to interrupt responses to immediate needs in light of long-term interests and goals. With reduced serotonin in this system, the PFC provides less interruption of emotion-driven responses, thus increasing the likelihood of either impulsive action or impulsive inaction (i.e. increasing the likelihood of RRE). In the Carver model, it is believed that the VMPFC, lateral temporal cortex, amygdala, and basal ganglia are activated as part of an automatic, reflexive mode, whereas rostral and dorsal areas of the ACC and the lateral and dorsal PFC are activated during a deliberative reflective mode (Casey, Tottenham, & Fossella, 2002; Posner & DiGirolamo, 2000; Satpute & Lieberman, 2006). The brain regions involved in the reflexive mode are also involved in externalizing and internalizing forms of psychopathology, potentially reflecting dominance of the reflexive over the reflective system present in both forms of dysfunction, as suggested by neuroanatomical studies looking at the interplay between the two (Brown, Manuck, Flory, & Hariri, 2006; Horn, Dolan, Elliott, Deakin, & Woodruff, 2003).

3.2. Neuromodulation of Serotonin

Although this work has typically been reported in separate literatures, serotonergic functioning has consistently been linked to impulsive action seen in externalizing dysfunction, and impulsive inaction seen in internalizing dysfunction. For example, high levels of serotonin in the PFC region of the brain are associated with socially adaptive behavior, while low levels are associated with aggression and socially maladjusted behavior in monkeys (Raleigh & Brammer, 1993). Furthermore, low serotonin, particularly in the ACC, is related to impulsive aggression and poor emotion regulation (Frankle et al., 2005). Additionally, serotonin reuptake inhibitors (SSRIs), which result in greater levels of serotonin in the synapse, have demonstrated reduction in both depressive symptoms (Arroll et al., 2005) and risky behaviors (Barbe, Rubovszky, Venturini-Andreoli, & Andreoli, 2005) in human, clinical samples. These findings have been replicated across multiple forms of externalizing and internalizing dysfunction in both human and animal models. Serotonergic functioning also has important implications for other neurotransmitter systems, for instance, the regulatory role it plays in inhibiting subcortical dopaminergic functioning (see Carver et al., 2008; Cyders & Smith, 2008b; Spoont, 1992 for reviews).

3.3. Genetic Influences on Serotonin and Urgency

Gene polymorphisms also appear to shape internalizing and externalizing indirectly, through their influence on serotonergic activity. Specifically, it appears that variations in the serotonin transporter gene, 5HTTLPR, are related to such variability, thus influencing presentation of impulsive action or inaction. The 5HTTLPR gene is triallelic, having one short allele, *S*, and two long alleles, *Lg* and *La* (Beitchman et al., 2006). The short allele and the *Lg* variant of the long allele on the 5HTTLPR gene are associated with lower neurotransmission of serotonin (Beitchman et al., 2006; Hu et al., 2005, 2006; Lakatos et al., 2003). Reduced serotonergic activity, as discussed above, has been implicated in a wide range of internalizing (e.g. anxiety, depression), and externalizing (e.g. substance dependence, conduct disorder) dysfunction. It is possible that one mechanism by which low serotonin increases risk is through urgency. Recently, the polymorphism on the 5HTTLPR gene shown to be associated with low serotonin levels was found to predict urgency levels (Carver et al., 2011). The serotonin transporter gene has been extensively targeted by psychopathology research; however, other gene polymorphisms, such as the dopamine receptor gene, BDNF (which encodes production of brain-derived neurotrophic factor), and others may be relevant (Carver, LeMoult, Johnson, & Joormann, 2014).

Cyders and Smith (2008b) present an account for the emergency of the trait of urgency that integrates genetic, neurotransmitter, and brain system research, along with research in temperament, personality, and psychosocial learning. Their account, together with that provided by Carver et al. (2008), provide a somewhat detailed account of the nature of one form of liability for, it appears, both externalizing and internalizing dysfunction.

4. Distinguishing Internalizing and Externalizing Dysfunction

Until this point, the present chapter has focused exclusively on factors that are indicated as common underpinnings of externalizing and internalizing dysfunction. These shared factors warrant this level of discussion, particularly given the traditional approach found across past psychopathology research, which often looked at these forms of dysfunction as separate constructs. However, despite the large overlap between these two domains of dysfunction, there is still a substantial amount of unshared variance between these two tendencies that remains unexplained. Individuals often do experience externalizing dysfunction without internalizing dysfunction and vice versa. For this reason, it is important to explore factors that uniquely contribute to one form of psychopathology but not the other. We consider two possible factors.

4.1. Reward and Punishment Sensitivity or Approach and Avoidance

From the Carver et al. (2008) perspective, what determines whether RRE is expressed as rash action or ill-advised inaction is determined by individual differences in reward and punishment sensitivity (Shankman, Klein, Tenke, & Bruder, 2007). Reward sensitivity is understood to reflect a strong responsiveness to reward, such that one's behavioral choices are heavily influenced by the pursuit of reward. A person high in reward sensitivity is thought to have a bias to engage in many behaviors, because of the possibility that they will bring reward. Punishment sensitivity is understood to reflect strong reactivity to, and hence concern about, punishment or possible negative outcomes of behavior. A person high in punishment sensitivity is thus thought to have a bias to avoid many behaviors, out of a concern that they might result in punishment. An individual who is high in RRE and who is also high in reward sensitivity may tend to choose reflexive responses to emotion that involve rash actions and risky behaviors, and therefore be at increased risk for externalizing dysfunction. In contrast, a high RRE, high punishment sensitive individual will tend to choose reflexive responses to emotion that are characterized by ill-advised inaction, and thus be at increased risk for internalizing dysfunction, such as depression.

A closely related possibility involves the concepts of approach temperament and avoidance temperament (Elliot & Thrash, 2002). Approach temperament is understood to refer to a fundamental sensitivity to positive or desirable stimuli, including perceptual vigilance for, emotional reactivity to, and behavioral predisposition toward rewarding stimuli (Elliot & Thrash, 2002). Avoidance temperament is understood to refer to a fundamental sensitivity to, or concern about, negative or undesirable stimuli, similarly accompanied by perceptual vigilance, for, emotional reactivity to, and behavioral disposition away from such stimuli (Elliot & Thrash, 2002). Interestingly, the two temperaments appear to be unrelated: in a series of six studies, the median correlation between measures of the two was $r = .02$. Perhaps, among individuals high in RRE, those high in approach temperament are prone to rash action and those high in avoidance temperament are prone to ill-advised inaction. These possibilities merit investigation by researchers.

The possibility of integrating RRE with Approach Temperament – Avoidance Temperament theory raises a number of interesting questions. What are the functional brain systems that underlie approach and avoidance temperaments? Is there a relationship between individual differences in RRE and individual differences in either approach or avoidance temperaments? If so, what is the nature of the relationship? Are certain patterns of RRE and temperament more likely than others? How might we understand the neuroanatomical structures that dispose individuals to elevations in both RRE and in approach or avoidance temperaments? Of course, one individual could be elevated in both approach and avoidance temperament. What would such a person's risk profile be like? Would that person have a tendency toward rash action accompanied by distress over their actions?

4.2. Gender, Externalizing, and Internalizing

Any effort to explain differential risk for externalizing and internalizing dysfunction must consider sex or gender. Males are much more likely to engage in externalizing dysfunction and females are much more likely to experience internalizing dysfunction (Grant & Weissman, 2007; Rutter, Caspi, & Moffitt, 2003; Widiger, 2007). There are many theories to explain this sex difference, ranging from evolutionary psychology theories (e.g. Ellis, 2011) that include proximal mechanisms such as higher exposure to prenatal testosterone in men and evolved propensities for empathy, cognitive rumination, and negative affect in women (Martel, 2013), to socialization theories of several kinds (cf. Keenan & Shaw, 1997; Maccoby, 2002). Perhaps in part due to hormonal differences during key developmental periods and in part due to different socialization processes for boys and girls, sex differences in dysfunction are striking. It thus seems likely that men high in RRE are more prone to externalizing problems and women high in RRE are more prone to internalizing problems.

5. Developmental Psychopathology and RRE

Study of the development of psychopathology is crucial for understanding the nature and etiology of dysfunction, as well as for developing effective prevention and intervention strategies. To the degree that impulsive action and impulsive inaction have a common antecedent, and thus to the degree that externalizing and internalizing dysfunction do as well, developmental researchers need to approach their understanding of psychopathology with this in mind. Thus, the Carver et al. (2008) model might inform developmental psychopathology research in profitable ways. One obvious implication of this model is that, in addition to studying the development of externalizing and internalizing dysfunction separately from each other, models that chart the development of high levels of RRE, and hence risk for both forms of dysfunction, may prove useful (Hussong, Jones, Stein, Baucom, & Boeding, 2011; Windle et al., 2008). Put differently, viewing development from the perspective of the Carver model may help clarify the risk process.

One example concerns the role of temperament in the development of risk. Infants differ in their ability to modify the duration and intensity of their emotions; some children are worse than others at using effective behavioral strategies, such as gaze aversion, self-soothing, or seeking proximity to a caregiver in order to reduce distress. These infants appear to be less likely to develop adaptive, effective emotion-regulation strategies (Buss & Goldsmith, 1998). Perhaps early individual differences in emotion-regulation strategies anticipate the emergence of reflexive versus reflected response to intense emotion. Consistent with this possibility, high levels of emotionality and low levels of behavioral regulation are very highly correlated in youth (Eisenberg et al., 2000; Rothbart, Ahadi, & Evans, 2000). Cyders and Smith (2008b) argued that this temperament profile may be a precursor to the development of urgency, and hence high RRE and low affect-guided planning.

Additional complexities concerning the developmental emergence of externalizing and internalizing behaviors need to be considered. Although the two types of dysfunction appear to share a common liability, it is also possible that each type of behavior influences the other over time. It is further possible that the two types of behaviors and RRE influence each other as well. Guller and Smith (2014) provided an example of such processes in a study of the emergence of problem drinking during adolescence. Using a longitudinal design, they found evidence for the following transactional processes between internalizing behaviors, externalizing behaviors, and RRE. Depressive symptom level in the spring of 5th grade predicted increases in negative urgency by the fall of 7th grade. Negative urgency, in turn, predicted drinking frequency by the fall of 8th grade. Drinking frequency predicted problem drinking by the spring of 8th grade, and then problem drinking predicted depression by the spring of 9th grade. In fact, there was reciprocal prediction between depression and problem drinking between grades 8 and 9. Each of these predictive paths operated above and beyond autoregressive prediction. As is consistently found in developmental psychopathology research (Cicchetti, 2006), development is complex and characterized by transactions among multiple factors, some of which share common antecedents. The possibility that two forms of dysfunction in this model, reflecting impulsive inaction and impulsive action respectively, stem from a common liability factor, offers an important direction for further research. If interventions are developed that alter RRE levels, it might be possible to lessen the magnitude of the transactional risk process described by Guller and Smith (2014). It might also be possible to interrupt that process at multiple points in time.

CONCLUSION

An important new direction in impulsivity research has been the development of a model identifying a common risk process for impulsive action and impulsive inaction. Choices to act, or not to act, in order to meet an immediate affective need at the expense of one's ongoing goals and interests can be considered rash, ill-advised, or impulsive. This model is supported by an elaborated model specifying the genetic, neurobiological and personality trait underpinnings to reflexive responsivity to emotion (RRE), the attribute thought to increase liability for impulsive choices. It is further supported by empirical work indicating that individual differences in RRE predict the emergence of individual differences in both externalizing and internalizing dysfunction over time. The frequent co-occurrence of externalizing and internalizing behaviors, though often not emphasized in the literature, is consistent with this model of a common liability for both. RRE and engagement in externalizing and internalizing behaviors transact over the course of development to increase risk for both types of dysfunction. There is a need for further research on the developmental course of those high in RRE.

REFERENCES

Arroll, B., Macgillivray, S., Ogston, S., Reid, I., Sullivan, F., Williams, B. & Crombie, I. (2005). Efficacy and tolerability of tricyclic antidepressants and SSRIs compared with placebo for treatment of depression in primary care: a meta-analysis. *Annals of Family Medicine*, *3*(5), 449–456. doi:10.1370/afm.349

Barbe, R. P., Rubovszky, G., Venturini-Andreoli, A. & Andreoli, A. (2005). The treatment of borderline personality disorder patients with current suicidal behaviour. *Clinical Neuropsychiatry: Journal of Treatment Evaluation*, *2*(5), 283–291.

Bechara, A. (2005). Decision making, impulse control and loss of willpower to resist drugs: a neurocognitive perspective. *Nature Neuroscience*, *8*(11), 1458–1463. doi: 10.1038/nn1584

Beitchman, J. H., Baldassarra, L., Mik, H., De Luca, V., King, N., Bender, D., Kennedy, J. L. (2006). Serotonin transporter polymorphisms and persistent, pervasive childhood aggression. *The American Journal of Psychiatry*, *163*(6), 1103–1105. doi:10.1176/appi.ajp.163.6.1103

Birkley, E. L. & Smith, G. T. (2011). Recent advances in understanding the personality underpinnings of impulsive behavior and their role in risk for addictive behaviors. *Current Drug Abuse Reviews*, *4*(4), 215–227.

Brown, S. M., Manuck, S. B., Flory, J. D. & Hariri, A. R. (2006). Neural basis of individual differences in impulsivity: contributions of corticolimbic circuits for behavioral arousal and control. *Emotion (Washington, D.C.)*, *6*(2), 239–245. doi:10.1037/1528-3542.6.2.239

Buss, K. A. & Goldsmith, H. H. (1998). Fear and anger regulation in infancy: effects on the temporal dynamics of affective expression. *Child Development*, *69*(2), 359–374.

Carver, C. S., Johnson, S. L. & Joormann, J. (2008). Serotonergic function, two-mode models of self-regulation, and vulnerability to depression: What depression has in common with impulsive aggression. *Psychological Bulletin*, *134*(6), 912–943. doi:10.1037/a0013740

Carver, C. S., Johnson, S. L., Joormann, J., Kim, Y. & Nam, J. Y. (2011). Serotonin transporter polymorphism interacts with childhood adversity to predict aspects of impulsivity. *Psychological Science*, *22*(5), 589–595. doi:10.1177/0956797611404085

Carver, C. S., LeMoult, J., Johnson, S. L. & Joormann, J. (2014). Gene Effects and G × E Interactions in the Differential Prediction of Three Aspects of Impulsiveness. *Social Psychological and Personality Science*, 1948550614527116. doi:10.1177/1948550614527116

Casey, B. J., Tottenham, N. & Fossella, J. (2002). Clinical, imaging, lesion, and genetic approaches toward a model of cognitive control. *Developmental Psychobiology*, *40*(3), 237–254.

Caspi, A., Houts, R. M., Belsky, D. W., Goldman-Mellor, S. J., Harrington, H., Israel, S., … Moffitt, T. E. (2013). The p Factor One General Psychopathology Factor in the Structure of Psychiatric Disorders? *Clinical Psychological Science*, 2167702613497473. doi:10.1177/2167702613497473

Cicchetti, D. (2006). Development and psychopathology. In D. Cicchetti & D. J. Cohen (Eds.), *Developmental psychopathology, Vol 1: Theory and method (2nd ed.).* (1–23). Hoboken, NJ US: John Wiley & Sons Inc.

Corbin, W. R., Iwamoto, D. K. & Fromme, K. (2011). A comprehensive longitudinal test of the acquired preparedness model for alcohol use and related problems. *Journal of Studies on Alcohol and Drugs*, *72*(4), 602–610.

Coskunpinar, A., Dir, A. L. & Cyders, M. A. (2013). Multidimensionality in impulsivity and alcohol use: A meta-analysis using the UPPS model of impulsivity. *Alcoholism: Clinical and Experimental Research*, *37*(9), 1441–1450. doi:10.1111/acer.12131

Cyders, M. A. & Smith, G. T. (2008a). Clarifying the role of personality dispositions in risk for increased gambling behavior. *Personality and Individual Differences*, *45*(6), 503–508. doi:10.1016/j.paid.2008.06.002

Cyders, M. A. & Smith, G. T. (2008b). Emotion-based dispositions to rash action: Positive and negative urgency. *Psychological Bulletin*, *134*(6), 807–828. doi:10.1037/a0013341

Davidson, R. J. (2003). Darwin and the neural bases of emotion and affective style. *Annals of the New York Academy of Sciences*, *1000*, 316–336.

Doran, N., Schweizer, C. A. & Myers, M. G. (2011). Do expectancies for reinforcement from smoking change after smoking initiation? *Psychology of Addictive Behaviors: Journal of the Society of Psychologists in Addictive Behaviors*, *25*(1), 101–107. doi:10.1037/a0020361

Elliot, A. J. & Thrash, T. M. (2002). Approach-avoidance motivation in personality: approach and avoidance temperaments and goals. *Journal of Personality and Social Psychology*, *82*(5), 804–818.

Ellis, L. (2011). Identifying and explaining apparent universal sex differences in cognition and behavior. *Personality and Individual Differences*, *51*(5), 552–561. doi:10.1016/j.paid.2011.04.004

Fischer, S., Peterson, C. M. & McCarthy, D. (2013). A prospective test of the influence of negative urgency and expectancies on binge eating and purging. *Psychology of Addictive Behaviors: Journal of the Society of Psychologists in Addictive Behaviors*, *27*(1), 294–300. doi:10.1037/a0029323

Fischer, S., Smith, G. T. & Cyders, M. A. (2008). Another look at impulsivity: a meta-analytic review comparing specific dispositions to rash action in their relationship to bulimic symptoms. *Clinical Psychology Review*, *28*(8), 1413–1425. doi:10.1016/j.cpr.2008.09.001

Frankle, W. G., Lombardo, I., New, A. S., Goodman, M., Talbot, P. S., Huang, Y., Siever, L. J. (2005). Brain Serotonin Transporter Distribution in Subjects With Impulsive Aggressivity: A Positron Emission Study With [11C]McN 5652. *American Journal of Psychiatry*, *162*(5), 915–923. doi:10.1176/appi.ajp.162.5.915

Ghashghaei, H. T. & Barbas, H. (2002). Pathways for emotion: interactions of prefrontal and anterior temporal pathways in the amygdala of the rhesus monkey. *Neuroscience*, *115*(4), 1261–1279.

Graber, J. A. & Brooks-Gunn, J. (1996). Transitions and turning points: Navigating the passage from childhood through adolescence. *Developmental Psychology*, *32*(4), 768–776. doi:10.1037/0012-1649.32.4.768

Grant, B. F. & Weissman, M. M. (2007). Gender and the prevalence of psychiatric disorders. In W. E. Narrow, M. B. First, P. J. Sirovatka, & D. A. Regier (Eds.), *Age and gender considerations in psychiatric diagnosis: A research agenda for DSM-V.* (pp. 31–45). Arlington, VA US: American Psychiatric Publishing, Inc.

Guller, L., Zapolski, T. C. B. & Smith, G. T. (2014, June). Integrating Externalizing and Internalizing Pathways to Problem Drinking Across Adolescence. Paper accepted for presentation at the annual Research Society on Alcoholism, Bellevue, Washington.

Horn, N. R., Dolan, M., Elliott, R., Deakin, J. F. W. & Woodruff, P. W. R. (2003). Response inhibition and impulsivity: an fMRI study. *Neuropsychologia, 41*(14), 1959–1966.

Hu, X. Z., Lipsky, R. H., Zhu, G., Akhtar, L. A., Taubman, J., Greenberg, B. D., Goldman, D. (2006). Serotonin Transporter Promoter Gain-of-Function Genotypes Are Linked to Obsessive-Compulsive Disorder. *American Journal of Human Genetics, 78*(5), 815–826.

Hu, X. Z., Oroszi, G., Chun, J., Smith, T. L., Goldman, D. & Schuckit, M. A. (2005). An expanded evaluation of the relationship of four alleles to the level of response to alcohol and the alcoholism risk. *Alcoholism, Clinical and Experimental Research, 29*(1), 8–16.

Hussong, A. M., Jones, D. J., Stein, G. L., Baucom, D. H. & Boeding, S. (2011). An internalizing pathway to alcohol use and disorder. *Psychology of Addictive Behaviors, 25*(3), 390–404. doi:10.1037/a0024519

Iacono, W. G., Malone, S. M. & McGue, M. (2008). Behavioral disinhibition and the development of early-onset addiction: common and specific influences. *Annual Review of Clinical Psychology, 4*, 325–348. doi:10.1146/annurev.clinpsy.4.022007.141157

Jacobson, N. S., Martell, C. R. & Dimidjian, S. (2001). Behavioral Activation Treatment for Depression: Returning to Contextual Roots. *Clinical Psychology: Science and Practice, 8*(3), 255–270. doi:10.1093/clipsy.8.3.255

Keenan, K. & Shaw, D. (1997). Developmental and social influences on young girls' early problem behavior. *Psychological Bulletin, 121*(1), 95–113. doi:10.1037/0033-2909.121.1.95

Krueger, R. F., Hicks, B. M., Patrick, C. J., Carlson, S. R., Iacono, W. G. & McGue, M. (2002). Etiologic connections among substance dependence, antisocial behavior, and personality: modeling the externalizing spectrum. *Journal of Abnormal Psychology, 111*(3), 411–424.

Krueger, R. F. & Markon, K. E. (2006). Reinterpreting Comorbidity: A Model-Based Approach to Understanding and Classifying Psychopathology. *Annual Review of Clinical Psychology, 2*(1), 111–133. doi:10.1146/annurev.clinpsy.2.022305.095213

Lakatos, K., Nemoda, Z., Birkas, E., Ronai, Z., Kovacs, E., Ney, K., Gervai, J. (2003). Association of D4 dopamine receptor gene and serotonin transporter promoter polymorphisms with infants' response to novelty. *Molecular Psychiatry, 8*(1), 90–97. doi:10.1038/sj.mp.4001212

Lewinsohn, P. M. (1975). Engagement in pleasant activities and depression level. *Journal of Abnormal Psychology, 84*(6), 729–731. doi:10.1037/0021-843X.84.6.729

Lewis, M. D. & Todd, R. M. (2007). The self-regulating brain: Cortical-subcortical feedback and the development of intelligent action. *Cognitive Development, 22*(4), 406–430. doi:10.1016/j.cogdev.2007.08.004

Lilienfeld, S. O. (2003). Comorbidity Between and Within Childhood Externalizing and Internalizing Disorders: Reflections and Directions. *Journal of Abnormal Child Psychology, 31*(3), 285–291. doi:10.1023/A:1023229529866

Maccoby, E. E. (2002). Gender and group process: A developmental perspective. *Current Directions in Psychological Science, 11*(2), 54–58. doi:10.1111/1467-8721.00167

Martel, M. M. (2013). Sexual selection and sex differences in the prevalence of childhood externalizing and adolescent internalizing disorders. *Psychological Bulletin*, *139*(6), 1221–1259. doi:10.1037/a0032247

Pearson, C. M., Combs, J. L., Zapolski, T. C. B. & Smith, G. T. (2012). A longitudinal transactional risk model for early eating disorder onset. *Journal of Abnormal Psychology*, *121*(3), 707–718. doi:10.1037/a0027567

Pearson, C. M., Riley, E. N., Davis, H. A. & Smith, G. T. (2014). Two pathways toward impulsive action: An integrative risk model for bulimic behavior in youth. *Journal of Child Psychology and Psychiatry.* Available online: doi: 10.1111/jcpp.12214.

Posner, M. I. & DiGirolamo, G. J. (2000). Cognitive neuroscience: origins and promise. *Psychological Bulletin*, *126*(6), 873–889.

Raleigh, M. I. & Brammer, G. L. (1993). Individual differences in serotonin-2 receptors and social behavior in monkeys. *Social Neuroscience Abstracts*, *19*, 592.

Riley, E.N., Combs, J.L., Jordan, C. E, & Smith, G.T. (2014, June). Negative urgency and depression: Trait-based predictors of self-injury over time. International Society for the Study of Self-Injury. Evanston, IL.

Rutter, M., Caspi, A. & Moffitt, T. E. (2003). Using sex differences in psychopathology to study causal mechanisms: unifying issues and research strategies. *Journal of Child Psychology and Psychiatry, and Allied Disciplines*, *44*(8), 1092–1115.

Satpute, A. B. & Lieberman, M. D. (2006). Integrating automatic and controlled processes into neurocognitive models of social cognition. *Brain Research*, *1079*(1), 86–97. doi:10.1016/j.brainres.2006.01.005

Settles, R. E., Fischer, S., Cyders, M. A., Combs, J. L., Gunn, R. L. & Smith, G. T. (2012). Negative urgency: a personality predictor of externalizing behavior characterized by neuroticism, low conscientiousness, and disagreeableness. *Journal of Abnormal Psychology*, *121*(1), 160–172. doi:10.1037/a0024948

Settles, R. F., Cyders, M. & Smith, G. T. (2010). Longitudinal validation of the acquired preparedness model of drinking risk. *Psychology of Addictive Behaviors: Journal of the Society of Psychologists in Addictive Behaviors*, *24*(2), 198–208. doi:10.1037/a0017631

Settles, R. E. & Smith, G. T. (2011, June). Toward a truly developmental model of adolescent problem drinking. Paper presented at the annual meeting of the Research Society on Alcoholism, Atlanta, GA.

Shankman, S. A., Klein, D. N., Tenke, C. E. & Bruder, G. E. (2007). Reward sensitivity in depression: A biobehavioral study. *Journal of Abnormal Psychology*, *116*(1), 95–104. doi:10.1037/0021-843X.116.1.95

Skinner, B. F. (1953). Some contributions of an experimental analysis of behavior to psychology as a whole. *American Psychologist*, *8*(2), 69–78. doi:10.1037/h0054118

Smith, G. T. & Guller, L. (in press). Psychological underpinnings to impulsive behavior. In M. L. Cooper & R. Larsen (Eds.), *APA Handbook of Personality and Social Psychology.*

Smith, G. T., Guller, L. & Zapolski, T. C. B. (2013). A Comparison of Two Models of Urgency: Urgency Predicts Both Rash Action and Depression in Youth. *Clinical Psychological Science*, *1*(3), 266–275. doi:10.1177/2167702612470647

Smyth, J. M., Wonderlich, S. A., Heron, K. E., Sliwinski, M. J., Crosby, R. D., Mitchell, J. E. & Engel, S. G. (2007). Daily and momentary mood and stress are associated with binge eating and vomiting in bulimia nervosa patients in the natural environment. *Journal of Consulting and Clinical Psychology*, *75*(4), 629–638. doi:10.1037/0022-006X.75.4.629

Spoont, M. R. (1992). Modulatory role of serotonin in neural information processing: Implications for human psychopathology. *Psychological Bulletin, 112*(2), 330–350. doi:10.1037/0033-2909.112.2.330

Stautz, K. & Cooper, A. (2013). Impulsivity-related personality traits and adolescent alcohol use: A meta-analytic review. *Clinical Psychology Review, 33*(4), 574–592. doi:10.1016/j.cpr.2013.03.003

Swendsen, J. D., Tennen, H., Carney, M. A., Affleck, G., Willard, A. & Hromi, A. (2000). Mood and alcohol consumption: an experience sampling test of the self-medication hypothesis. *Journal of Abnormal Psychology, 109*(2), 198–204.

Whiteside, S. P. & Lynam, D. R. (2001). The Five Factor Model and impulsivity: using a structural model of personality to understand impulsivity. *Personality and Individual Differences, 30*(4), 669–689. doi:10.1016/S0191-8869(00)00064-7

Widiger, T. A. (2007). DSM's approach to gender: History and controversies. In W. E. Narrow, M. B. First, P. J. Sirovatka, & D. A. Regier (Eds.), *Age and gender considerations in psychiatric diagnosis: A research agenda for DSM-V.* (pp. 19–29). Arlington, VA US: American Psychiatric Publishing, Inc.

Windle, M., Spear, L. P., Fuligni, A. J., Angold, A., Brown, J. D., Pine, D., Dahl, R. E. (2008). Transitions Into Underage and Problem Drinking: Developmental Processes and Mechanisms Between 10 and 15 Years of Age. *PEDIATRICS, 121* (Supplement), S273–S289. doi:10.1542/peds.2007-2243C

Zapolski, T. C. B., Cyders, M. A. & Smith, G. T. (2009). Positive urgency predicts illegal drug use and risky sexual behavior. *Psychology of Addictive Behaviors: Journal of the Society of Psychologists in Addictive Behaviors, 23*(2), 348–354. doi:10.1037/a0014684

In: Psychology of Impulsivity
Editor: Mary C. Olmstead

ISBN: 978-1-63321-879-6

Chapter 7

BIOMARKERS OF IMPULSIVITY

***Dubravka Svob Strac*[1], *Matea Nikolac Perkovic*[1], *Gordana Nedic Erjavec*[1], *Evelyn Kiive*[2], *Katarina Dodig Curkovic*[3], *Mario Curkovic*[4], *Dubravka Kocijan Hercigonja*[5], *Jaanus Harro*[2], *Dorotea Muck-Seler*[1] *and Nela Pivac*[1*]**

[1]Division of Molecular Medicine, Rudjer Boskovic Institute, Zagreb, Croatia
[2]Department of Psychology, Estonian Centre for Behavioural and Health Sciences, University of Tartu, Estonia
[3]University Department of Child and Adolescent Psychiatry, University Hospital Osijek, School of Medicine Josip Juraj Strossmayer University of Osijek, Osijek, Croatia
[4]Department of Family Medicine, School of Medicine Josip Juraj Strossmayer University of Osijek, Osijek, Croatia
[5]Polyclinic Kocijan/Hercigonja, Zagreb, Croatia

ABSTRACT

Impulsivity represents a complex human behavior characterized by little or no forethought, reflection, or consideration of the consequences. The definitions of impulsivity include a number of subtraits, such as risk taking, lack of planning, making up one's mind quickly, acting on the spur of the moment (motor activation), not focusing on the task at hand (attention), and not planning and thinking carefully (lack of planning). Evidence from different genetic and neuroimaging studies suggest that biopsychosocial factors and their interaction affect the development of impulsivity; however the underlying biological substrates are not yet fully defined. Biological factors are greatly influenced by a variety of genetic and non-genetic factors. Although impulsivity represents one of the diagnostic criteria for several psychiatric disorders, its complex role is still not fully clarified. There is a large body of behavioral, personality, psychological, biological and neurological research on impulsivity, with a great interest in identifying

[*]Corresponding author: Prof. Nela Pivac, PhD; Senior Scientist, Laboratory for Molecular Neuropsychiatry, Division of Molecular Medicine, Rudjer Boskovic Institute, Zagreb, Croatia, Phone: +385-1-457-1207; Fax: + 385 1 456 1010, E-mail: npivac@irb.hr.

biomarkers associated with this trait. Impulsivity is moderated through a network of different cortical regions such as medial and dorsolateral prefrontal cortices, and the subcortical ventral striatum. These results suggest that structures mediating reward related decision-making are associated with impulsivity. Biomarkers are objective, quantifiable characteristics of biological processes. As impulsive behavior has been associated, primarily, with functional changes in serotonergic, dopaminergic, and noradrenergic systems, our aim was to investigate the biological and genetic markers of impulsivity, especially those related to dopaminergic and serotonergic systems in children and adolescents. In this chapter we have presented the results regarding association of impulsivity with peripheral biochemical markers such as platelet serotonin (5-HT) concentration and platelet monoamine oxidase (MAO-B) activity. Moreover, we have investigated the potential genetic markers of impulsivity, such as different variants of the genes encoding catechol-o-methyl transferase (COMT), dopamine-beta-hydroxylase (DBH), monoamine oxidase type B (MAO-B), dopamine receptor type 4 (DRD4) and serotonin transporter (5-HTT). Our findings might contribute to a more complete understanding of the etiology of impulsive behavior and lead to improvements in the treatment of a variety of psychiatric disorders.

1. Introduction

1.1. Impulsivity

Impulsivity has been broadly defined as a part of human behavior which is characterized by the lack of adequate thought, the tendency to act and go into swift action with less forethought or conscious judgment, the tendency to take unnecessary risks with no planning and quickly making up one's mind (Eysenck and Eysenck, 1977; Moeller et al., 2001). An impulsive person will react rapidly to internal or external stimuli without regard for the negative consequences of these reactions (Chamberlain and Sahakian, 2007; Chamorro et al., 2012; Moeller et al., 2001). This complex behavior is composed of different domains encompassing behavioral disinhibition, risky decision-making, inattention and delay discounting abnormalities (Cho et al., 2013; Dom et al., 2006; Reynolds et al., 2006; Schwann et al., 2002). While inattention involves the inability to maintain alertness and receptivity for a particular set of stimuli or stimuli changes over time, impulsive disinhibition represents dysregulation of inhibitory processes in the case of inappropriate or unwanted behaviors.

Socially, impulsivity has been considered as a learned behavior, coming from a family environment in which the child learns to "react immediately to obtain what is desired for gratification" (L'Abate, 1993). In addition, various genetic (Bevilacqua et al., 2010; Terracciano et al., 2011) and neuroimaging (Kim and Lee, 2011) studies suggest a neurobiological basis for impulsivity. Although particular biological and genetic markers of impulsivity have been detected (Coccaro et al., 1989; Evans et al., 2000; Mann and Arango; 1992; Schalling et al., 1988; Suominen et al., 1997), the neurobiology of this complex behavior is still not clear. The involvement of particular areas of the brain such as dorsolateral and medial prefrontal cortices, orbitofrontal cortex, anterior cingulate cortex and ventral striatum has been shown to be crucial for impulsive behavior (Bechara and Van Der Linden, 2005; Cho et al., 2013; Stuss et al., 1992; Rolls, 2004). Structural changes at the cortical and subcortical levels may be responsible for different degrees of impulsive behavior (Bjork et al.,

2009; Boes et al., 2009; Matsuo et al., 2009; McAlonan et al., 2007; Yu, 2012). Behavior resilience and the capacity to control impulsivity is greatly influenced by the balance between various neurotransmitters and neuromodulators in the brain (Pavlov et al., 2012; Winstanley et al., 2006). Namely, impulsive behavior has been associated primarily with functional changes in serotonergic, dopaminergic, and noradrenergic systems (Pattij and Vanderschuren, 2008). Moreover, the complex background of impulsivity involves different genetic and non-genetic factors.

There are three main ways to measure impulsivity: self-report measures, behavioral laboratory measures, and event-related cortical potentials (Dom et al., 2006; Moeller et al., 2001). Impulsivity or diminished inhibition of behavior is a central deficit in various psychiatric disorders (substance use disorders, antisocial personality disorder, borderline personality disorder, attention-deficit/hyperactivity disorder (ADHD) and pathological behaviors (self-injurious, violent and suicidal behavior, risk-taking behaviors, risky driving and risky sexual behaviors, domestic violence, gambling and kleptomania) (Chamorro et al., 2012; Pattij and Vanderschuren, 2008). All these risky behaviors, impulsive actions and impulsive decision making, associated with the one's increased preference for immediate reward, might lead to driving accidents, increased risk of exposure to HIV, undesired pregnancies, criminal behavior and arrest (Chamorro et al., 2012; Pattij and Vanderschuren, 2008). Impulsive behavior can be present also in healthy persons; however, the lack of behavioral inhibition is one of the key elements in patients with personality disorders, mania and substance dependence (Bagby et al., 2007; Fillmore and Rush, 2002; Hegerl et al., 2010; Hopwood et al., 2007; Mitchell, 1999; Moeller et al., 2001). Current diagnostic criteria do not differentiate between impulsive and non-impulsive individuals within diagnostic groups (Moeller et al., 2001). Impulsivity, as a part of symptom clusters in different psychiatric disorders, affects different aspects of cognition, it is associated with a greater motor activation, less attention, or decreased planning (Moeller et al., 2001), and is related to a treatment response.

In addition to further research, the integration of data accumulated from behavioral, biological, social, and environmental areas may lead to a better understanding of the relationship between impulsivity and behavioral disorders, identification of novel biomarkers associated with this complex behavior, as well as to improvements in the treatment of a variety of psychiatric disorders (Barratt, 1993; Barratt and Slaughter; 1998; Corruble et al., 2003; Moeller et al., 2001). In addition, genetic factors are presumed to be related to behavioral dimensions, such as impulsivity, rather than with clinical definitions of specific psychiatric disorders (Moeller et al., 2001; Pavlov et al., 2012).

1.2. Impulsivity and ADHD

Impulsivity is a key symptom in ADHD. In addition to symptoms of impulsivity, inattention and hyperactivity and cognitive disturbances (Bidweell et al., 2007), aggressive behavior (Schulz et al., 2001) also frequently occurs in ADHD. Affected children show difficulties in educational, academic and social functioning, as well as in skill and language development (Biederman, 2005). The diagnosis of ADHD, according to DSM-IV criteria (APA, 1994), includes the presence of six or more of the inattention symptoms that have been present for at least six months to a point that is disruptive and inappropriate for developmental level, or six or more of the symptoms of hyperactivity-impulsivity that have been present for at least six months to an extent that these symptoms are disruptive and inappropriate for the child's age.

A person with inattention symptoms often displays the following problems: does not pay close attention to details or makes careless mistakes in schoolwork, work, or other activities; has trouble keeping attention on tasks or play activities; does not seem to listen when spoken to directly; does not follow instructions and fails to finish schoolwork, chores, or duties in the workplace; has trouble organizing activities; avoids, dislikes, or doesn't want to do things that take a lot of mental effort for a long period of time; loses things needed for tasks and activities; and is easily distracted and forgetful in daily activities. A person with symptoms of hyperactivity often fidgets or squirms in their seat, gets up from their seat when remaining in seat is expected, runs around or climbs when and where it is not appropriate, has trouble playing or enjoying leisure activities quietly, and is often "on the go" or acts and talks as if "driven by a motor". A person with symptoms of impulsivity often blurts out answers before questions have been finished, has trouble waiting one's turn and interrupts or intrudes on others.

For a clinical diagnosis, these symptoms should be present before the age of 7 years, and the impairment caused by these symptoms should be present in two or more settings (e.g. at school/work and at home). This strong impairment must be clearly evidenced in social, school, or work functioning. A diagnosis of ADHD is excluded if these symptoms occur during the course of other psychiatric disorders, such as pervasive developmental disorder, schizophrenia, other psychotic disorder, mood disorder, anxiety disorder, dissociative disorder, or a personality disorder.

Therefore, according to DSM-IV criteria, three types of ADHD exist:

1. ADHD, Combined Type: six or more of the symptoms of innatention, hyperactivity and impulsivity are present for the past six months
2. ADHD, Predominantly Inattentive Type: six or more of the symptoms of innatention are present for the past six months
3. ADHD, Predominantly Hyperactive-Impulsive Type: six or more of the symptoms of hyperactivity and impulsivity are present for the past six months

ADHD is a complex and multifactorial neurodevelopmental childhood psychiatric disorder, whose etiology involves interactions between different demographic, psychosocial, psychiatric, cognitive, genetic and environmental factors (Biederman, 2005; Faraone and Khan, 2006). Although, according to DSM-IV criteria, the unusual pattern of behavior has to be noted before 7 years of age, in some cases this disturbed behavior might be evident in teenagers or young adults. The prevalence of ADHD is 5% (Faraone et al., 2005) and ADHD is sex-dependent, i.e. it develops more frequently in boys than in girls (Wallis, 2010). ADHD rarely develops alone and is more frequently associated with different comorbidities such as oppositional defiant disorder, conduct disorder, unipolar and bipolar affective disorders and anxiety disorders (Biederman, 2005). Unfortunately, high rate of criminality, increased substance (drug or alcohol) abuse, disturbed family relationships including family breakups and driving accidents also accompany ADHD (Gizer et al., 2009; Sharp et al., 2009).

Genetic origin of the etiology of ADHD comes from data obtained from the family, twins and adoption studies. All of these findings suggest that ADHD is a hereditable and polygenic disorder (Derks et al., 2008; Nemoda et al., 2011). Although the neurobiology of ADHD is not completely clear (Biederman, 2005), the main neurotransmitter systems that are disturbed in ADHD are dopaminergic, noradrenergic and serotoninergic systems (Biederman and Faraone, 2005; Chamberlain et al., 2007; Comings, 2001; Faraone and Khan, 2006; Oades, 2002a). Therefore, genetic studies focused on the genes controlling the proteins involved in the synthesis, degradation and function of these neurotransmitter systems as candidate genes for ADHD. To date, the results of ADHD candidate gene association studies have been inconclusive (Franke et al., 2009; Gizer et al., 2009; Reuter et al., 2006; Sharp et al., 2009). The discrepancies in these studies might be a consequence of the inadequate sample size, population stratification, lack of statistical power, differences in allelic frequencies between different populations, heterogeneity and complexity of ADHD, or gender differences (Wallis, 2010).

1.3. Biomarkers of Impulsivity

1.3.1. Serotonin (5-hydroxytryptamine, 5-HT)

Serotonin (5-hydroxytryptamine, 5-HT), an important neurotransmitter and neuromodulator in the central nervous system (CNS), is involved in the regulation of different brain functions and behaviors (Lesch and Merschdorf, 2000; Lucki, 1998), particularly cognitive functions such as learning and memory (Schmitt et al., 2006). Several studies suggest the association between impulsivity and low serotonergic function (Cherek and Lane, 1999; Murphy et al., 2002; Walderhaug et al., 2002). Impulsive behavior has been associated with serotonergic disfunction in animal models (Evenden, 1999; Fairbanks et al., 2001) and in humans (Brown et al., 1982; Nelson, 2005). Namely, in the cerebrospinal fluid (CSF) of violent criminals (Nelson, 2005) and impulsive suicide committers (Brown et al., 1982), lower concentrations of 5-hydroxyindoleacetic acid (5-HIAA), the main metabolite of 5-HT, have been detected. Furthermore, the deficiency of tryptophan, a precursor of 5-HT, results in the higher impulsivity (Walderhaug et al., 2002) and altered attention (Schmitt et al., 2000) in healthy subjects, and this reduced tryptophan concentration most likely affects cognitive processes like behavioral inhibition or attention. Elevated concentrations of 5-HT are associated with decreased impulsivity (Cherek and Lane, 1999).

In addition to impulsivity (Pattij and Vanderschuren, 2008), 5-HT also regulates other behaviors and traits which are often disturbed in ADHD, such as hostility, aggression and extreme violence (Askenazy et al., 2000; Dolan et al., 2002; Manuck et al., 1998; Schulz et al., 2001). Low 5-HT concentration in the brain has been usually associated with ADHD (Comings, 2001). In line with these findings, an association between ADHD and polymorphisms in the serotonin transporter (5-HTT) gene (Retz et al., 2002), and serotonergic 5-HT1B receptor (Quist et al., 2001) was found. As cognitive disturbances (Bidweell et al., 2007) and aggressive behavior (Schulz et al., 2001) frequently occur in ADHD, it is suggested that neurobiological basis of ADHD involves an imbalance of the CNS serotonergic system (Comings, 2001; Oades et al., 2002b). However, as numerous methodological complexities are associated with the determination of brain serotonergic function, such as sampling of 5-HT metabolites from the cerebrospinal fluid, or hormonal responses to pharmacologic treatment of ADHD, the assessment of peripheral, i.e. platelet 5-

HT has been proposed as a limited peripheral model for studies of serotonergic function in CNS (Goveas et al., 2004; Hrdina, 1994; Stahl, 1985).

Blood platelets share some similarities as well as some differences with serotonergic neurons in the brain (Goveas et al., 2004; Hrdina, 1994; Stahl, 1985). Although some authors have found altered platelet 5-HT concentration in impulsive and aggressive behavior (Askenazy et al., 2000; Dolan et al., 2002; Goveas et al., 2004), findings from the ADHD studies demonstrated lower, unaltered, or increased concentrations of platelet 5-HT and tryptophan in the whole blood in ADHD compared to healthy control subjects (Comings, 2001; Hercigonja Novkovic et al., 2009).

1.3.2. Serotonin transporter (5-HTT)

The serotonin transporter (5-HTT) is a monoamine transporter protein that transports 5-HT from the synaptic cleft to the presynaptic neuron, and therefore is the main regulator of 5-HT concentration in a synapse (Lesch and Gutknecht, 2005). Development as well as plasticity of various brain circuits critically depends on the expression of the 5-HTT gene (SLC6A4), located on chromosome 17 (Lesch and Gutknecht, 2005). There is a functional insertion–deletion polymorphism (5-HTTLPR) in the promoter region of the 5HTT gene, consisting of a 20-23 base pair sequence, which is repeated 14 (short variation) or 16 (long variation) times. The S allele of this variable locus has lower transcriptional activity than the long (L) allele, and that SS and SL genotypes display similar transcriptional activity, while the LL genotype has higher activity (Lesch et al., 1996).

Lower serotonergic innervation was also observed in the anterior cingulate cortex of impulsive aggressive individuals (Frankle et al., 2005). Carrying the S allele has been associated with higher impulsivity in healthy subjects (Paaver et al., 2007; 2008). Higher frequency of the S allele was observed in impulsive suicide attempters (Baca-Garcia et al., 2005; Li and He, 2007), violent alcoholics (Hallikainen et al., 1999), substance abusers (Gerra et al., 2005a,b; Uher and McGuffin, 2008), manic individuals (Masoliver et al., 2006), subjects with aggressive behavior (Haberstick et al., 2006) and subjects with increased novelty seeking (Gerra et al., 2005a,b).

1.3.3. Dopamine

Dopamine is an important neurotransmitter that acts via fronto-striato-cerebellar circuits. It is involved in modulation of emotional and reward responses, behavior and cognitive functions (Robbins, 2005) and hence considered to influence impulsivity (Congdon and Canli, 2005; Lee et al., 2009). Inadequate activity of D2-like receptors induces impulsive responses (Lee et al., 2009). Namely, administration of dopaminergic agonists reduces impulsive responses in humans (Aron et al., 2003; Tannock et al., 1989), and animals (van Gaalen et al., 2006; Wade et al., 2000), while D2/D3 receptor blockade impairs the inhibition of responses in various species (Lee et al., 2007; Ridley et al., 1981). Negative correlation of novelty seeking with D2/D3 receptor availability in right insular cortex (Suhara et al., 2001) and midbrain was demonstrated in healthy subjects (Zald et al., 2008), while some studies suggested a relationship of striatal D2/D3 receptors and impulsiveness (Brennan and Arnsten, 2008; Dalley et al., 2008; Lee et al., 2009).

A relationship between dopamine transporter (DAT) and dopaminergic receptor type 4 (DRD4) with ADHD has been reported (Daly et al., 1999; Dougherty et al., 1999; Krause et al., 2000; Smalley et al., 1998) and increased brain activity of dopamine-synthesizing enzymes was found in children diagnosed with ADHD (Ernst et al., 1999). Namely, the dysfunctions of frontal cortex dopaminergic system are related to ADHD and cognitive dysfunctions (Caspi et al., 2008; Cheuk and Wong, 2006; Genro et al., 2010). As changes in dopamine signaling might be associated with the number of ADHD symptoms (Arnsten and Li; 2005; Biederman and Faraone, 2005; Solanto, 2002), especially with hyperactivity and inattention, two subdomains of ADHD that are linked to dopamine function, dopaminergic system often represents target for pharmacotherapy of ADHD (Antshel et al., 2011). Both impulsiveness and ADHD are associated with gene variants controlling proteins that regulate dopaminergic activity (Biederman and Faraone, 2005; Congdon and Canli, 2005; Cook et al., 1995a; Eisenberg et al., 2007; Faraone et al., 2001; 2005; LaHoste et al., 1996; Limosin et al., 2003; Nemoda et al., 2011; Schinka et al., 2002; White et al., 2008).

1.3.4. Monoamine oxidase (MAO)

Enzyme monoamine oxidase (MAO) catalyzes oxidative deamination of monoamines dopamine, serotonin and noradrenaline. In humans there are two isoenzymes of MAO: MAO-A and MAO-B, encoded by two adjacent genes located on chromosome X, which differ from each other in localization, substrates and inhibitors. Both MAO enzymes are vital to the inactivation of monoaminergic neurotransmitters, however they display different specificities. The preferential substrates for MAO-A are serotonin, melatonin, noradrenaline and adrenaline, while MAO-B catalyzes dopamine, phenylethylamine, benzylamine, tyramine and typtamine.

Outside the CNS, MAO-B is mostly found in blood platelets (Oreland, 2004). Platelet MAO-B activity has been proposed to serve as peripheral marker of a variety of personality traits and behaviors such as addiction, gambling, sensation seeking, and vulnerability to psychiatric disorders (Eensoo et al., 2004; Oreland, 2004; Ruchkin et al., 2005; Schalling et al., 1988). Low platelet MAO-B activity has been associated with aggressive, impulsive, criminal and violent behaviors (Eensoo et al., 2004; Kiive et al., 2005; 2007; Oreland, 2004; Paaver et al., 2006; 2007) and self-reported impulsiveness or novelty seeking (Oreland, 2004; Ruchkin et al., 2005; Schalling et al., 1988). Altered platelet MAO-B activity has been also related to anxiety (Irving et al., 1989) and neuroticism (Kirk et al., 2001), while children with ADHD might have low platelet MAO activity (Nedic et al., 2010; Shekim et al., 1982; 1984; 1986). Several factors including gender (Malmberg et al., 2008; Roth et al., 1976), smoking (Eensoo et al., 2007; Kiive et al., 2002; Pivac et al., 2008), older age, ethnicity and race (Sobell et al., 1997), some neurodegenerative disorders, pernicious anemia, and psychotropic drugs (Ertugrul et al., 2007; Meszaros et al., 1998; Muck-Seler et al., 2008; Oreland et al., 2004; Pivac et al., 2003) affect platelet MAO-B activity.

As some MAO-B polymorphisms were found to be associated with ADHD (Ribases et al., 2008), MAO-B gene was suggested as an interesting candidate gene for ADHD. Among numerous polymorphisms found in human MAO-B, there is a single nucleotide polymorphism (rs1799836) in the MAO-B gene, located on X chromosome, which is shown to be associated with varying enzyme activity. Namely, G allele of this polymorphism might be associated with lower activity of brain MAO-B activity (Baldiuniene et al., 2002), although some reports demonstrated lack of this association (Pivac et al., 2006a; 2007). Our previous study failed to find significant association between MAO-B gene variants and ADHD (Nikolac Perkovic et al., 2014).

1.3.5. Catecholamine-O-methyltransferase (COMT)

Catecholamine-O-methyltransferase (COMT) is an enzyme catalyzing the catecholamines such as dopamine, noradrenaline and adrenaline. The most common functional polymorphism in the human COMT gene, located on chromosome 22, is a G/A transition (rs4680) in the exon 4 which is responsible for Valine (Val) to Methionine (Met) substitution at codon 108 of the predominant soluble COMT and at codon 158 of the membrane bound COMT.

The carriers of Val/Val genotype have 3-4 times greater COMT activity then Met/Met genotype carriers (Lachman et al., 1996). Consequently, faster degradation of dopamine in Val/Val genotype carriers results in lower dopamine levels, particularly in the prefrontal cortex, where dopamine transporter is not abundant (Chen et al., 2004). COMT Val108/158Met polymorphism affects executive functions moderated by prefrontal cortex circuits (Egan et al., 2001), and executive functions are disturbed in patients with ADHD. Therefore, COMT variants influence hyperactivity and attention, both in healthy subjects as well as in patients with ADHD (Nikolac Perkovic et al., 2013; 2014). Although studies suggested that COMT is a candidate gene in ADHD, the results of the association studies are not clear (Gizer et al., 2009).

1.3.6. Dopamine beta-hydroxylase (DBH)

Dopamine beta-hydroxylase (DBH) is an enzyme which converts dopamine to noradrenaline, acting as a link between dopaminergic and noradrenergic system. It is expressed in noradrenergic nerve terminals of the central and peripheral nervous systems, as well as in adrenal medulla. The activity of DBH in plasma is under the influence of a −1021C/T polymorphism in the promoter region of DBH gene (rs1611115), where CC genotype carriers have higher plasma DBH activity than TT genotype carriers (Cubells et al., 2000). Decreased plasma DBH activity could consequently result in deficiency of noradrenaline, while noradrenergic dysfunction is associated with ADHD. Although lower plasma DBH activity was found in conduct disorders (Bowden, 1998), and the association of T allele with lower DBH plasma activity was detected (Mustapic et al., 2007; Zabetian et al., 2001), some studies have not observed the association of −1021C/T DBH polymorphism with ADHD (Nikolac Perkovic et al., 2014).

1.3.7. Dopamine receptor D4 (DRD4)

Dopamine receptors are membrane receptors located in the CNS and some other tissues (kidney, blood vessels, heart, and smooth muscles). At least five subtypes of dopamine receptors (D1–D5) could be distinguished, which are subdivided into D1-like (D1 and D5) and D2-like (D2, D3, and D4) subfamily of receptors. Dopamine receptor type 4 (DRD4) is a G protein-coupled receptor with seven transmembrane spanning domains, and it is expressed in the limbic system, frontal cortex and globus pallidus (Van Tol, 1996). This receptor is encoded by DRD4 gene located on chromosome 11.

The polymorphism in the third exon of the DRD4 gene, consisting of a variable number of tandem repeats (VNTR), is a 48 bp long repeat motif, which is in humans present in 1–11 tandem copies (Chang et al., 1996; Lichter et al., 1993; Van Tol et al., 1992). VNTR variants of DRD4 gene might affect second messenger coupling or signal transduction (Van Tol et al., 1992). Namely, long repeat allele reduces DRD4 gene expression and consequently dopaminergic regulation of the cognitive functions. Various studies reported the association of both short and long repeat alleles of the DRD4 gene with ADHD (Faraone et al., 2001; Nikolac Perkovic et al., 2014; Swanson et al., 1998), as well as with the behavioral (Swanson et al., 2000), and attentional (Bellgrove et al., 2005; Langley et al., 2004; Manor et al., 2002) performance of patients with ADHD.

2. Aims and Hypothesis

The aims of this study were to determine the biological and genetic markers of impulsivity, especially those related to dopaminergic and serotonergic systems in children and adolescents.

The hypothesis of this study is that peripheral biochemical markers such as platelet 5-HT concentration and platelet MAO-B activity, as well as genetic markers such as variants of the genes encoding COMT, DBH, MAO-B, DRD4 and 5-HTT might be associated with impulsivity. Therefore, these biomarkers might contribute to a more complete understanding of the etiology of impulsive behavior and lead to improvements in the treatment of a variety of psychiatric disorders.

3. Methods

3.1. Participants

All participants were sampled in two places: Estonia and in Croatia. The participants of Estonian origin were enrolled in the Estonian Children Personality, Behavioural and Health Study (Irving et al., 1989; Kiive et al., 2005; 2007), while Croatian participants were sampled by the Department of Family Medicine and University Department of Child and Adolescent Psychiatry at University Hospital Osijek, School of Medicine, Josip Juraj Strossmayer University of Osijek and in Polyclinic Kocijan/Hercigonja, Zagreb, Croatia.

Children with suspected ADHD were referred by their parents, teachers, family doctors and pediatricians, but all participants met DSM-IV criteria for ADHD as assessed by a psychiatric interview (APA, 1994), a physical examination, and the Conners Rating Scale for Parents (CRS-P) and Teachers (CRS-T) -short version (Conners, 1989). ADHD was diagnosed by experienced child and adolescent psychiatrists, who conducted separate interviews with the children and their parents, while psychological interview and psychological tests were performed by a psychologist. According to the DSM-IV criteria (APA, 1994) and based on their predominant symptoms, the participants were subdivided into groups having inattentive, hyperactive, or combined subtype of ADHD. In order to be classified as the inattentive or hyperactive-impulsive subtype of ADHD, children had to have six or more of the symptoms present for at least six months. The symptoms had to be so severe that the behavior was disruptive and inappropriate for each developmental level. The combined subtype of ADHD included children with both criteria met for the past six months (APA, 1994).

Children with ADHD included in the study were medication free, while healthy unmedicated children, attending their regular physical exams, served as controls. All participants were asked about their smoking habits. The healthy children were matched in age to the patient's sample. The age of all participants ranged from 4-18 years. In the Croatian sample in the studies measuring platelet 5-HT levels and platelet MAO-B activity the average age of participants with ADHD was 9.35 ± 2.40 (4-14) and of healthy participants was 8.90 ± 3.09 (5-14). In the genetic studies the average age of Croatian participants with ADHD was 9.23 ± 2.54 (males) and 9.38 ± 2.10 (females) and healthy participants was 11.44 ± 3.34 (males) and 11.92 ± 2.99 (females), respectively. Hence, only in the genetic studies age was significantly different between Croatian boys and girls in the control and ADHD group (P = 0.001, ANOVA). Tukey's test revealed that Croatian healthy boys (P = 0.001) and healthy girls (P = 0.024) were significantly older than boys and girls with ADHD, but within groups age did not differ significantly. The participants of Estonian origin were enrolled in longitudinal study where platelet MAO-B activity was measured in the same participants at the average age 15.4 ± 0.5 and then again at 18.2 ± 0.5. In genetic study investigating association of 5HTTLPR and impulsivity the average age was 15.3 ± 0.5.

Both healthy and ADHD children were Caucasians of urban origin attending kindergartens or primary schools, with average intellectual abilities. Exclusion criteria were co-morbid depression, schizophrenia, oppositional defiant disorder, conduct disorder, borderline personality disorder and evidence of major neurological conditions and somatic disorders, all assessed by psychiatric interview based on DSM-IV criteria (APA, 1994) and the Child Symptoms Inventory-4. Written informed consent was obtained from all participants, or from the children's parents, after explaining the aims and procedures of the study. Before starting the study, permission were obtained from the local Ethics Committees. All human studies have been executed with the full cooperation of participants, adequate understanding, and have therefore been performed in accordance with the ethical standards outlined in the 1964 Declaration of Helsinki.

3.2. Impulsivity Assessment

The scales used for determination of impulsivity symptoms were: Swanson, Nolan and Pelham Questionnaire IV (SNAP-IV), Thoughtlessness and Disinhibition, Fast Decision-Making and Excitement Seeking and Barratt Impulsiveness Scale (BIS-11). The SNAP-IV scale evaluates a symptom of DSM-IV for ADHD and these scores indicate whether the participants exhibits the symptom "not at all" (score=0), "just a little" (score=1), "pretty much" (score=2) or "very much" (score=3). These SNAP-IV scores are subdivided into inattention and hyperactivity/impulsivity subscale scores. Based on the SNAP-IV subscale scores, participants were subdivided into those without any hyperactive-impulsive and inattentive symptoms, participants with moderate hyperactive-impulsive symptoms (more than 0, less than 1.78 scores on SNAP-IV hyperactivity/impulsivity subscale), participants with severe hyperactive-impulsive symptoms (1.78 or more scores on SNAP-IV hyperactivity/impulsivity subscale), participants with moderate inattentive symptoms (more than 0, less than 2.56 scores on SNAP-IV inattention subscale), and participants with severe inattentive symptoms (more than 2.56 scores on SNAP-IV inattention subscale).

Scores in the Thoughtlessness and Disinhibition scales measure the maladaptive types of impulsivity, while Fast Decision-Making and Excitement Seeking scores measure the adaptive types of impulsivity. These subscales were based on the Dickman impulsivity inventory (Dickman; 1990), which assess functional and dysfunctional impulsivity, and on the impulsivity related subscales of NEO-PI (Neuroticism, Extraversion, Openness, Personality Inventory (Costa and McCrae, 1989; Pulver, 1995). The BIS-11 scale (Patton, 1995) is a questionnaire designed to assess the personality/behavioral construct of impulsiveness. It consists of three subscales: motor (motor and perseverance), non-planning (self-control and cognitive complexity), and attentional (attention and cognitive instability). BIS-11 is composed of 30 items describing impulsive or non-impulsive behaviors and preferences. Items are scored on a 4-point scale: 1 score (rarely/never); 2 scores (occasionally); 3 scores (often); and 4 scores (almost always/always). The participants were subdivided according to total BIS-11 scores (Patton, 1995) and into two groups, group with $\geq$ 69 scores and group with $\leq$ 70 (that likely indicates an impulse-control disorder or pathological impulsivity). Moreoever, the data regarding the number of stressful life events (SLE) of participants was collected.

3.3. Biochemical and Genetic Analysis

Blood samples (4 ml) were taken during usual laboratory routine tests from a forearm vein into a plastic syringe with 1 ml of acid citrate dextrose anticoagulant at 08.00 a.m. after overnight fasting.

3.3.1. Determination of the platelet 5-HT concentration

Platelet 5-HT concentration was determined in platelet pellets by the spectrofluorimetric method, as described previously (Pivac et al., 2006b). Platelet-rich plasma (PRP) was obtained a centrifugation (935 x g) for 70 s at room temperature. PRP was further centrifuged at 10,000 x g for 5 min. The platelet pellet was washed with saline and centrifuged again. Platelets were lysed by sonication (20 Hz, amplitude 8 x 10-3 mm for 30 s). Following sonication, specimens of standard, blank (water) and platelet sonicates were analyzed in duplicate. All samples were deproteinized with 1 ml of 10% $ZnSO_4$ and 0.5 ml of 1 N NaOH. For the preparation of fluorophore, 0.2 ml of L-cysteine (0.1%) and 1.2 ml of orthophthalaldehyde (0.05%) were added to deproteinized samples. The measurement of the 5-HT fluorescence was performed on a Varian Spectrophotofluorimeter Cary Eclipse, on an exciting wavelength of 345 nm and emitted wavelength of 485 nm. The detection limit of the method was 10.0 ng/ sample, and intra- and inter-assay coefficients of variation were 3.66% and 8.69%, respectively. Platelet protein concentrations were measured by the method of Lowry et al. (Lowry et al., 1951).

3.3.2. Determination of platelet MAO-B activity

Platelet MAO-B activity (expressed as nmol 4OHQ/mg protein/h) was determined spectrofluorometrically, using a kynuramine as a substrate, by a slight modification of the method of Krajl (Krajl, 1965) in the Croatian sample. PRP was obtained by a centrifugation (935 x g) for 70 s at room temperature. PRP was further centrifuged at 10,000 x g for 5 min.

The platelet pellet was washed with saline and centrifuged again. Platelets were lysed by sonication (20 Hz, amplitude 8 x 10-3 mm for 30 s). Aliquots of standard, blank (water) and platelet sonicates (100 μl) in duplicates were incubated 60 min on 37° C with kynuramine. The reaction was stopped by adding an ice-cold 1 N NaOH. The fluorescence of 4-hydroxyquinoline (4-HOQ), a product of kynuramine, was measured on a Varian Cary Eclipse spectrofluorimeter, with an exciting wavelength of 310 nm and emitted wavelength of 380 nm. The detection limit of the method was 1 nmol/ sample and intra- and inter-assay coefficients of variation were 4.4% and 5%, respectively. In the Estonian sample, platelet MAO-B activity was analyzed from the blood sampled with EDTA as an anticoagulant in platelet-rich plasma by a radio-enzymatic method with ß-phenylethylamine. All samples were analyzed in duplicate. Platelet MAO activity was determined using (^{14}C)-ß-phenylethylamine (β-PEA) as the substrate according to the procedure described by Hallman et al. (Hallman et al., 1987) after modification described in the paper of Harro et al. (Harro et al., 2001).

3.3.3. Genotyping

Genomic DNA was extracted from peripheral blood using a salting out method (Miller et al., 1988). Genotyping of the 5-HTTLPR was done using PCR from genomic DNA. The polymorphic region was amplified using the primers 5-HTTLPR-F: CAA CCT CCC AGC AAC TCC CTG TA, 5-HTTLPR-R: GAG GGA CTGAGC TGG ACA ACC AC. The forward primer was fluorescently labeled with a 5'-FAM. Reagents and conditions for the PCR reaction were: 1 x PCR buffer (Perkin Elmer, AmpliTaq Gold buffer II), 200 μM dNTP with 50% of dGTP replaced with 7-deaza-dGTP, 2 mM $MgCl_2$, 1 μM of each primer, 1 UTaq polymerase (Perkin Elmer, AmpliTaq Gold), and 20 ng genomic DNA, in a total reaction volume of 10 μL. The reaction started with 10 min at 95° C, followed by 40 cycles with 30 s at 95° C, 30 s at 59° C, 30 s at 72° C, and ended with 7 min at 72° C. PCR products were then run on an ABI PRISM 3700 DNA analyzer (Applied Biosystems, U.S.A.), and analyzed using the software Gene-Marker 1.5 (SoftGenetics, U.S.A.). Genotypes were checked on chromatograms to detect inconsistencies, and where needed, amplified and scored a second time.

Genotyping of DRD4 VNTR was done using polymerase chain reaction and primers 5' AGG ACC CTC ATG GCC TTG 3' and 5' GCG ACT ACG TGG TCT ACT CG 3', followed by 2% agarose gel electrophoresis. PCR was performed in total volume of 15 μL containing 150 ng DNA, 0,8 μM of each specific primer (Sigma Aldrich, USA), 1 U Tfi polymerase (Invitrogen, USA), 0,2 mM of each dNTP (Invitrogen, USA), 1 mM $MgCl_2$ (Invitrogen, USA) and 1 X PCR buffer (200 mM Hepes-KOH (pH 8.1), 75 mM KCl, 75 mM $(NH4)_2SO_4$, 10% Glycerol and Proprietary stabilizers) (Invitrogen, USA). Cycle conditions consisted of an initial denaturation at 94° C for 10 min, followed by 35 cycles of denaturation at 94° C for 30 s, 30 s annealing at 54° C, extension at 72° C for 1 min as well. A final extension was carried out at 72° C for 10 min. According to DRD4 VNTR individuals were categorized into long (L) allele carriers (possessing at least one copy of 7 or more repeats allele) and short (SS) homozygotes (possessing 2 copies of 2-6 repeats allele).

Genotyping of the COMT Val108/158Met (rs4680), DBH -1021C/T (rs1611115) and MAO-B intron 13 polymorphism (rs1799836) was done in all participants by ABI Prism 7300

Sequencing Detection System apparatus (ABI) using a Taqman-based allele-specific polymerase chain reaction assays, according to the procedures described by Applied Biosystems (Foster City, CA, USA). The primers and probes were purchased from Applied Biosystems as TaqMan® Drug Metabolism Genotyping Assay or TaqMan® SNP Genotyping Assay. Participants were categorized into COMT AA (Met/Met) homozygous genotype vs. G (Val) carriers (the combined AG (Met/Val) and GG (Val/Val) genotype), DBH CC vs. T carriers (the combined CT and TT genotype) and MAO-B A or G carriers. Five percent of all samples (blind duplicates) were genotyped again as a quality control.

3.4. Statistical Analysis

Statistical analysis of the data was conducted using Sigmastat 2.0 (Jandell Scientific Corp. San Raphael, California, USA), GraphPad Prism (GraphPad Software, San Diego, CA, USA) and MedCalc. The results, expressed as means ± standard deviations (SD), were evaluated with Student t-test, or by using one-way or two-way analysis of variance (ANOVA), followed by Tukey's test. Analysis of covariance (ANCOVA) was used with BIS-11 scores as a dependent variable, 5-HTTLPR genotypes and stressful life events as factors, and gender as covariate. The differences in the genotype frequencies and the Hardy-Weinberg equilibrium (HWE) were evaluated with a χ^2 test with Yates correction for continuity. To establish what category was a major contributor to rejecting the null hypothesis, standardized residuals (*R*) were calculated (Field et al., 2012). The correlation between parameters was determined by a Pearson´s coefficient of correlation. The level of significance was set to P lower than 0.05.

4. RESULTS

4.1. Platelet 5-HT

Platelet 5-HT concentration was determined among boys and girls with characteristic symptoms (inattention, hyperactivity, and impulsivity) and clinical subtypes (predominantly hyperactive, predominantly inattentive, and combined subtype) of ADHD, as well as in healthy children. No significant differences in age (P = 0.055, ANOVA) between boys and girls with ADHD, or healthy boys and girls were detected. As shown in Table 1, there were no differences in platelet 5-HT concentration between boys and girls with ADHD, and healthy boys and girls (P = 0.4837, ANOVA). Two-way ANOVA showed no significant effect of diagnosis (P = 0.9668), no significant effect of sex (P = 0.1568), and no significant interaction between diagnosis and sex (P = 0.881) on platelet 5-HT concentration.

When children were subdivided according to the subtype of ADHD, platelet 5-HT concentrations were not significantly (P = 0.0674) different between children with hyperactive/impulsive, inattentive and combined subtype of ADHD (Figure 1).

Table 1. Platelet 5-HT concentration in healthy children and children with ADHD subdivided according to gender

Platelet 5-HT concentration (nmol/mg protein)	Boys	Girls
Healthy children	1.43 ± 0.49 (16)	1.28 ± 0.48 (14)
Children with ADHD	1.44 ± 0.53 (72)	1.25 ± 0.26 (12)

Values are expressed as mean ± S.D., while the numbers in parentheses represent the number of children per group.

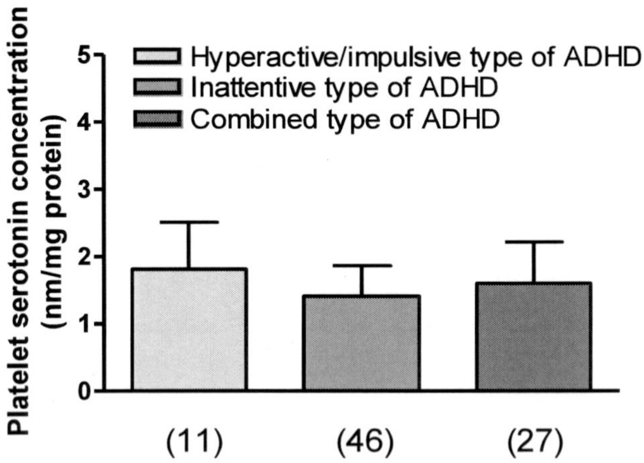

Values are expressed as mean ± S.D., while the numbers in parentheses represent the number of children per group.

Figure 1. Platelet 5-HT concentration in children with ADHD subdivided according to type of ADHD.

According to DSM-IV criteria, children with ADHD had an average number of symptoms of impulsivity, hyperactivity and inattention of 1.25 ± 1.20 (range 1-3), 4.22 ± 1.41 (range 1-6) and 5.92 ± 1.95 (range 2-9), respectively. Pearson coefficient of correlation demonstrated that platelet 5-HT concentration was significantly and positively correlated with impulsive symptoms (R = 0.271, P = 0.0125), but not with symptoms of hyperactivity (R = 0.156, P = 0.157) or symptoms of inattention (R = 0.152, P = 0.167).

Table 2. Platelet 5-HT concentration in children with ADHD without impulsive symptoms and with impulsive symptoms subdivided according to presence of 1, 2 or 3 impulsive symptoms

Platelet 5-HT concentration	(nmol/mg protein)
Children without impulsive symptoms	1.22 ± 0.43 (26)
Children with impulsive symptoms	1.52 ± 0.51 (58)*
Children with 1 impulsive symptom	1.50 ± 0.52 (27)
Children with 2 impulsive symptoms	1.54 ± 0.45 (15)
Children with 3 impulsive symptoms	1.72 ± 0.54 (16)**

Values are expressed as mean ± S.D., while the numbers in parentheses represent the number of children per group. * P < 0.013 vs. the group without impulsive symptoms (Student t-test); ** P < 0.010 vs. the group without impulsive symptoms (ANOVA followed by the Tukey´s test).

As platelet 5-HT concentration was significantly correlated only with impulsive symptoms, children with ADHD were subdivided according to the presence (scores 1-3) or absence (score 0) of impulsive symptoms (Table 2). There was a significant difference in platelet 5-HT concentration (P = 0.0108, Student t-test) between children without impulsive symptoms and children with impulsive symptoms.

As shown in Table 2, platelet 5-HT concentration differed significantly in children with ADHD without impulsive symptoms and impulsive children with ADHD, subdivided according to the number of impulsive symptoms into children with 1, 2 or 3 symptoms present (P = 0.0127, ANOVA). Namely, children without impulsive symptoms had significantly (P < 0.01, Tukey´s test) lower platelet 5-HT levels than children with 3 impulsive symptoms (Table 2).

4.2. 5-HTTLPR Polymorphism

In order to determine whether certain types of impulsivity are higher in carriers of 5-HTTLPR short (S) allele, a genotype leading to a less efficient 5-HT system, the association of different 5-HTTLPR genotypes with scores of Thoughtlessness, Disinhibition, Fast Decision-Making, Excitement Seeking and Barratt Impulsiveness Scale, as well as with the number of Stressful life events (SLE) was studied.

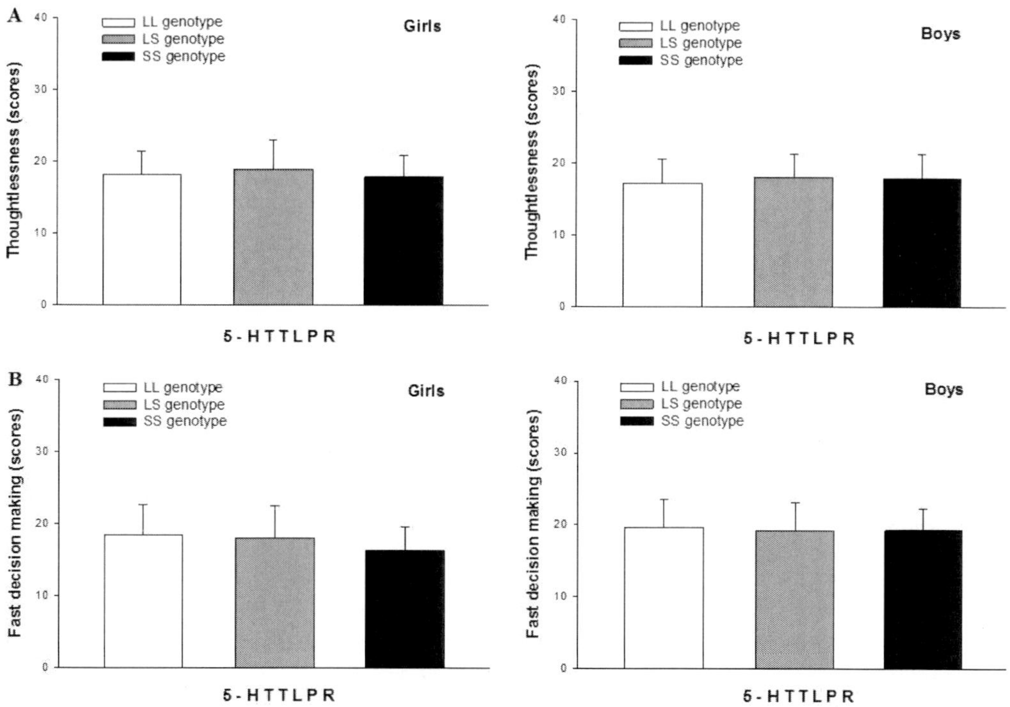

Values are expressed as mean ± S.D.

Figure 2. The scores of Thoughtlessness (A) and Fast decision making (B) in adolescent girls and boys subdivided according to different 5-HTTLPR genotype.

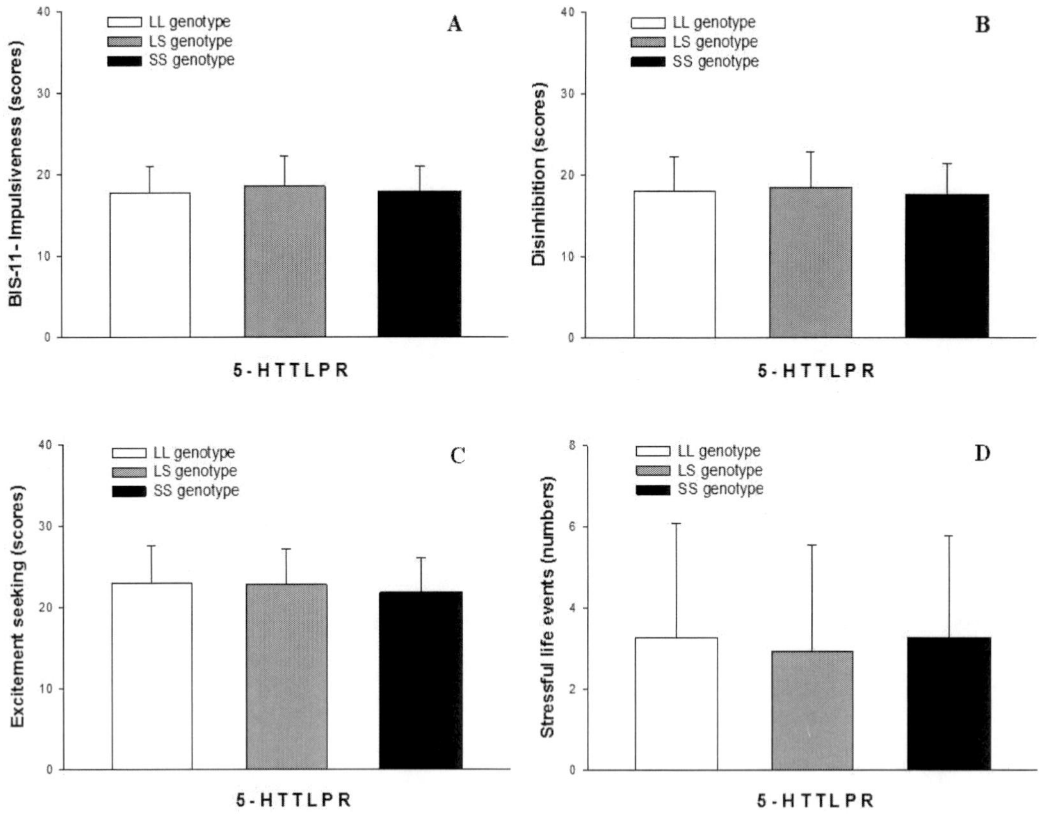

Source: Values are expressed as mean ± S.D.

Figure 3. The scores of BIS-11 impulsiveness (A), Disinhibition (B) and Excitement seeking (C) and the number of Stressful life events (D) in participants subdivided according to different 5-HTTLPR genotype.

Our results showed no significant differences in the frequency of various 5-HTTLPR genotypes ($\chi2$ = 0.075; P = 0.9633), as well as in the distribution of LL homozygotes vs. S allele carriers ($\chi2$ = 0.002; P = 0.967) between adolescent boys and girls. However, as significant sex differences were revealed in the scores of Thoughtlessness (P = 0.007, ANOVA), as well as in the scores of Fast decision making (P < 0.001, ANOVA), in the analysis of the association between these measures of impulsivity and 5-HTTLPR genotypes, the children were subdivided according to gender (Figure 2).

As shown in Figure 2A, there were no significant differences in the scores on Thoughtlessness scale between girls (P = 0.217, ANOVA) or boys (P = 0.208, ANOVA) carrying different 5-HTTLPR genotypes. Moreover, the Fast decision making scores were not significantly different between adolescent girls (P = 0.077, ANOVA) or between adolescent boys (P = 0.734) with various 5-HTTLPR genotypes (Figure 2B).

Scores in the BIS-11 impulsiveness (P = 0.689), Disinhibition (P = 0.300) and Excitement seeking (P = 0.164) scale, as well as the number of Stressful life events (P = 0.285) (ANOVA), did not differ between gender, therefore the data from adolescent boys and girls were collapsed (Figure 3).

As shown in Figure 3A, the BIS-11 scores were not significantly (P = 0.872) different between participants who were carriers of LL, SL and SS genotype of the 5-HTTLPR. In addition, participants subdivided according to 5-HTTLPR genotypes did not differ significantly (P = 0.486) in the Disinhibition scores (Figure 3B). As shown in Figure 3C, ANOVA revealed no significant differences in the Excitement seeking scores between carriers of different 5-HTTLPR genotypes (P = 0.164, ANOVA). The average number of stressful life events (SLE) was 3.26 for the LL genotype, 2.91 for the LS genotype and 3.26 for the SS genotype, respectively (Figure 3D), and ANOVA showed no significant differences in the number of SLE (P = 0.396, ANOVA) between participants with different 5-HTTLPR genotypes.

When evaluating the association between the number of SLE and 5-HTTLPR genotypes, there were significant differences ($\chi 2$ = 10.704; P = 0.030) in the distribution of the 5-HTTLPR genotypes when participants were subdivided according to the number of SLE into the group with the number of SLE from 0-1, the group with the number of SLE of 2-4, and a group of 5 and more (Figure 4).

The group of participants carrying SS homozygous genotype with the number of SLE from 2-4 had contributed significantly to these differences, since the R value was 1.99, showing the significant influence of this genotype on SLE. To further investigate this effect, participants were subdivided into two groups: the group with the number of SLE from 0-1, and the group with the number of SLE of 2 and more and subdivided according to their 5-HTTLPR genotype. A $\chi 2$ test revealed significant ($\chi 2$ = 6.509; P = 0.035) differences in the frequency of the 5-HTTLPR genotypes between the stressed (i.e. with 2 and more SLE) and non-stressed (i.e. with 0-1 SLE) groups, however the R value (R = 1.54), lower than 2, could not indicate which genotype was responsible for these significant differences.

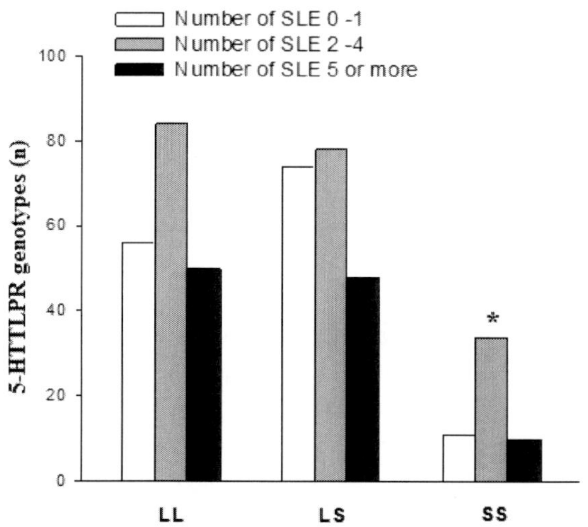

The participants were subdivided according to SLE into 3 groups: number of SLE 0-1, number of SLE 2-4, and number of SLE 5 and more than 5. Values represent numbers of carriers of different genotypes. (*$\chi 2$ = 10.740; P = 0.030).

Figure 4. Frequencies of 5-HTTLPR genotypes in participants subdivided according to the number of SLE.

To elucidate whether the exposure to SLE was associated with impulsivity and 5-HTTLPR genotype, participants exposed to varying number of SLE were subdivided according to their genotype and the number of SLE. ANCOVA with BIS-11 total scores as dependent variable revealed that 5-HTTLPR genotypes were not significantly ($P = 0.718$) associated with impulsivity, SLE were significantly ($P = 0.020$) associated with impulsivity, but there was no significant ($P = 0.098$) interaction between impulsivity, 5-HTTLPR genotypes and SLE. In addition, when all participants were subdivided into those with BIS-11 scores ≥ 69 scores and BIS-11 scores ≤ 70, the frequency of the LL, LS or SS genotypes was not significantly ($\chi 2 = 2.943$; $P = 0.087$) different between these two groups. Therefore, impulsivity scores were not significantly associated with 5-HTTLPR genotypes.

4.3. Platelet MAO-B Activity

Platelet MAO-B activity was evaluated in healthy adolescent boys and girls and in boys and girls with ADHD. The activity of MAO-B in platelets was measured in healthy children at age 15 years and again at 18 years. Our results, demonstrated that platelet MAO-B activity significantly increased from age 15 to age 18 years ($P = 0.0332$, Student t-test). When participants were subdivided according to gender, one-way ANOVA showed significant differences between groups ($P < 0.0001$, ANOVA). Namely, platelet MAO-B activity was significantly lower in adolescent boys when compared to girls, at the age of 15 years ($P < 0.05$; Tukey´s test), and was also significantly lower in male than in female participants at the age of 18 years ($P < 0.001$; Tukey´s test).

Further analysis revealed significant differences in platelet MAO-B activity between healthy participants subdivided according to the smoking status, at the age of 15 years, as well at the age of 18 years ($P < 0.0001$; ANOVA). Namely, Tukey's post-hoc test revealed that smokers had significantly lower platelet MAO-B activity than nonsmokers, and this difference was present both at the age 15 years ($P < 0.05$) and at the age of 18 years ($P < 0.01$). This difference was also significant when data were adjusted for gender ($P < 0.01$ and $P < 0.05$ at the age of 15 and 18 years, respectively).

Moreover, when participants were subdivided according to the low (< 25th percentile), medium (25 - 75th percentile) and high (> 75th percentile) platelet MAO-B activity, multiple linear regression model revealed an association ($P = 0.04$) between platelet MAO-B activity measured at age 15 and motor restlessness at age 18 (Figure 5A). This model demonstrated that 11% of the variance in motor restlessness scores was due to a gender, smoking status and platelet MAO-B activity of participants at the age 15, and that male sex, low MAO activity and smoking at the age of 15 were associated with 1.3 fold increase in the motor restlessness score at the age of 18.

The model of multiple linear regression also demonstrated an association ($P = 0.05$) between platelet MAO-B activity measured at the age of 15 and inattention at the age of 18 (Figure 5B). However, as shown in Figure 5C, the influence of MAO-B activity measured at the age of 15 on SNAP-IV total scores was not significant ($P = 0.10$). Both male sex and low platelet MAO-B activity at the age of 15 were associated with 1.3-fold increase in the SNAP-IV total scores at the age of 18, while smoking at the age of 15 was associated with 2.0-fold increase in the SNAP-IV total scores at the age of 18.

As shown in Table 3, platelet MAO-B activity was significantly ($P < 0.0001$, Student t-test) lower in 9 years old children with ADHD when compared to control healthy children.

Table 3. Platelet MAO-B activity in healthy children and children with ADHD subdivided according to gender

Platelet MAO-B activity (nmol 4-OHQ/mg p/h)	Total	Boys	Girls
Healthy children	28.84 ± 8.46 (64)	27.33 ± 9.32 (32)	30.35 ± 7.34 (32)
Children with ADHD	21.10 ± 10.13 (84)**	21.42 ± 10.12 (72)*	26.74 ± 13.01 (12)

Values are expressed as mean ± S.D., while the numbers in parentheses represent the number of children per group. **P < 0.0001 vs. control children (Student t-test); *P < 0.05 (ANOVA followed by the Tukey's test).

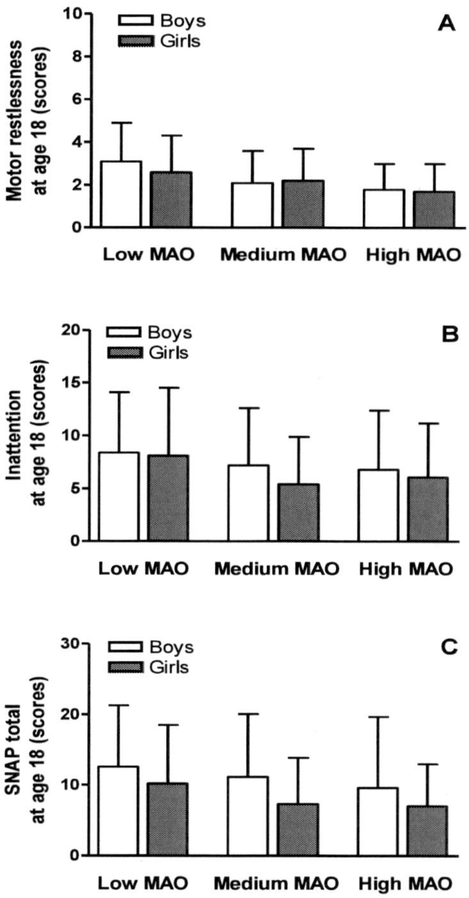

Boys and girls were subdivided according to the the low (< 7.3), medium (7.3-11.2) and high (> 11.2 nmol x 10^{10} platelets $^{-1}$ x min $^{-1}$) platelet MAO activity at the age of 15. Motor restlessness scores are determined at the age of 18. Values are expressed as mean ± S.D.

Figure 5. Motor restlessness (A), inattention (B) and total SNAP (C) scores at the age of 18 in healthy children subdivided according to gender and platelet MAO activity at the age of 15.

In children subdivided according to gender, significantly lower (P < 0.05, one-way ANOVA followed by the Tukey´s test) platelet MAO-B activity was observed in boys with ADHD in comparison to healthy boys, while no differences were found between girls with ADHD and girls in control group (Table 3). Two-way ANOVA revealed significant effects of diagnosis (P < 0.01) and gender (P < 0.04), but no significant interaction (P = 0.553) between diagnosis and gender on platelet MAO-B activity.

According to DSM-IV criteria and average number of particular symptoms of hyperactivity-impulsivity and inattention, children with ADHD were subdivided into groups with predominantly hyperactive-impulsive (number of hyperactive-impulsive symptoms: 7.2 ± 1.4; number of inattentive symptoms: 4.1 ± 1.0, n= 11), predominantly inattentive (number of hyperactive-impulsive symptoms: 3.6 ± 1.5; number of inattentive symptoms: 7.2 ± 1.3, n= 46), and combined (number of hyperactive-impulsive: 7.8 ± 1.4; number of inattentive symptoms: 7.1 ± 1.3, n= 27) subtype of ADHD.

Table 4. Platelet MAO-B activity in healthy children and children subdivided according to the type of with ADHD

Platelet MAO-B activity	(nmol 4-OHQ/mg p/h)
Healthy children	28.84 ± 8.47 (64)
Children with hyperactive/impulsive type of ADHD	20.27 ± 9.25 (11)*
Children with inattentive type of ADHD	22.29 ± 8.42 (46)**
Children with combined type of ADHD	21.78 ± 8.74 (27)*

Values are expressed as mean ± S.D., while the numbers in parentheses represent the number of children per group. In the group with predominantly hyperactive-impulsive type of ADHD all participants were boys, in the group with predominantly inattentive type of ADHD there were 38 boys and 8 girls, and in the group with predominantly combined type of ADHD there were 23 boys and 4 girls *P < 0.05– 0.01, **P < 0.001 vs. control children (ANOVA followed by the Tukey's test).

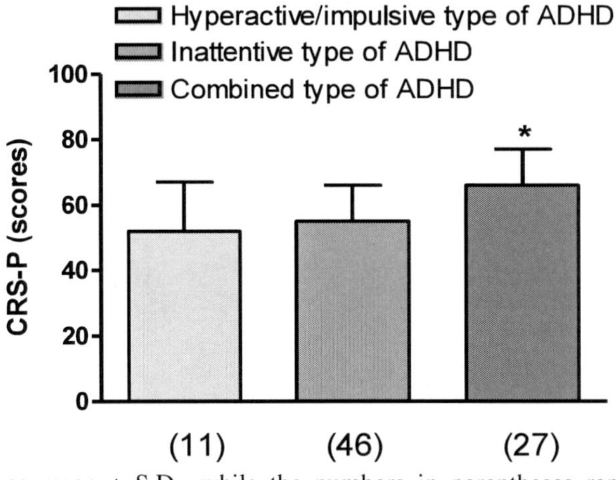

Values are expressed as mean ± S.D., while the numbers in parentheses represent the number of children per group. *P < 0.01-0.001 vs. all other groups (ANOVA followed by the Tukey's test).

Figure 6. CRS-P scores in children with predominantly hyperactive-impulsive, inattentive and combined type of ADHD.

Significant differences were also observed when platelet MAO-B activity of healthy children was compared to platelet MAO-B activity in children subdivided according to the subtype of ADHD ($P < 0.0001$, ANOVA). Platelet MAO-B activity was significantly lower (Tukey´s test) in children with predominantly hyperactive-impulsive ($P < 0.05$), inattentive ($P < 0.001$) and combined ($P < 0.01$) subtype of ADHD than in healthy children (Table 4).

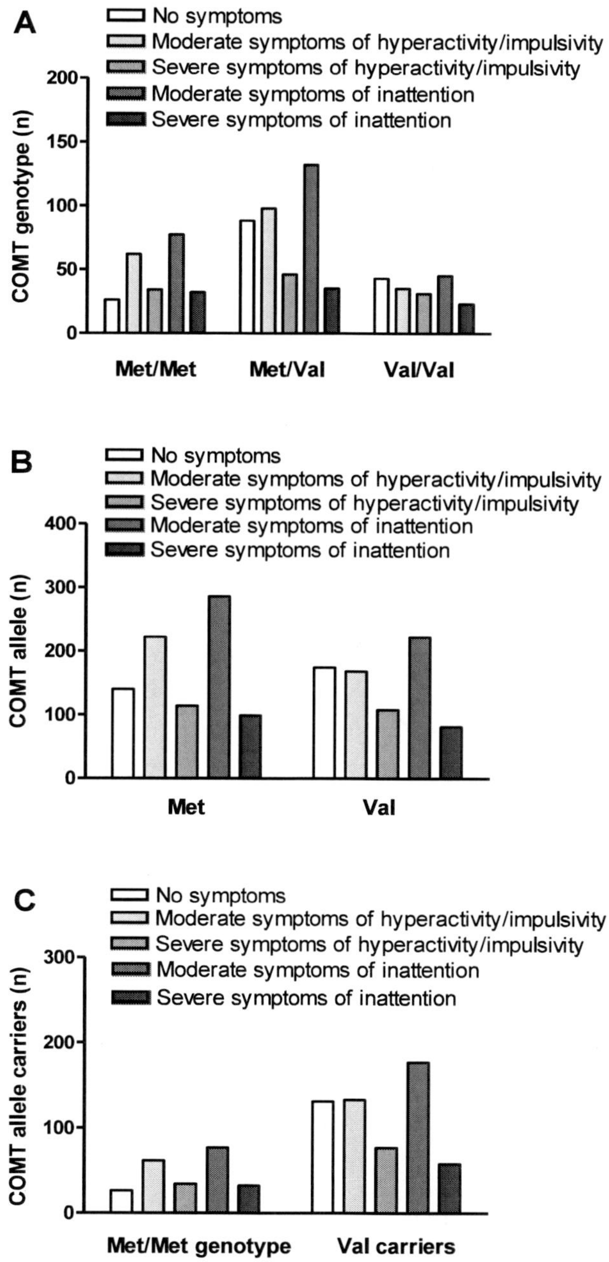

Values represent numbers of carriers of different genotypes or alleles.

Figure 7. The frequencies of the COMT Val108/158Met genotypes (A), alleles (B) and carriers (C) in the male participants subdivided according to the hyperactive-impulsive and inattentive symptoms.

ANOVA revealed significant differences in the CRS-P scores ($P < 0.0002$) between children with predominantly hyperactive-impulsive, inattentive and combined type of ADHD (Figure 6). Namely, children with combined type of ADHD had significantly higher CRS-P scores than children with hyperactive-impulsive ($P < 0.01$) or inattentive ($P < 0.001$) type of ADHD (Tukey´s test).

No significant differences ($P = 0.0842$) in age were found between children with ADHD and control children (Student t-test), or between children with predominantly hyperactive-impulsive, predominantly inattentive or combined type of ADHD ($P = 0.0589$, ANOVA).

There was no significant correlation (Pearson´s correlation coefficient) of platelet MAO-B activity with age in healthy children ($R = 0.028$, $P = 0.827$), or in children with ADHD ($R = -0.125$, $P = 0.194$). Moreover, when children with ADHD were subdivided according to age into 6 groups: 4-5, 6-7, 8-9, 10-11, 12-13 and 14-15 years of age, no significant differences in platelet MAO-B activity were observed between groups ($P = 0.2627$, ANOVA).

4.4. Gene Variants Encoding Dopaminergic Systems

The association between COMT Val108/158Met gene polymorphism (rs4680) with hyperactive-impulsive and inattentive symptoms, in the group of male boys and adolescents was evaluated. The genotype frequencies of the COMT polymorphism in the participants enrolled in the study were in the expected HWE ($\chi2 = 0.036$; $P = 0.849$). Age of the group was significantly different ($P < 0.001$), as participants with severe hyperactive-impulsive and inattentive symptoms were younger than individuals in other groups, however there was no significant correlation between age and SNAP-IV scores ($R = 0.02$; $P = 0.670$).

The distribution of the COMT Met/Met, Met/Val or Val/Val genotypes ($\chi2 = 23.751$; $P = 0.003$), Met or Val alleles ($\chi2 = 14.020$; $P = 0.007$) and Met/Met genotype carriers vs Val carriers ($\chi2 = 14.833$; $P = 0.005$) was significantly different in participants without the hyperactive-impulsive and inattentive symptoms when compared to participants with moderate and severe hyperactive-impulsive symptoms and participants with moderate and severe inattentive symptoms (Figure 7). The Met/Met genotype ($R = 2.83$) or the Met allele ($R = 2.27$) contributed to these significant differences, since they were less frequent in participants without the hyperactive-impulsive and inattentive symptoms than in other groups. On the other hand, the frequency of COMT genotypes between participants with lower (< 1.78) and higher (> 1.78) hyperactive-impulsive scores, as well as between participants with lower (< 2.56) and higher (> 2.56) inattentive scores was similar.

When all participants were subdivided according to the COMT genotypes, the results demonstrated significant differences in the hyperactive-impulsive ($P < 0.05$, ANOVA) (Figure 8A) and inattentive scores ($P < 0.006$, ANOVA) (Figure 8B). Namely, higher hyperactive-impulsive scores were observed in participants carrying the Met/Met genotype vs. Met/Val genotype ($P < 0.05$, Tukey's test) and in participants carrying the Met/Met genotype vs. Val carriers ($P < 0.05$, Student t-test). Moreover, participants carrying the Met/Met genotype had significantly higher number of inattentive scores compared to the Met/Val ($P < 0.01$) and Val/Val ($P < 0.05$) genotypes (Tukey's test). The same result, higher number of inattentive scores, was detected when Met carriers were compared to the Val carriers ($P = 0.001$; Student t-test).

In order to test the hypothesis that specific variants of selected candidate genes of dopaminergic system might be associated with the subtype of ADHD in boys and girls, the association of single nucleotide polymorphisms (SNP) of the COMT, DBH and MAO-B genes as well as a variable number of tandem repeats (VNTR) polymorphism of the DRD4 gene, with the subtype of ADHD was evaluated. The genotype frequencies of all SNP analyzed, in healthy children and in children with ADHD, did not deviate from HWE.

To elucidate the association of the diagnosis (ADHD vs. healthy children) as the dependent variable with gender, age and particular genotype as independent variables, logistic regression analyses were used. These analyses revealed a significant association of diagnosis with gender ($P < 0.001$), age ($P < 0.001$) and COMT Met/Val ($P = 0.029$) and Val/Val genotype ($P = 0.048$), and an association with the DRD4 VNTR long (L) allele variant ($P = 0.020$), but no association with -1021C/T DBH genotype (CT genotype: $P = 0.509$; TT genotype: $P = 0.552$) (Figure 9).

Significant differences in the frequency of the COMT Met/Met, Met/Val and Val/Val genotypes ($\chi^2 = 6.031$; $P = 0.049$), and in the Val carriers (the combined Met/Val and Val/Val genotypes) and the Met/Met homozygotes ($\chi^2=5.246$; $P = 0.022$) between healthy children and children with ADHD. The value of the standardized residuals for the Met/Met genotype in ADHD group was $R = 1.74$, suggesting that this genotype was presumably responsible for significant differences. In addition, significant differences were detected also in the frequency of the DRD4 long (L) allele carriers and non-carriers between children with ADHD and control children ($\chi^2 = 7.023$; $P = 0.008$).

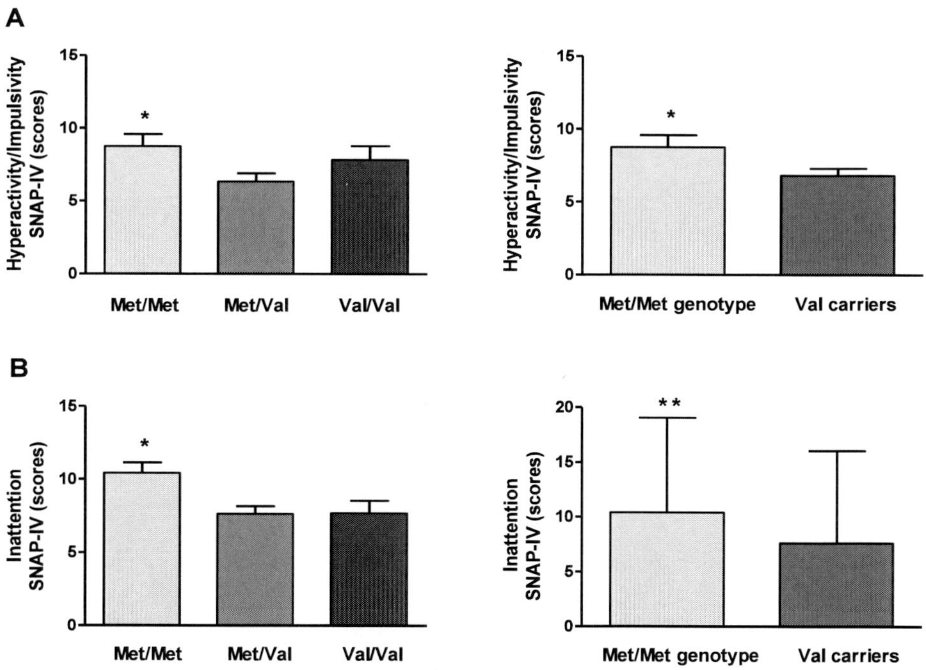

Values are expressed as mean ± S.D. *$P < 0.05$ or $P < 0.01$ (ANOVA followed by the Tukey's test or Student t-test); **$P = 0.001$, Student t-test.

Figure 8. The hyperactivity/impulsivity (A) and inattention (B) SNAP-IV scores in the male participants subdivided according to COMT Val108/158Met genotypes.

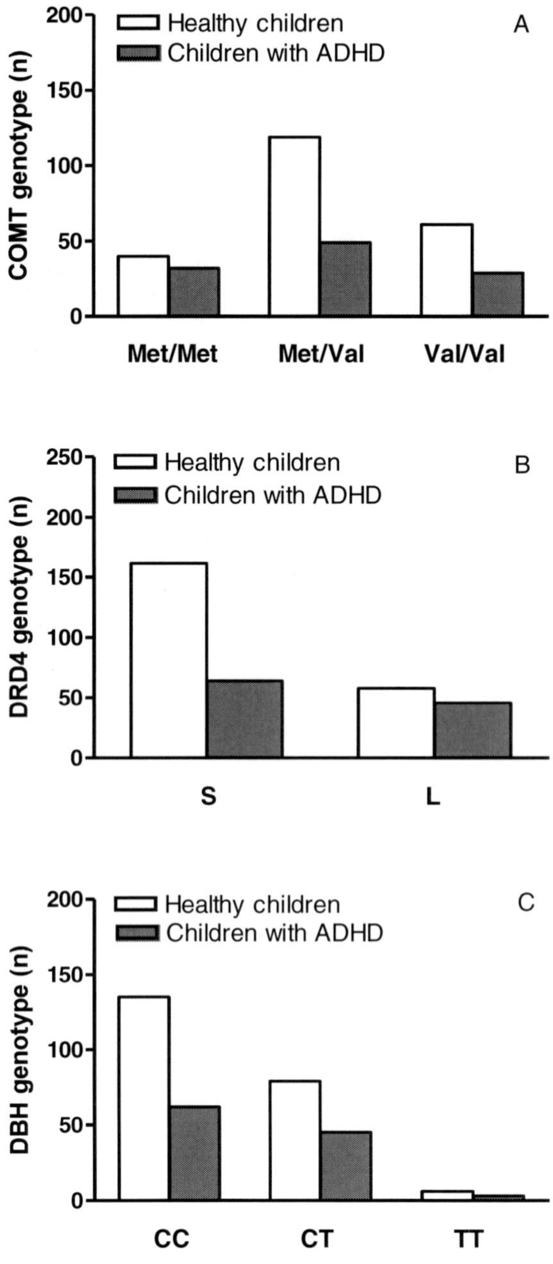

Values represent numbers of carriers of different genotypes or alleles (S - short allele, L -long allele).

Figure 9. Frequencies of COMT (A), DRD4 (B) and DBH (C) genotypes in healthy children and children with ADHD.

Since MAO-B intron 13 polymorphism is X-linked, male and female participants were evaluated separately, and there was a significant association of diagnosis with age in boys and girls ($P < 0.01$), but no association with MAO-B intron 13 polymorphism in boys (A genotype: $P = 0.469$) or in girls (GA and AA genotype: $P = 0.994$) (Figure 10).

Table 5. The frequency of gene variants of COMT, DBH, MAO-B and DRD4 in healthy children and children with different subtypes of ADHD

	Healthy children	ADHD Combined type	ADHD Inattentive type	ADHD Hyperactive-impulsive type
	N (%)	N (%)	N (%)	N (%)
COMT genotype				
Met/Met	40 (18.2)	23 (37.7)	6 (23.1)	3 (13.0)
Met/Val	119 (54.1)	21 (34.4)	15 (57.7)	13 (56.5)
Val/Val	61 (27.7)	17 (27.9)	5 (19.2)	7 (30.4)
X^2= 14.016; d.f.=6; P = 0.029, Power=0.814				
DRD4 genotype				
Short allele carriers	162 (73.6)	36 (59.0)	15 (57.7)	13 (56.5)
Long allele carriers	58 (26.4)	25 (41.0)	11 (42.3)	10 (43.5)
X^2= 8.167; d.f.=3; P = 0.043, Power=0.660				
DBH genotype				
CC	135 (61.4)	38 (62.3)	11 (42.3)	13 (56.5)
CT	79 (35.9)	23 (37.7)	13 (50.0)	9 (39.1)
TT	6 (2.7)	0 (0.0)	2(7.7)	1 (4.3)
X^2= 7.008; d.f.=6; P = 0.320, Power= 0.459				
MAO-B genotype				
Male				
G	51 (46.4)	20 (35.7)	11 (55.0)	8 (34.8)
A	59 (53.6)	36 (64.3)	9 (45.0)	15 (65.2)
X^2= 3.528; d.f.=3; P = 0.317, Power= 0.308				
Female				
GG	22 (20.0)	0 (0.0)	0 (0.0)	0 (0.0)
GA	55 (50.0)	4 (80.0)	2 (33.3)	0 (0.0)
AA	33 (30.0)	1 (20.0)	4 (66.7)	0 (0.0)
X^2=6.071; d.f.=4; P = 0.194, Power= 0.465				

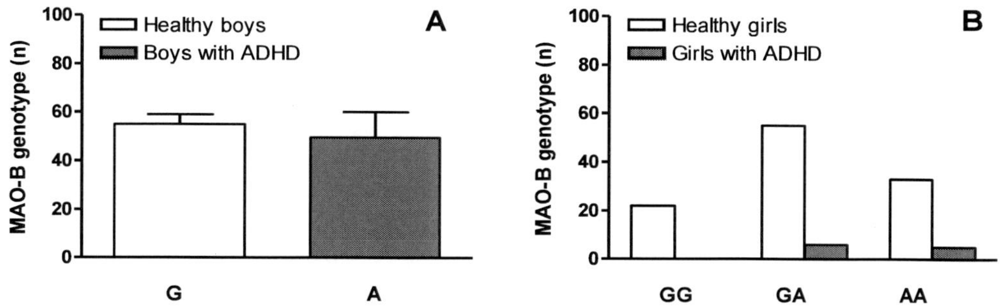

Values represent numbers of carriers of different genotypes or alleles.

Figure 10. Frequencies of MAO-B genotypes in healthy and ADHD boys (A) and girls (B).

As shown in Table 5, χ^2 test detected significant differences in the frequencies between gene variants of the COMT Val108/158Met (P = 0.029) and DRD4 VNTR (P = 0.043) between healthy children and the combined subtype of ADHD, while the distribution of the gene variants of the -1021C/T DBH or MAO-B intron 13 polymorphism did not differ significantly between healthy children and children with combined, inattentive and hyperactive/impulsive subtype of ADHD.

Results demonstrated significantly different distribution (χ^2 = 11.793; P = 0.008) of Met/Met homozygotes vs. Val carriers between healthy children and children with the three subtypes of ADHD. Since the value of standardized residuals was R = 2.66 for the Met/Met homozygous genotype in the combined subtype of ADHD, these data verified the over-expression of the Met/Met genotype in the combined subtype of ADHD.

Logistic regression was used to assess the gene-gene interaction on the risk for ADHD. The interaction effect of COMT Val108/158Met genotype (Met/Met and Val carriers) and DRD4 genotype (long allele carriers and non-carriers) on the ADHD risk was not significant (P = 0.108). However, significant interactions were found for COMT Val108/158Met genotype (Met/Met and Val carriers) and -1021C/T DBH (TT and C carriers), (P = 0.009), and for COMT Val108/158Met genotype (Met/Met and Val carriers) and MAO-B intron 13 polymorphism (AA and G carriers), (P = 0.000), respectively.

The significant interaction effects were detected for DRD4 genotype (long allele carriers and non-carriers) and -1021C/T DBH (TT and C carriers), (P = 0.005), and for DRD4 genotype (long allele carriers and non-carriers) and MAO-B intron 13 (GG and A carriers), (P = 0.035), on the ADHD risk.

Since the COMT Val108/158Met and DRD4 VNTR were significantly associated with the combined subtype of ADHD, to elucidate their relationship with particular symptoms, only children with the combined subtype were subdivided into two groups defined by presence/absence of the COMT Met/Met genotype and DRD4 7-repeat allele, and symptoms of impulsivity and hyperactivity/inattention were evaluated with one-way ANOVA. No significant differences were detected in the number of symptoms of inattention (P = 0.903) or hyperactivity/impulsivity (P = 0.360) between carriers of the Met/Met genotype vs. Val carriers of the COMT, or in the symptoms of inattention (P = 0.069) or hyperactivity/impulsivity (P = 0.813) between DRD4 long allele carriers and non-carriers group. Two-way ANOVA revealed a significant effect of diagnosis (P = 0.001), no significant effect of gender on age, or interaction between age, diagnosis and gender.

4. Discussion

Our results showing no significant differences in platelet 5-HT concentration between children with ADHD and healthy children are in line with findings demonstrating similar concentration of 5-HT in the blood between controls and ADHD patients (Cook et al., 1995a; Hercigonja Novkovic et al., 2009; Unis et al., 1997). However, some studies found lower platelet 5-HT concentration in children with ADHD (Comings, 1993), as well as lower (Rapoport et al., 1974) or higher (Rogeness et al., 1992) peripheral indices of serotonergic function in ADHD. These discrepancies between these results might be explained by the racial and ethnic differences in platelet 5-HT concentration observed in prepubertal psychiatric patients, as well as healthy children (Pfeffer et al., 1998). Significant differences in platelet 5-HT concentration between control and ADHD children, that we failed to detect in this present study, might be due to a relatively small number of control children, and lack of statistical power. Since the healthy children and children with ADHD were matched by age, the lack of differences in platelet 5-HT concentration between groups was not associated with possible age related changes in serotonergic function (Halperin et al., 1997).

No differences observed in platelet 5-HT concentration between children with predominantly hyperactive, predominantly inattentive, and combined subtype of ADHD, suggest that different platelet 5-HT concentration does not characterize various subtypes of ADHD. However, platelet 5-HT concentration was significantly higher in ADHD children with impulsive, but not hyperactive symptoms, in comparison to children without symptoms, as previously reported (Hercigonja Novkovic et al., 2009). Moreover, platelet 5-HT was significantly positively correlated with the number of impulsive symptoms, but not with symptoms of hyperactivity or inattention in children with ADHD. These results are consistent with the findings obtained in depressed adult patients (Mann et al., 1992), juvenile offenders (Pliszka et al., 1992; Unis et al., 1997), non-patient sample (Manuck et al., 1998), or in offenders with diagnosed personality disorders (Dolan et al., 2001), demonstrating correlation of impulsivity with central serotonergic function. The results of our study are also in line with findings of the association between cognitive impulsivity and altered affinity of the 5-HTT transporter binding site in children with ADHD (Oades et al., 2002b), and a high positive correlation between a clinical measure of impulsivity and platelet 5-HT concentration (Askenazy et al., 2000). Our data support the hypothesis that increased platelet 5-HT concentration might be a trait marker predictive of impulsivity in ADHD (Askenazy et al., 2000; Peirson et al., 1999), and that platelet 5-HT concentration might be an index of altered serotonergic function in impulsivity (Pattij and Vanderschuren, 2008; Lesch and Merschdorf, 2000). However, this biological marker may be more closely related to basic psychopathologic dimension of impulsivity, than to specific current diagnostic category of ADHD (Askenazy et al., 2000; Goveas et al., 2004; Manuck et al., 1998; Mueller-Oerlinghausen et al., 2004; Schmitt et al., 2006).

Platelet 5-HT concentration might be influenced by various factors such as age, gender, drug treatment, and different co-morbid psychiatric diagnoses (Kovacic et al., 2008; Muck-Seler et al., 1996; Mueller-Oerlinghausen et al., 2004) However, previous data have suggested that smoking (Kovacic et al., 2008), as well as seasonality (Jakovljevic et al., 1997) does not affect platelet 5-HT concentration, and platelet 5-HT concentrations are rather stable (Pick et al., 1999). On the other hand, increased platelet 5-HT concentration might be related to the presence of psychotic symptoms (Kovacic et al., 2008; Muck-Seler et al., 1996), or delusions (Pivac et al., 2006b), therefore diagnostic instruments including clinical interview, physical examination and Conner Rating Scale for Parents and Teachers, excluded children with these symptoms. In addition, children enrolled in the study and the exclusion criteria used in the present study excluded the possible influence of various factors affecting platelet 5-HT concentration (Muck-Seler et al., 2005; Sagud et al., 2008; Southam et al., 1998).

Our results demonstrating no significant differences in the scores of thoughtlessness, disinhibition, fast decision-making, excitement seeking and BIS-11 scale in children subdivided according to different 5-HTTLPR genotypes are in line with the findings showing that 5-HTTLPR alone has no significant effect on impulsiveness in children (Paaver et al., 2007; Preuss et al., 2000). Namely, Paaver and colleagues (Paaver et al., 2007) demonstrated that the effect of 5-HTTLPR S allele on the impulsivity depends on the presence of low platelet MAO-B activity. This interaction on impulsiveness might be an explanation for the contradictory data in the literature. Namely, some authors reported no effect of S allele on impulsive responding in laboratory disinhibition task (Clark et al., 2005) and so called Go/No-go task (Fallgatter et al., 1999). On the other hand, a variety of studies suggests the association of 5-HTTLPR S allele with suicide behavior (Baca-Garcia et al., 2005), violence in alcoholism (Hallikainen et al., 1999), anxiety and neuroticism (Lesch et al., 1996), which are all characterized with pronounced impulsive behavior (Brotman et al., 2006; Costa and McCrae, 1989). Controdictory data also exist, and some authors reported that participants carrying SS genotype have less depression in comparison to the LL genotype (Taylor et al., 2007). In the present study the effect of possible anxiety and depression was not studied. However, their prevalence in a community-based group of healthy adolescents was probably not high enough to significantly impact the development of impulsivity. Adolescent brain is known to be more vulnerable to risk-taking and impulsive behaviour, due to high sensitivity to reward. It is possible that environmental factors such as stress (Caspi et al., 2003) or family environment (Kaufman et al., 2006; Paaver et al., 2008; Taylor et al., 2007) in the interaction with the 5-HTTLPR S allele, which might be responsible for the impulsive tendencies, might result in adaptive or maladaptive impulsivity in adulthood, especially as our results demonstrated that the number of stressful life events was significantly different in participants carrying different 5-HTTLPR genotypes. This effect was not clear, since the SS homozygous genotype in participants exposed to 2-4 stressful life events, but not 5 or more, contributed significantly to these differences. To elucidate this association, all participants were subdivided into groups with 0-1 stressful life events and the other groups with more than 2 stressful life events, and the frequency of the 5-HTTLPR genotypes was significantly different among these groups, but the effect of the SS genotype on SLE was still unclear. This lack of significant interaction between the SS genotype and a higher number of SLE is at present difficult to explain. In evaluating further the association between impulsivity, 5-HTTLPR genotypes and SLE, our results revealed that SLE were associated with impulsivity, assessed with BIS-11 total scores, but that 5-HTTLPR genotypes were not, and we failed to detect any significant interaction between impulsivity, SLE and 5-HTTLPR genotypes. In addition, there was no significant difference in the frequency of the LL, LS or SS genotypes between all participants subdivided into less and more impulsive (i.e. according to the BIS-11 scores $\geq$ 69 scores and BIS-11 scores $\leq$ 70). These results suggested that in our participants presumably the interaction between family environment (Kaufman et al., 2006; Paaver et al., 2008; Taylor et al., 2006) and the risk allele of the 5-HTTLPR might be more important in development of impulsivity than the association between 5-HTTLPR genotypes and SLE. The mechanism of the previously observed cumulative effect of the environment and the S allele on behavioral problems is still unclear. Maternal separation in the early age is suggested to be significant factor, as it may lead to lower expression of the serotonin transporter and serotonergic 5-HT1A receptor in the brain (Lee et al., 2007). As 5-HTTLPR genotypes were found to have a significant effect on the development of cortico-limbic structures (Hariri et al., 2003) involved in impulsivity (Liotti and Panksepp, 2004), serotonin transporter may have role in an inhibition of impulsive behavior (Lesch and Merschdorf, 2000). It could be further speculated that environmental stress factors may have more prominent effect on S allele carriers, as various studies demonstrated higher activity of amygdala to negative emotional stimuli, and lower neuronal densities in impulse regulating regions like cingulate and prefrontal cortex in individuals with S allele (Graff-Guerrero et al., 2005; Heinz et al., 2005; Pezawas et al., 2005). Therefore, carrying the S allele of the 5-HTTLPR might present a vulnerability factor to higher impulsivity when associated with SLE.

The activity of platelet MAO-B has been previously shown to be rather stable over period of 8-10 weeks (Bagdy and Rihmer, 1986; Murphy et al., 1976). In our study a significant correlation was observed between MAO-B activity measured twice in a period of three years, which might be due to the possibility that platelet MAO-B activity has not stabilized at age 15 (Kiive et al., 2007). The observed sex differences in the platelet MAO-B activity are in line with previous findings (Bagdy and Rihmer, 1986; Kiive et al., 2002; Murphy et al., 1976). Our findings demonstrating lower platelet MAO-B activity in smokers in comparison to non-smokers are in accordance with other studies which found that smoking decreases platelet MAO-B activity (Berlin and Anthenelli, 2001; Kiive et al., 2002; 2005; Oreland et al., 2002; Pivac et al., 2005; 2007; 2008; Whitfield et al., 2000). Therefore, the effects of smoking on platelet MAO-B activity has to be considered as serious confounding factor in the studies investigating platelet MAO-B activity in various personality traits, behaviors and psychiatric disorders. The study revealed that low MAO-B activity at age 15 is associated with high scores of motor restlessness and inattention at age 18. While motor restlessness declined with age, it declined in a reduced amount among participants with low platelet MAO-B activity. These results suggest that platelet MAO-B activity, which might reflect central serotonergic activity (Oreland, 2004), is associated with specific parameters of hyperactivity and attention deficit in adolescence (Kiive et al., 2007). Some previous studies also observed significant association between low platelet MAO-B activity and impulsivity, while others failed to detect any significant association (Kiive et al., 2005; 2007; Klinteberg et al., 1987; Oreland, 2004; Paaver et al., 2006; Ruchkin et al., 2005).

MAO-B metabolizes dopamine and trace amines, while predominantly dopaminergic, and to a lesser extent noradrenergic and serotonergic dysfunctions are involved in the ADHD (Biederman, 2005; Comings, 2001; Waldman and Gizer, 2006). In addition to disturbances in dopaminergic system, serotonergic activity may modulate features of the ADHD. However, as serotonergic activity depends on the status of dopaminergic activity, it could be suppressed as well as enhanced in ADHD. Our results showing low platelet MAO-B activity in children with all three subtypes of ADHD might indicate that central serotonergic activity is altered in ADHD, and suggest that this peripheral biological marker may represent a nonspecific marker indicating predisposition to distress or psychopathology (Dolan et al., 2001). Our findings are in line with previous reports of lower platelet MAO-B activity in hyperactive children with ADHD compared to healthy children (Shekim et al., 1982; 1986). Together, these results suggest an association between low platelet MAO-B activity and a behavioral state of over-activity, short attention span, and impulsivity (Shekim et al., 1982), or performance on the Matching familiar figures test and the Continuous performance test, which yield scores sensitive to impulsivity and inattention (Shekim et al., 1986). Our data are in agreement with the findings showing negative correlation of platelet MAO-B activity with difficulties in concentration, which are also the key symptoms in ADHD (Kiive et al., 2005). Lower platelet MAO-B activity has been also associated with personality traits such as impulsivity, sensation seeking, monotony avoidance, risk taking behavior, antisocial and high risk traffic behavior (Eensoo et al., 2007; Oreland, 2004).

Previous studies demonstrated that lower platelet MAO-B activity has been related to impulsivity in adolescent girls, but not boys, with high traffic risks (Eensoo et al., 2007), or in girls with behavioral disorders, attention deficit disorders and/or alcohol and hashish abuse, showing more deviant personalities (Cederblad et al., 1992). In contrast, our previous (Hercigonja Novkovic et al., 2009) and present study showed that platelet MAO-B activity was lower in both boys and girls with predominantly hyperactive, predominantly inattentive, and combined subtype of ADHD than in healthy children. Some authors found that platelet MAO-B activity in children was not significantly affected by gender (Pfeffer et al., 1998; Shekim et al., 1982; 1984), in contrast to other reports (Murphy et al., 1976; Roth et al., 1976). The findings from the larger cohort of adolescents (Kiive et al., 2007; Paaver et al., 2007) demonstrated significant gender related differences, i.e. higher platelet MAO-B activity in girls than in boys who were 15 years old. These gender related differences in platelet MAO-B activity, which differ from our results, might be explained by the fact that children in this part of our study with ADHD or matched controls were significantly younger (children in this part of our study were on average 9 years old, i.e. just before the puberty), while 15-years old children in the other studies were in the last stages of their puberty. However, in a large sample of children and adolescents, boys had significantly lower MAO-B activity when compared with girls both before and during puberty (Harro et al., 2001). Hence, the lack of gender differences in our study might be due to the small number of children, especially girls. More boys than girls with ADHD were included in our study, presumably due to the fact that boys with ADHD have more pronounced hyperactivity symptoms, which induce more obstruction in the school or more problems in kindergartens. On the other hand, girls usually have more inattention symptoms in ADHD, and these symptoms are frequently under-recognized and attributed to laziness or being a day dreamer or in love. The average age of the children with ADHD or control children included in this part of our study was 9 years, and children of this age have been reported to have lower (Harro et al., 2001; Kiive et al., 2005), as well as higher (Kiive et al., 2005) platelet MAO-B activity compared to 15-years old adolescents. Therefore, the differences in age, even if they existed, were presumably not responsible for the lower platelet MAO-B activity found in children with ADHD. Hence, the possible effect of age on platelet MAO-B activity might be excluded.

It is known that smoking decreases platelet MAO-B activity in adults (Fowler et al., 2003; Oreland, 2004; Pivac et al., 2005; 2007; 2008) or adolescents (Eensoo et al., 2007; Kiive et al., 2002). However, as children included in this part of our study and their parents reported that they were non-smokers, the inhibitory effect of smoking on platelet MAO activity, even if it existed, was negligible. Moreover, children in this part of our study denied that they abused alcohol. This is in line with studies reporting that in the age up to 10 years less than 2% of children are smoking or drinking alcohol (Macleod et al., 2008). In addition, the results obtained from a large cohort of children, who were on average 9-years old, showed that platelet MAO-B activity did not differ significantly between smokers and non-smokers (Harro et al., 2001). No significant association was found between alcohol illicit drug use and platelet MAO-B activity in preadolescents (Merenakk et al., 2003). As platelet MAO-B activity is influenced by various psychotropic treatments, in our study we enrolled only medication-free children in order to exclude possible effects of medication (Oreland, 2004), such as haloperidol (Meszaros et al., 1998), clozapine (Ertugrul et al., 2007), antidepressants (Pivac et al., 2003) or lamotrigine (Muck-Seler et al., 2008). Moreover, as platelet MAO-B activity might be affected by the ethnicity and race (Sobell et al., 1997), boys and girls in our study were all ethnically uniform Caucasian children of the Croatian origin.

In our present and previous study (Nikolac Perkovic et al., 2013) Met/Met genotype and the Met allele of the COMT Val108/158Met were more frequently found in participants with hyperactive-impulsive and inattentive symptoms compared to control participants. However, COMT genotypes were similarly distributed among participants who had moderate compared to severe hyperactive-impulsive or inattentive symptoms (characteristic for ADHD), suggesting that hyperactive-impulsive and inattentive symptoms were more frequently associated with one or two Met allele of the COMT Val108/158Met. Although these results are in line with previously shown association between the Met allele and ADHD (Biederman et al., 2008; DeYoung et al., 2010; Reuter et al., 2006; Qian et al., 2009), our findings might explain conflicting findings regarding involvement of COMT polymorphism in ADHD (Cheuk and Wong, 2006; Das et al., 2011; Faraone et al., 2005; Gizer et al., 2009; Halleland et al., 2009). Namely, the presence of hyperactive-impulsive or inattentive symptoms, and not the intensity of these symptoms, and/or ADHD diagnosis, was significantly related to COMT Val108/158Met polymorphism. Moreover, the discrepancies between studies might be explained by the different diagnostic instruments used to assess ADHD, the effect of age and gender, differences in the study designs, methodology and sample sizes.

Our results might suggest that in participants with the over-representation of the Met/Met genotype and hyperactive-impulsive and inattentive symptoms, lower COMT activity associated with decreased dopaminergic degradation and consequently increased dopamine, differently affected development of neuronal circuits involved in cognition, working memory and executive function (Egan et al., 2001), primarily in the prefrontal cortex. In line with this hypothesis, the Mel allele was suggested to be associated with sustained attention capacity and was suggested to impair prefrontally mediated cognition in ADHD (Bellgrove et al., 2005). This finding, that carriers of the Met/Met genotype had significantly higher hyperactive-impulsive and inattentive scores than carriers of other genotypes (Nikolac Perkovic et al., 2013), agree with some (Bellgrove et al., 2005; Reuter et al., 2006), but not with other (Caspi et al., 2008) reports. It might be speculated that carriers of the Met/Met genotype, with lower COMT activity and consequently higher dopaminergic activity of prefrontal circuits, have decreased cognitive functioning and more negative emotional states compared to Val carriers. As a consequence, they develop more pronounced hyperactivity and inattention, resulting in ADHD. However, the finding that COMT haplotype related to higher COMT activity was significantly associated with hyperactivity-impulsivity in adults (Halleland et al., 2009), might suggest that both hyper- and hypo-dopaminergic function in prefrontal cortex might be associated with hyperactivity and attention, major aspects in ADHD.

As ADHD is heterogeneous disorder with a large phenotypic heterogeneity, different subtypes and comorbidities, in our study we examined the association between the COMT Val108/158Met polymorphism and the different subtypes of ADHD. In line with our data, showing significant association between the Met/Met genotype of the COMT Val108/158Met and ADHD (Nikolac Perkovic et al., 2014), some authors reported that adult carriers of the Met allele had the highest ADHD self-reported scale scores and the hyperactivity/impulsivity scores compared to Val allele carriers (Ettinger et al., 2006; Halleland et al., 2009). Moreover, children carrying the Met allele demonstrated higher symptom severity of ADHD (Palmason et al., 2010), while youth with problem behaviors, who were Met carriers, had higher scores of aggression (Albaugh et al., 2010) in comparison to Val homozygotes. The opposite results also exist, and some authors observed higher frequency of the Met carriers than the Val/Val genotype in children with predominantly inattentive subtype of ADHD (Qian et al., 2009), or in ADHD adults with higher inattention scores (Reuter et al., 2006).

The results of the logistic regression revealing that COMT Val108/158Met polymorphism was significantly affected by gender, are confirmed by the reports of association between the Met allele and ADHD in only male (Nikolac Perkovic et al., 2014), but not in samples with mixed gender (Biederman et al., 2008; Cheuk and Wong, 2006), or in incarcerated adolescent male delinquents (DeYoung et al., 2010). As the number of girls included in the study was too small, it is not surprising that we could not detect significant gender related differences in the frequency of the genotypes of the COMT Val108/158Met. In our present and previous (Nikolac Perkovic et al., 2014) study, COMT Val108/158Met genotypes were not significantly associated with the particular symptoms of impulsivity and/or hyperactivity/inattention in the combined subtype of ADHD. Similar finding were reported by Caspi et al. (Caspi et al., 2008), showing no significant association between COMT Val108/158Met and ADHD symptom severity. As prefrontal cognition, especially performance related to attention phenotypes in ADHD was found to be affected by the presence of the Met allele in children and adolescents (Bellgrove et al., 2005), it has been suggested that prefrontal actions of the lower activity COMT variant could induce hyperdopaminergia. Met carriers have increased activation of prefrontal cortex which maintains the excitation of the limbic system, resulting in a higher sensitivity to adverse stimuli (Smolka et al., 2005). Bilder et al. (Bilder et al., 2004) suggested that in subcortical regions the Met carriers will have increased tonic and decreased phasic dopamine function, while in prefrontal cortex the Met carriers will have increased dopamine concentrations.

Various studies reported the association of both short and long repeat alleles of the DRD4 with ADHD (Faraone et al., 2001; Swanson et al., 1998), and with the behavioral (Swanson et al., 2000), and attentional (Bellgrove et al., 2005; Langley et al., 2004; Manor et al., 2002) performance in ADHD. In line with our findings from the present and our previous (Nikolac Perkovic et al., 2013) study, other studies also reported the association of DRD4 long allele with ADHD (Faraone et al., 2001; Gizer et al., 2009), as well as significant association between DRD4 VNTR and impulsive behavioral aggression, a characteristic feature of the combined type of ADHD (Oades et al., 2008). However, similar to some other previous reports (Langley et al., 2004), the average number of symptoms of impulsivity and hyperactivity/inattention did not differ significantly between carriers of the long and short allele of the DRD4.

Although the activity of DBH in plasma is under the influence of −1021C/T polymorphism in DBH gene (Cubells et al., 2000), our present and previous results (Nikolac Perkovic et al., 2013) as well as some other studies (Bhaduri and Mukhopadhyay, 2006; Gizer et al., 2009; Hawi et al., 2005), demonstrated no significant association of -1021C/T DBH genotypes with ADHD, or with the combined, inattentive and hyperactive/impulsive subtype of ADHD.

Genes encoding MAO enzyme are interesting candidates for association with ADHD (Waldman and Gizer, 2006). The association between genes encoding MAO-A and MAO-B subtypes and the corresponding enzyme activities has been confirmed and questioned (Garpenstrand et al., 2000; Girmen et al., 1992; Jansson et al., 2005; Pivac et al., 2006a). In line with data showing no association between other MAO-B polymorphisms with ADHD, such as rs1799836 and ADHD (Domschke et al., 2005), and no major influence of the MAO-B CA(n) microsatellite (rs3838196) on ADHD (Jiang et al., 2001), our present and previous

(Nikolac Perkovic et al., 2013) study found no significant association between MAO-B intron 13 polymorphism and ADHD, or between this polymorphism and the combined, inattentive and hyperactive/impulsive subtype of ADHD.

However, as ADHD is a complex and polygenetic disorder, it is not surprising that single risk allele was not associated with ADHD. On the other hand, gene-gene interaction was found in previous (Nikolac Perkovic et al., 2013) and present study, since significant interaction effects was observed between DRD4 long allele carriers and non-carriers and TT and C carriers of the -1021C/T DBH or GG and A carriers of the MAO-B intron 13 on the ADHD risk. These findings confirmed the important role of dopaminergic system and its candidate genes in the etiology of ADHD (Biederman and Faraone, 2005; Nemoda et al., 2011). Our present and previous results, showing significant association between COMT Val108/158Met and DRD4 VNTR with ADHD (Nikolac Perkovic et al., 2013), support the hypothesis that a complex set of connections of small genetic variations are involved in the disturbance of neural circuits underlying ADHD (Konrad and Eickhoff, 2010).

Conclusion

Recently (Franke et al., 2009), the direct involvement of classic neurotransmitter (dopaminergic, noradrenergic and serotonergic) pathways in impulsivity, the key symptom in ADHD, has been questioned. However, the results of our studies investigating platelet 5-HT concentration and platelet MAO-B activity, as well as different variants of the genes encoding COMT, DBH, MAO-B, DRD4 and 5-HTT, support their association with impulsivity. In addition, our findings demonstrate that the presence of specific impulsive symptoms, and not the diagnosis of ADHD itself, is significantly associated with peripheral biochemical and genetic markers of serotonergic and dopaminergic system. Finally, this review, together with other data accumulated from behavioral, biological, social and environmental studies, might contribute to a more complete understanding of the etiology of impulsive behavior, and might lead to identification of novel biomarkers that will result in improvements in the treatment of a variety of psychiatric disorders associated with impulsivity.

References

Albaugh, MD; Harder, VS; Althoff, RR; Rettew, DC; et al. COMT Val108/158Met genotype as a risk factor for problem behaviors in youth. *J Am Acad Child Adol Psychiatry*, 2010, 49, 841-849.

American, Psychiatric Association: Diagnostic and Statistical Manual of Mental Disorders, 1994, 4th ed. *American Psychiatric Press*, Washington, DC.

Antshel, KM; Hargrave, TM; Simonescu, M; Kaul, P; et al. Advances in understanding and treating ADHD. *BMC Medicine*, 2011, 9, 72.

Arnsten, AF; Li, BM. Neurobiology of executive functions: catecholamine influences on prefrontal cortical functions. *Biol Psychiatry*, 2005, 57, 1377-1384.

Aron, AR; Dowson, JH; Sahakian, BJ; Robbins, TW. Methylphenidate improves response inhibition in adults with attention-deficit/hyperactivity disorder. *Biol Psychiatry*, 2003, 54, 1465–1468.

Askenazy, F; Caci, H; Myquel, M; Darcourt, G; Lecrubier, Y. Relationship between impulsivity and platelet serotonin content in adolescents. *Psychiatry Res*, 2000, 94, 19-28.

Baca-Garcia, E; Salgadoa, BR; Segala, HD; Lorenzo, CV; Acosta, MN; Romeroa, MA; Hernandez, MD; Ruiza, JS; Piqueras, JF; de Leone, J. A pilot genetic study of the continuum between compulsivity and impulsivity in females: The serotonin transporter promoter polymorphism. *Prog Neuropsychopharmacol Biol Psychiatry*, 2005, 29, 713-717.

Bagby, RM; Vachon, DD; Bulmash, EL; Toneatto, T; Quilty, LC; Costa, PT. Pathological gambling and the five-factor model of personality. *Pers Individ Dif*, 2007, 43, 873–880.

Bagdy, G; Rihmer, Z. Measurement of platelet monoamine oxidase activity in healthy human volunteers. *Acta Physiol Hung*, 1986, 68, 19-24.

Baldiuniene, J; Emilsson, L; Oreland, L; Pettersson, U; Jazin, E: Investigation of the functional effect of monoamine oxidase polymorphisms in human brain. *Hum Genet*, 2002, 110, 1-7.

Barratt, ES; Slaughter, L. Defining, measuring, and predicting impulsive aggression: a heuristic model. *Behav Sci Law*, 1998, 16, 285–302.

Barratt, ES. Impulsivity: integrating cognitive, behavioral, biological, and environmental data, in The Impulsive Client. Edited by McCown WG, Johnson JL, Shure MB. Washington, DC, *American Psychological Association*, 1993, pp 39–53.

Bechara, A; Van Der Linden, M. Decision-making and impulse control after frontal lobe injuries. *Curr Opin Neurol*, 2005, 18, 734–739.

Bellgrove, MA; Hawi, Z; Lowe, N; Kirley, A; et al. DRD4 gene variants and sustained attention in attention deficit hyperactivity disorder (ADHD): effects of associated alleles at the VNTR and -521 SNP. *Amer J Med Genet Part B, Neuropsych Genet*, 2005, 136B, 81-86.

Berlin, I; Anthenelli, RM. Monoamine oxidases and tobacco smoking. *Int J Neuropsychopharmacol*, 2001, 4, 33-42.

Bevilacqua, L; Doly, S; Kaprio, J; Yuan, Q; Tikkanen, R; Paunio, T; et al. A population-specific HTR2B stop codon predisposes to severe impulsivity. *Nature*, 2010, 468, 1061–1066.

Bhaduri, N; Mukhopadhyay, K. Lack of significant association between -1021C-->T polymorphism in the dopamine beta hydroxylase gene and attention deficit hyperactivity disorder. *Neurosci Lett*, 2006, 402, 12-16.

Bidweell, LC; Willcutt, EG; DeFries, JC; Pennington, BF. Testing for Neuropsychological Endophenotypes in Siblings Discordant for Attention-Deficit/Hyperactivity Disorder. *Biol Psychiatry*, 2007, 62, 991-998.

Biederman, J; Faraone, SV. Attention-deficit hyperactivity disorder. *Lancet*, 2005, 366, 237-248.

Biederman, J; Kim, JW; Doyle, AE; Mick, E; et al. Sexually dimorphic effects of four genes (COMT, SLC6A2, MAOA, SLC6A4) in genetic associations of ADHD: a preliminary study. *Amer J Med Genet. Part B, Neuropsych Genet*, 2008, 147B, 1511-1518.

Biederman, J. Attention-Deficit/Hyperactivity Disorder: A Selective Overview. *Biol Psychiatry*, 2005, 57, 1215-1220.

Bilder, RM; Volavka, J; Lachman, HM; Grace, AA. The catechol-O-methyltransferase polymorphism: relations to the tonic-phasic dopamine hypothesis and neuropsychiatric phenotypes. *Neuropsychopharmacology*, 2004, 29, 1943-1961.

Bjork, JM; Momenan, R; Hommer, DW. Delay discounting correlates with proportional lateral frontal cortex volumes. *Biol Psychiatry*, 2009, 65, 710–713.

Boes, AD; Bechara, A; Tranel, D; Anderson, SW; Richman, L; Nopoulos, P. Right ventromedial prefrontal cortex: a neuroanatomical correlate of impulse control in boys. *Soc Cogn Affect Neurosci*, 2009, 4, 1–9.

Bowden, CL. New concepts in mood stabilization: evidence for the effectiveness of valproate and lamotrigine. *Neuropsychopharmacology*, 1998, 19, 194-199.

Brennan, AR; Arnsten, AF. Neuronal mechanisms underlying attention deficit hyperactivity disorder: the influence of arousal on prefrontal cortical function. *Ann N Y Acad Sci*, 2008, 1129, 236–245.

Brotman, MA; Schmajuk, M; Rich, BA; Dickstein, DP; Guyer, AE; Costello, EJ; Egger, HL; Angold, A; Pine, DS; Leibenluft, E. Prevalence, clinical correlates, and longitudinal course of severe mood dysregulation in children. *Biol Psychiatry*, 2006, 60, 991-997.

Brown, GI; Ebert, M; Goyer, PF; Jimerson, DC; Klwin, WJ; Bunney, WE; Goodwin, FK. Agression, suicide, and serotonin: relationships to CSF amine metabolites. *Am J Psychiatry*, 1982, 60, 991-997.

Caspi, A; Langley, K; Milne, B; Moffitt, TE; et al. A replicated molecular genetic basis for subtyping antisocial behavior in children with attention-deficit/hyperactivity disorder. *Arch Gen Psychiatry*, 2008, 65, 203-210.

Caspi, A; Sugden, K; Moffitt, TE; Taylor, A; Craig, IW; Harrington, H; McClay, J; Mill, J; Martin, J; Braithwaite, A; Poulton, R. Influence of life stress on depression: moderation by a polymorphism in the 5-HTT. *Science*, 2003, 301, 386-389.

Cederblad, M; Oreland, L; Zachrisson, E. Thrombocyte monoamine oxidase activity and behavior deviances in adolescence. *Develop Pharmacol Ther*, 1992, 18, 184-190.

Chamberlain, SR; Robbins, TW; Sahakian, BJ. The neurobiology of attention-deficit/hyperactivity disorder. *Biol Psychiatry*, 2007, 61, 1317-1319.

Chamberlain, SR; Sahakian, BJ. The neuropsychiatry of impulsivity. *Curr Opin Psychiatry*, 2007, 20, 255–61.

Chamorro, J; Bernardia, S; Potenza, MN; Grante, JE; Marsh, R; Wang, S; Blanco, C. Impulsivity in the general population: A national study. *J Psychiatr Res*, 2012, 46, 994–1001.

Chang, FM; Kidd, JR; Livak, KJ; Pakstis, AJ; et al. The world-wide distribution of allele frequencies at the human dopamine D4 receptor locus. *Hum Genet*, 1996, 98, 91-101.

Chen, J; Lipska, BK; Halim, N; Ma, QD; Matsumoto, M; Melhem, S; Kolachana, BS; Hyde TM; Herman, MM; et al. Functional analysis of genetic variation in catechol-O-methyltransferase (COMT): effects on mRNA, protein, and enzyme activity in postmortem human brain. *Am J Hun Genet*, 2004, 75, 807-21.

Cherek, DR; Lane, SD. Effects of d,l-fenfluramine on aggressive and ipulsive responding in adult males with a history of conduct disorder. *Psychopharmacology (Berl)*, 1999, 146, 473-481.

Cheuk, DK; Wong, V. Meta-analysis of association between a catechol-O-methyltransferase gene polymorphism and attention deficit hyperactivity disorder. *Behav Genet*, 2006, 36, 651-659.

Cho, SS; Pellecchia, G; Aminian, K; Ray, N; Segura, B; Obeso, I; Strafella, AP. Morphometric correlation of impulsivity in medial prefrontal cortex. *Brain Topogr*, 2013, 26, 479-87.

Clark, L; Roiser, JP; Cools, R; Rubinsztein, DC; Sahakian, BJ; Robbins, TW. Stop signal response inhibition in not modulated by tryptophan depletion or the serotonin transporter polymorphism in healthy volunteers: implications for the 5-HT theory of impulsivity. *Psychopharmacology (Berl)*, 2005, 182, 570-578.

Coccaro, EF; Siever, LJ; Klar, HM; Maurer, G; Cooper, TB; Mohs, RC. Serotonergic studies in patients with affective and personality disorders. Correlates with suicidal and impulsive aggressive behaviour. *Arch Gen Psychiatry*, 1989, 46, 587–599.

Comings, DE. Clinical and Molecular Genetics of ADHD and Tourette Syndrome: Two Related Polygenic Disorders. *Ann NY Acad Sci*, 2001, 931, 50-83.

Comings, DE. Serotonin and the biochemical genetics of alcoholism: lessons from studies of attention deficit hyperactivity disorder (ADHD) and Tourette syndrome. *Alc Alcoholism*, 1993, 2, 237-241.

Congdon, E; Canli, T. The endophenotype of impulsivity: reaching consilience through behavioral, genetic, and neuroimaging approaches. *Behav Cogn Neurosci Rev*, 2005, 4, 262–281.

Conners, CK. Manual for Conners' Rating Scales. 1989; N. Tonawanda, NY: Multi-Health Systems.

Cook, EHJ; Stein, MA; Krasowski, MD; Cox, NJ; Olkon DM; Kieffer, JE; et al. Association of attention-deficit disorder and the dopamine transporter gene. *American J Hum Genet*, 1995a, 56, 993–998.

Corruble, E; Benyamina, A; Bayle, F; Falissard, B; Hardy, P. Understanding impulsivity in severe depression? A psychometrical contribution. *Prog Neuropsychopharmacol Biol Psychiatry*, 2003, 27, 829-33.

Costa, PT; Jr, McCrae, RR. The NEO-PI/NEO-FFI manual supplement. *Psycholical Assessment Resources*, 1989, Odessa, FL.

Cubells, JF; Kranzler, HR; McCance-Katz, E; Anderson, GM; et al. A haplotype at the DBH locus, associated with low plasma dopamine beta-hydroxylase activity, also associates with cocaine-induced paranoia. *Mol Psychiatry*, 2000, 5, 56-63.

Dalley JW; Mar, AC; Economidou, D; Robbins, TW. Neurobehavioral mechanisms of impulsivity: frontostriatal systems and functional neurochemistry. *Pharmacol Biochem Behav*, 2008, 90, 250–260.

Daly, G; Hawi, Z; Fitzgerald, M; Gill, M. Mapping susceptibility loci in attention deficit hyperactivity disorder: preferential transmission of parental alleles at DAT1, DBH and DRD5 to affected children. *Mol Psychiatry*, 1999, 4, 192–196.

Das, M; Das Bhowmik, A; Bhaduri, N; Sarkar, K; et al. Role of gene-gene/gene-environment interaction in the etiology of eastern Indian ADHD probands. *Prog Neuropsychopharmacol Biol Psychiatry*, 2011, 35, 577-587.

Derks, EM; Hudziak, JJ; Dolan, CV; van Beijsterveldt, TC; Verhulst, FC; Boomsma, DI. Genetic and environmental influences on the relation between attention problems and attention deficit hyperactivity disorder. *Behav Genet*, 2008, 38, 11-23.

DeYoung, CG; Getchell, M; Koposov, RA; Yrigollen, CM; et al. Variation in the catechol-O-methyltransferase Val 158 Met polymorphism associated with conduct disorder and ADHD symptoms, among adolescent male delinquents. *Psych Genet*, 2010, 20, 20-24.

Dickman, SJ. Functional and dysfunctional impulsivity: personality and cognitive correlates. *J Pers Soc Psychology*, 1990, 58, 95–102.

Dolan, M; Anderson, IM; Deakin, JFW. Relationship between 5-HT function and impulsivity and aggression in male offenders with personality disorders. *Br J Psychiatry*, 2001, 178, 352-359.

Dolan, M; Deakin, WJF; Roberts, N; Anderson, I. Serotonergic and cognitive impairments in impulsive aggressive personality disordered offenders: are there implications for treatment? *Psychol Med*, 2002, 32, 105–117.

Dom, G; De Wilde, B; Hulstijn, W; van den Brink, W; Sabbe, B. Behavioural aspects of impulsivity in alcoholics with and without a cluster-B personality disorder. *Alc Alcoholism*, 2006, 41, 412–420.

Domschke, K; Sheehan, K; Lowe, N; Kirley, A; et al. Association analysis of the monoamine oxidase A and B genes with attention deficit hyperactivity disorder (ADHD) in an Irish sample: preferential transmission of the MAO-A 941G allele to affected children. Am Journal Med Genet. Part B, *Neuropsychiat Genet*, 2005, 134B, 110-114.

Dougherty, DD; Bonab, AA; Spencer, TJ; Rauch, SL; Madras, BK; Fischman, AJ. Dopamine transporter density in patients with attention deficit hyperactivity disorder. *The Lancet*, 1999, 354, 2132−2133.

Eensoo, D; Harro, M; Pullmann, H; Allik, J; Harro, J. Association of traffic behavior with personality and platelet monoamine oxidase activity in school children. *J Adol Health*, 2007, 40, 311-317.

Eensoo, D; Paaver, M; Pulver, A; Harro, M; Harro, J. Low platelet MAO activity associated with high dysfunctional impulsivity and antisocial behavior: evidence from drunk drivers. *Psychopharmacology (Berl)*, 2004, 172, 356-8.

Egan, MF; Goldberg, TE; Kolachana, BS; Callicott, JH; Mazzanti, CM; Straub, RE; Goldman, D; Weinberger, DR. Effect of COMT Val108/158 Met genotype on frontal lobe function and risk for schizophrenia. *Proc Natl Acad Sci USA*, 2001, 98, 6917-22.

Eisenberg, DT; Mackillop, J; Modi, M; Beauchemin, J; Dang, D; Lisman, SA; Lum, JK; Wilson, DS. Examining impulsivity as an endophenotype using a behavioral approach: a DRD2 TaqI A and DRD4 48-bp VNTR association study. *Behav Brain Funct*, 2007, 3, 2.

Ernst, M; Zametkin, AJ; Matochik, JA; Pascualvaca, D; Jons, PH; Cohen, RM. High midbrain [^{18}F]DOPA accumulation in children with attention deficit hyperactivity disorder. *Am J Psychiatry*, 1999, 156, 1209–1215.

Ertugrul, A; Ucar, G; Basar, K; Demir, B; Yabanoglu, S; Ulug, B. Influence of clozapine on platelet serotonin, monoamine oxidase and plasma serotonin levels. *Psychiatry Res*, 2007, 149, 49-57.

Ettinger, U; Joober, R; R DEG, O'Driscoll, GA. Schizotypy, attention deficit hyperactivity disorder, and dopamine genes. *Psych Clin Neurosci*, 2006, 60, 764-767.

Evans, J; Reeves, B; Platt, H; Leibenau, A; Goldman, D; Jefferson, K; Nutt, D. Impulsiveness, serotonin genes and repetition of deliberate self-harm (DSH). *Psychol Med*, 2000, 30, 1327–1334.

Evenden, JL. Varieties of imulsivity. *Psychopharmacology (Berl)*, 1999, 146, 348-361.

Eysenck, SB; Eysenck, HJ. The place of impulsiveness in a dimensional system of personality description. *Br J Soc Clin Psychol*, 1977, 16, 57-68.

Fairbanks, LA; Melega, WP; Jorgensen, MJ; Kaplan, KR; McGuire, MT. Social impulsivity inversly associated with CSF 5-HIAA and fluoxetine exposure in velvet monkeys. *Neuropsychopharmacology*, 2001, 24, 370-378.

Fallgatter, AJ; Jatzke, S; Bartsch, AJ; Hamelbeck, B; Lesch, KP. Serotonin transporter polymorphism influences topography of inhibitory motor control. *Int J Neuropsychopharmacology*, 1999, 2, 115-120.

Faraone, S; Perlis, RH; Doyle, SE; Smoller, JW; Jennifer, J; Goralnick, JJ; Holmgren, MA; Sklar, P. Molecular genetics of attention-deficit/hyperactivity disorder. *Biol Psychiatry*, 2005; 57, 1313-1323.

Faraone, SV; Doyle, AE; Mick, E; Biederman, J. Meta-analysis of the association between the 7-repeat allele of the dopamine D(4) receptor gene and attention deficit hyperactivity disorder. *Am J Psychiatry*, 2001, 158, 1052–1057.

Faraone, SV; Khan, SA. Candidate gene studies of attention-deficit/hyperactivity disorder. *J Clin Psychiatry*, 2006, 67, 13-20.

Field, AP; Miles, J; Field, F. Discovering statistics using R. 2012; SAGE publications, Ltd., London, UK.

Fillmore, MT; Rush, CR. Impaired inhibitory control of behavior in chronic cocaine users. *Drug Alcoh Depend*, 2002, 66, 265–273.

Fowler, JS; Logan, J; Wang, GJ; Volkow, ND. Monoamine oxidase and cigarette smoking. *Neurotoxicology*, 2003, 24, 75-82

Franke, B, Neale, BM; Faraone, SV. Genome-wide association studies in ADHD. *Human Genetics*, 2009, 126, 13-50.

Frankle, WG; Lombardo, I; New, AS; Goodman, M; Talbot, PS; Huang, YH; Hwang, DR; Slifstein, M; Curry, S; Abi-Dargham, A; Laruelle, M; Siever, LJ. Brain serotonin transporter distribution in subjects with impulsive aggressivity: a positron emission study with [^{11}C] mcn 5662. *Am J Psychiatry*, 2005, 5, 915-923.

Garpenstrand, H; Ekblom, J; Forslund, K; Rylander, G; Oreland, L. Platelet monoamine oxidase activity is related to MAOB intron 13 genotype. *J Neural Transm*, 2000, 107, 523-530.

Genro, JP; Kieling, C; Rohde, LA; Hutz, MH. Attention-deficit/hyperactivity disorder and the dopaminergic hypotheses. *Exp Rev Neurother*, 2010, 10, 587-601.

Gerra, G; Garofano, L; Castaldini, L; Rowetto, F; Zaimovic, A; Moi, G; et al. Serotonin transporter promoter polymorphism genotype is associated with temperament, personality traits and illegal drugs use among adolescents. *J Neural Transm*, 2005a, 112, 1397-410.

Gerra, G; Garofano, L; Zaimovic, A; Moi, G; Branchi, B; Bussandri, M; et al. Association of the serotonin transporter promoter polymorphism with smoking behavior among adolescents. *Am J Med Genet B Neuropsychiatr Genet*, 2005b, 5, 73-8.

Girmen, AS; Baenziger, J; Hotamisligil, GS; Konradi, C; Shalish, C; Sullivan, JL; et al. Relationship between platelet monoamine oxidase B activity and alleles at the MAO-B locus. *J Neurochem*, 1992, 59, 2063-2066.

Gizer, IR; Ficks, C; Waldman, ID. Candidate gene studies of ADHD: a meta-analytic review. *Hum Genet*, 2009, 126, 51-90.

Goveas, JS; Csernansky, JG; Coccaro, EF. Platelet serotonin content correlates inversely with life history of aggression in personality-disordered subjects. *Psychiatry Res*, 2004, 126, 23-32.

Graff-Guerrero, A; De la Fuente-Sandoval, D; Camarena, B; Gomez-Martin, D; Apiquian, R; Fesan, A; et al. Frontal and limbic metabolic differences in subjects selected according to genetic variation of the SCL6A4 gene polymorphism. *NeuroImage*, 2005, 25, 1197-204.

Halleland, H; Lundervold, AJ; Halmoy, A; Haavik, J; et al. Association between catechol O-methyltransferase (COMT) haplotypes and severity of hyperactivity symptoms in adults. *Amer J Med Genet. Part B, Neuropsych Genet,* 2009, 150B, 403-410.

Hallikainen, T; Saito, T; Lachman, HM; Volavka, J; Pojhanen, T; Ryynanen, OP; Kauhanen, J; Syvalahti, E; Hietala, J; Tiihonen, J. Association between low activity serotonin transporter promoter genotype and early onset alcoholism with habitual impulsive violent behavior. *Mol Psychiatry*, 1999, 4, 385-388.

Hallman, J; Oreland, L; Edman, G; Schalling, D. Thrombocyte monoamine oxidase activity and personality traits in women with severe premenstrual syndrome. *Acta Psychiatr Scand*, 1987, 76, 225–234.

Halperin, JM; Newcorn, JH; Schwartz, ST; Sharma, V; Siever, LJ; Koda, VH; Gabriel, S: Age-related changes in the association between serotonergic function and aggression in boys with ADHD. *Biol Psychiatry*, 1997, 41, 682–689.

Hariri, AR; Mattay, VS; Tessitore, A; Fera F; Weinberger DR. Neocortical modulation of the amygdala response to fearful stimuli. *Biol Psychiatry*, 2003, 53, 494-501.

Harro, M; Eensoo, D; Kiive, E; Merenäkk, L; Alep, J; Oreland, L; Harro, J. Platelet monoamine oxidase in healthy 9- and 15-years old children: the effect of gender, smoking and puberty. *Prog Neuropsychopharmacol Biol Psychiatry*, 2001, 25, 1497–1511.

Hawi, Z; Segurado, R; Conroy, J; Sheehan, K; et al. Preferential transmission of paternal alleles at risk genes in attention-deficit/hyperactivity disorder. *Am J Hum Genet*, 2005, 77, 958-965.

Hegerl, U; Himmerich, H; Engmann, B; Hensch, T. Mania and attention-deficit/hyperactivity disorder: Common symptomatology, common pathophysiology and common treatment? *Curr Opin Psychiatry*, 2010, 23, 1–7.

Heinz, A; Braus, DF; Smolka, MN; Wrase, J; Puls, I; Hermann, D; et al., Amygdala-prefrontal coupling depends on a genetic variation of the serotonin transporter. *Nat Neurosci*, 2005, 8, 20-1.

Hercigonja Novkovic, V; Rudan, V; Pivac, N; Nedic, G; Muck-Seler, D. Platelet serotonin concentration in children with attention-deficit/hyperactivity disorder. *Neuropsychobiology.*, 2009, 59, 17-22.

Hopwood, CJ; Morey, LC; Skodol, AE; Stout, RL; Yen, S; Ansell, EB; et al. Five-factor model personality traits associated with alcohol related diagnoses in a clinical sample. *J Stud Alcohol Drugs*, 2007, 68, 455–460.

Hrdina, PD. Platelet serotonergic markers in psychiatric disorders: use, abuse and limitations. *J Psychiatry Neurosci*, 1994, 19, 87-88.

Irving, JB; Coursey, RD; Buchsbaum, MS; Murphy, DL. Platelet monoamine oxidase activity and life stress as predictors of psychopathology and coping in a community sample. *Psychol Med*, 1989, 19, 79–90.

Jakovljevic, M; Muck-Seler, D; Pivac, N; Ljubicic, D; Bujas, M; Dodig, G. Seasonal influence on platelet 5-HT levels in patients with recurrent major depression and schizophrenia. *Biol Psychiatry*, 1997, 41, 1028-1034.

Jansson, M; McCarthy, S; Sullivan, PF; Dickman, P; Andersson, B; Oreland, L; et al. MAOA haplotypes associated with thrombocyte-MAO activity. *BMC Genetics*, 2005, 6, 46

Jiang, S; Xin, R; Lin, S; Qian, Y; et al. Linkage studies between attention-deficit hyperactivity disorder and the monoamine oxidase genes. *Am J Med Genet*, 2001, 105, 783-788.

Kaufman, J; Yang, BZ; D-Palumberi, H; Grasso, D; Lipschitz, D; Houshyar, S; et al. Brain-derived neurotrophic factor- 5-HTTLPR gene interactions and environmental modifiers of depression in children. *Biol Psychiatry*, 2006, 59, 673-80.

Kiive, E; Eensoo, D; Harro, M; Harro, J. Platelet monoamino oxidase activity in association with aggressive and hyperactive behavior: the effect of smoking? *Pers Ind Differ*, 2002, 33, 355-363.

Kiive, E; Fischer, K; Harro, M; Harro, J. Platelet monoamino oxidase activity in association with adolescent inattentive and hyperactive behaviour: A prospective longitudinal study. *Pers Ind Differ*, 2007, 43, 155-166.

Kiive, E; Merenäkk, L; Harro, M; Harro, J. Changes in platelet monoamine oxidase activity, cholesterol levels and hyperactive behaviour in adolescents over a period of three years. *Neurosci Lett*, 2005, 384, 310-5.

Kim, S; Lee, D. Prefrontal cortex and impulsive decision making. *Biol Psychiatry*, 2011, 69, 1140–1146.

Kirk, KM; Whitfield, JB; Pang, D; Heath, AC; Martin, NG. Genetic covariation of neuroticism with monoamine oxidase activity and smoking. *Am J Med Gen*, 2001, 105, 700–706.

Klinteberg, B; Levander, SE; Oreland, L; Asberg, M; Schalling, D. Neuropsychological correlates of platelet monoamine oxidase (MAO) activity in female and male subjects. *Biol Psychol*, 1987, 24, 237-252.

Konrad, K; Eickhoff, SB. Is the ADHD brain wired differently? A review on structural and functional connectivity in attention deficit hyperactivity disorder. *Hum Brain Mapp*, 2010, 31, 904-916.

Kovacic, Z; Henigsberg, N; Pivac, N; Nedic, G; Borovecki, A. Platelet serotonin concentration and suicidal behaviour in combat related posttraumatic stress disorder. *Prog Neuropsychopharmacol Biol Psychiat*, 2008, 32, 544-551.

Krajl, M. A rapid microfluorimetric determination of monoamine oxidase. *Biochem Pharmacol*, 1965, 14, 1683-1685.

Krause, KH; Dresel, SH; Krause, J; Kung, HF; Tatsch, K. Increased striatal dopamine transporter in adult patients with attention deficit hyperactivity disorder: Effects of methylphenidate as measured by single photon emission computed tomography. *Neurosci Lett*, 2000, 285, 107−110.

L'Abate, L. A family theory of impulsivity, in The Impulsive Client. Edited by McCown, WG; Johnson, JL; Shure, MB. Washington, DC; *American Psychological Association*, 1993, pp 93–117.

Lachman, HM; Papolos, DF; Saito, T; Yu, YM; Szumlanski CL; Weinshilboum RM. Human catechol-O-methyltransferase pharmacogenetics: description of a functional polymorphism and its potential application to neuropsychiatric disorders. *Pharmacogenetics*, 1996, 6, 243-50.

LaHoste, GJ; Swanson, JM; Wigal, SB; Glabe, C; Wigal, T; King, N; et al. Dopamine D4 receptor gene polymorphism is associated with attention deficit hyperactivity disorder. *Mol Psychiatry*, 1996, 1, 121–124.

Langley, K; Marshall, L; van den Bree, M; Thomas H; et al. Association of the dopamine D4 receptor gene 7-repeat allele with neuropsychological test performance of children with ADHD. *Am J Psychiatry*, 2004, 161, 133-138.

Lee, B; Groman, S; London, ED; Jentsch, JD. Dopamine D(2)/D(3) Receptors Play a Specific Role in the Reversal of a Learned Visual Discrimination in Monkeys. *Neuropsychopharmacology*, 2007, 32, 2125–2134.

Lee, B; London, ED; Poldrack, RA; Farahi, J; Nacca, A; Monterosso, JR; Mumford, JA; Bokarius, AV; Dahlbom, M; Mukherjee, J; Bilder, RM; Brody, AL; Mandelkern, MA. Striatal dopamine d2/d3 receptor availability is reduced in methamphetamine dependence and is linked to impulsivity. *J Neurosci*, 2009, 29, 14734-40.

Lesch, KP; Bengel, D; Heils, A; Sabol, SZ; Greenberg, BD; Petri, S; Banjamin, J; Muller, CR; Hamer, DH; Murphy, DL. Association of anxiety-related traits with a polymorphism in the serotonin transporter gene regulatory region. *Science*, 1996, 274, 1527-1531.

Lesch, KP; Gutknecht, L. Pharmacogenetics of the serotonin transporter. Prog Neuropsychopharmacology *Biol Psychiatry*, 2005, 29, 1062-1073.

Lesch, KP; Merschdorf, U. Impulsivity, Aggression, and Serotonin: A Molecular Psychobiological Perspective. *Behav Sci Law*, 2000, 18, 581–604.

Li, D; He, L. Meta-analysis supports association between serotonin transporter (5-HTT) and suicidal behavior. *Mol Psychiatry*, 2007, 12, 47-54.

Lichter, JB; Barr, CL; Kennedy, JL; Van Tol, HH; et al. A hypervariable segment in the human dopamine receptor D4 (DRD4) gene. *Hum Mol Genetics*, 1993, 2, 767-773.

Limosin, F; Loze, JY; Dubertret, C; Gouya, L; Ades, J; Rouillon, F; Gorwood, P. Impulsiveness as the intermediate link between the dopamine receptor D2 gene and alcohol dependence. *Psychiatr Genet*, 2003, 13, 127–129.

Liotti, M; Panksepp, J. Imaging human emotions and affective feelings: implications for biological psychiatry. In: Panksepp J. editor. *Textbook of Biological Psychiatry*. New Jersey Hoboken: Wiley-Liss Inc, 2004, 33-66.

Lowry, OH; Rosenbrough, NS; Farr, AC; Randall, RJ. Protein measurement with the Folin phenol reagent. *J Biol Chem*, 1951, 193, 265-75.

Lucki, I. The spectrum of behaviours influenced by serotonin. *Biol Psychiatry*, 1998, 44, 151-162.

Macleod, J; Hickman, M; Bowen, E; Alati, R; Tilling, K; Smith, GD. Parental drug use, early adversities, later childhood problems and children's use of tobacco and alcohol at age 10, birth cohort study. *Addiction*, 2008, 103, 1731-43.

Malmberg, K; Wargelius, HL; Lictenstein, P; Oreland, L; Larsson, JO. ADHD and Disruptive behavior scores-associations with MAO-A and 5-HTT genes and with platelet MAO activity in adolescents. *BMC Psychiatry*, 2008, 8, 28.

Mann, JJ; Arango, V. Integration of neurobiology and psychopathology in a unified model of suicidal behavior. *J Clin Psychopharmacol*, 1992, 12, 2-7.

Mann, JJ; McBride, PA; Anderson, GM; Mieczkowski, TA. Platelet and whole blood serotonin content in depressed inpatients: correlations with acute and lifetime psychopathology. *Biol Psychiatry*, 1992, 32, 243-257.

Manor, I; Tyano, S; Eisenberg, J; Bachner-Melman, R; et al. The short DRD4 repeats confer risk to attention deficit hyperactivity disorder in a family-based design and impair performance on a continuous performance test (TOVA). *Mol Psychiatry*, 2002, 7, 790-794.

Manuck, SB; Flory, JD; McCaffery, JM; Matthews, KA; Mann, JJ; Muldoon, MF: Aggression, impulsivity, and central nervous system serotonergic responsivity in a nonpatient sample. *Neuropsychopharmacology*, 1998, 19, 287-299.

Masoliver, E; Menoyo, A; Perez, V. Serotonin transporter linked promoter (polymorphism) in the serotonin transporter gene may be associated with antidepressant-induced mania in bipolar disorder. *Psychiatr Genet*, 2006, 16, 25-9.

Matsuo, K; Nicoletti, M; Nemoto, K; Hatch, JP; Peluso, MA; Nery, FG; Soares, JC. A voxel-based morphometry study of frontal gray matter correlates of impulsivity. *Hum Brain Mapp*, 2009, 30, 1188–1195.

McAlonan, GM; Cheung, V; Cheung, C; Chua, SE; Murphy, DGM; Suckling, J; Tai, KS; Yip, LKC; Leung, P; Ho, TP. Mapping brain structure in attention deficit-hyperactivity disorder: a voxel-based MRI study of regional grey and white matter volume. *Psychiatry Res*, 2007, 154, 171-180.

Merenakk, L; Harro, M; Kiive, E; Laidra, K; Eensoo, D; Allik, J; et al. Association between substance use, personality traits, and platelet MAO activity in preadolescents and adolescents. *Add Behav*, 2003, 28, 1507–1514.

Meszaros, Z; Borsiczky, D; Mate, M; Tarcali, J; Szombathy, T; Tekes, K; et al.. Platelet MAO-B activity and serotonin content in patients with dementia: effect of age, medication and disease. *Neurochem Res*, 1998, 23, 863-868.

Miller, SA; Dykes, DD; Polesky, HF. A simple salting out procedure for extracting DNA from human nucleated cells. *Nucl Acid Res*, 1988, 16, 1215-1215.

Mitchell, S. Measures of impulsivity in cigarette smokers and non-smokers. *Psychopharmacology*, 1999, 146, 455–464.

Moeller, FG; Barratt, ES; Dougherty, DM; Schmitz, JM; Swann, AC. Psychiatric Aspects of Impulsivity. *Am J Psychiatry*, 2001, 158, 1783-1793.

Muck-Seler, D; Jakovljevic, M; Pivac, N. Platelet 5-HT concentrations and suicidal behaviour in recurrent major depression. *J Affect Disord*, 1996, 39, 73-80.

Muck-Seler, D; Pivac, N; Sagud, M; Mustapic, M; Jakovljevic, M. The effects of serotonin uptake inhibitors on platelet serotonin: From basic to clinical research, in Shirley AC (ed) Trends in Serotonin uptake inhibitors research. New York, *Nova Science Publishers*, 2005, pp 29-53.

Muck-Seler, D; Sagud, M; Mustapic, M; Nedic, G; Babic, A; Mihaljevic Peles, A; et al. The effect of lamotrigine on platelet monoamine oxidase type B activity in patients with bipolar depression. *Prog Neuropsychopharmacol Biol Psychiatry*, 2008, 32, 1195-1198.

Mueller-Oerlinghausen, B; Roggenbach, J; Franke, L. Serotonergic platelet markers of suicidal behaviour – do they really exist? *J Affect Disord*, 2004, 79, 13-24.

Murphy, DL; Wright, C; Buchsbaum, M; Nichols, A; Costa, JL; Wyatt, RL. Platelet and plasma monoamine oxidase activity in 680 normals: Sex and age differences and stability over time. *Biochem Med*, 1976, 16, 254-256.

Murphy, FC; Smith, KA; Cowen, PJ; Robbins, TW; Sahakian, BJ. The effects of tryptophan depletion on cognitive and affective processing in healthy volunteers. *Psychopharmacology* (Berl), 2002, 163, 42-53.

Mustapic, M; Pivac, N; Kozaric-Kovacic, D; Dezeljin, M; et al. Dopamine beta-hydroxylase (DBH) activity and -1021C/T polymorphism of DBH gene in combat-related post-traumatic stress disorder. *Amer J Med Genet. Part B, Neuropsych Genet*, 2007, 144B, 1087-1089.

Nedic, G; Pivac, N; Hercigonja, DK; Jovancevic, M; Curkovic, KD; Muck-Seler, D. Platelet monoamine oxidase activity in children with attention-deficit/hyperactivity disorder. *Psychiatry Res*, 2010, 175, 252-5.

Nelson, RJ. Biology of agression. Oxford University Press, Cary, NC, USA, 2005, 79-84.

Nemoda, Z; Szekely, A; Sasvari-Szekely, M. Psychopathological aspects of dopaminergic gene polymorphisms in adolescence and young adulthood. *Neurosc Biobehav Rev*, 2011, 35, 1665-86.

Nikolac Perkovic, M; Kiive, E; Nedic Erjavec, G; Veidebaum, T; Curkovic, M; Dodig-Curkovic, K; Muck-Seler, D; Harro, J; Pivac, N. The association between the catechol-O-methyltransferase Val108/158Met polymorphism and hyperactive-impulsive and inattentive symptoms in youth. *Psychopharmacology* (Berl) 2013, 230, 69-76.

Nikolac Perkovic, M; Nedic Erjavec, G; Stefulj, J; Muck-Seler, D; Pivac, N; Kocijan Hercigonja, D; Hranilovic, D; Curkovic, M; Dodig-Curkovic, K. Association between the polymorphisms of the selected genes encoding dopaminergic system with ADHD and autism. *Psychiatry Res*, 2014, 215, 260-1.

Oades, RD; Lasky-Su, J; Christiansen, H; Faraone, SV; et al. The influence of serotonin- and other genes on impulsive behavioral aggression and cognitive impulsivity in children with attention-deficit/hyperactivity disorder (ADHD): Findings from a family-based association test (FBAT) analysis. *Behav Brain Funct*, 2008, 4, 48.

Oades, RD; Slusarek, M; Velling, S; Bondy, B. Serotonin platelet-transporter measures in childhood attention-deficit/hyperactivity disorder (ADHD): Clinical versus experimental measures of impulsivity. *World J Biol Psychiatry*, 2002b, 3, 96-100.

Oades, RD. Dopamine may be «hyper» with respect to noradrenaline metabolism, but «hypo» with respect to serotonin metabolism in children with attention deficit hyperactivity disorder. *Behav Brain Res*, 2002a, 130, 97-102.

Oreland, L; Damberg, M; Hallman, J; Garpenstrand, H. Smoking only explains part of associations between platelet monomine oxidase activity and personality. *J Neur Transm*, 2002, 109, 963-975.

Oreland, L. Platelet monoamine oxidase, personality and alcoholism: the rise, fall and resurrection, *Neurotoxicity*, 2004, 25, 79-89.

Paaver, M; Eensoo, D; Pulver, A; Harro, J. Adaptive and maladaptive impulsivity, platelet monoamine oxidase (MAO) activity and risk-admitting in different types of risky drivers. *Psychopharmacology*, (Berl) 2006, 186, 32-40.

Paaver, M; Kurrikoff, T; Nordquist, N; Oreland, L; Harro, J. The effect of 5-HTT gene promoter polymorphism on impulsivity depends on family relations in girls. *Prog Neuropsychopharmacol Biol Psychiatry*, 2008, 32, 1263-8.

Paaver, M; Nordquist, N; Parik, J; Harro, M; Oreland, L; Harro, J. Platelet MAO activity and the 5-HTT gene promoter polymorphism are associated with impulsivity and cognitive style in visual information processing. *Psychopharmacology*, 2007, 194, 545–554.

Palmason, H; Moser, D; Sigmund, J; Vogler, C; et al. Attention-deficit/hyperactivity disorder phenotype is influenced by a functional catechol-O-methyltransferase variant. *J Neural Trans*, 2010, 117, 259-267.

Pattij, T; Vanderschuren, LJMJ. The neuropharmacology of impulsive behaviour. *Trends Pharmacol Sci*, 2008, 29, 192-199.

Patton, JH; Stanford, MS; Barratt, ES. Factor structure of the Barratt Impulsiveness Scale. *J Clin Psychology*, 1995, 51, 768–774.

Pavlov, KA; Chistiakov, DA; Chekhonin, VP. Genetic determinants of aggression and impulsivity in humans. *J Appl Genet*, 2012, 53, 61-82.

Peirson, AR; Heuchert, JW; Thomala, L; Berk, M; Plein, H; Cloninger, CR. Relationship between serotonin and the Temperament and character inventory. *Psychiatry Res*, 1999, 89, 29-37.

Pezawas, L; Meyer-Lindenberg, A; Drabant, EM; Verchinski, BA; Munoz, KE; Kolachana, BS; et al. 5-HTLPR polymorphism impacts human cingulate-amygdala interactions: a genetic susceptibility mechanism for depression. *Nat Neurosci*, 2005, 8, 828-34.

Pfeffer, CR; McBride, PA; Anderson, GA; Kakuma, T; Fensterheim, L; Khait, V. Peripheral serotonin measures in prepubertal psychiatric inpatients and normal children: associations with suicidal behaviour and its risk factors. *Biol Psychiatry*, 1998, 44, 568-577.

Pick, LH; Halperin, JM; Schwartz, ST; Newcorn, JH. A longitudinal study of neurobiological mechanisms in boys with attention-deficit hyperactivity disorder: preliminary findings. *Biol Psychiatry*, 1999, 45, 371-373.

Pivac, N; Knezevic, J; Kozaric-Kovacic, D; Dezeljin, M; Mustapic, M; Rak, D; Matijevic, T; Pavelic, J; Muck-Seler, D. Monoamine oxidase (MAO) intron 13 polymorphism and platelet MAO-B activity in combat-related posttraumatic stress disorder. *J Affect Disord*, 2007, 103, 131-8.

Pivac, N; Knezevic, J; Mustapic, M; Dezeljin, M; Muck-Seler, D; Kozaric-Kovacic, D; Balija, M; Matijevic, T; Pavelic, J. The lack of association between monoamine oxidase (MAO) intron 13 polymorphism and platelet MAO-B activity among men. *Life Sci*, 2006a, 79, 45-9.

Pivac, N; Kozaric-Kovacic, D; Mustapic, M; Dezeljin, M; Borovecki, A; Grubisic-Ilic, M; Muck-Seler, D. Platelet serotonin in combat related posttraumatic stress disorder with psychotic symptoms. *J Affect Disord*, 2006b, 93, 223-227.

Pivac, N; Kozaric-Kovacic, D; Mustapic, M; Dezeljin, M; Nenadic-Sviglin, K; Muck-Seler, D. Peripheral biological markers in alcoholism. New York: *Nova Science Publishers*, 2008.

Pivac, N; Muck-Seler, D; Mustapic, M; Kozaric-Kovacic, D; Nenadic-Sviglin, K; Dezeljin, M. Platelet monoamine oxidase in alcoholism. *Psychopharmacology*, 2005, 182, 194-196.

Pivac, N; Mück-Seler, D; Sagud, M; Jakovljevic, M; Mustapic, M; Mihaljevic-Peles, A. Long-term sertraline treatment and peripheral biochemical markers in female depressed patients. Prog. Neuro-Psychopharmacol. *Biol Psychiatry*, 2003, 27, 759-765.

Pliszka, SR; Rogeness, GA; Renner, P; Sherman, J; Broussard, T. Plasma neurochemistry in juvenile offenders. *Am Acad Child Adolesc Psych*, 1988, 255, 588–594.

Preuss, UW; Soyka, M; Bahlmann, M; Wenzel, K; Behrens, S; Jonge, S; Kruger, M; Bondy, B. Serotonin transporter gene regulatory region polymorhism (5-HTTLPR),

[^{3}H]paroxetine binding in healthy control subjects and alcohol-dependent patients and their relationships to impulsivity. *Psychiatry Res*, 2000, 96, 51-61.

Pulver, A; Allik, J; Pulkkinen, L; Hämäläinen, M. A big five personality inventory in two non-indo-european languages. *Eur J Personality*, 1995, 9, 109-124.

Qian, QJ; Liu, J; Wang, YF; Yang, L; et al. Attention Deficit Hyperactivity Disorder comorbid oppositional defiant disorder and its predominately inattentive type: evidence for an association with COMT but not MAOA in a Chinese sample. *BehaviorBrain Funct*, 2009, 5, 8.

Quist, JL; Barr, CL; Schachar, R; Roberts, W; Malone, M; Tannock, R; et al. The serotonin 5-HT1B receptor gene and attention deficit hyperactivity disorder. *Mol Psychiatry*, 2003, 8, 98−102.

Rapoport, J; Quinn, N; Scribanu, N; Murphy, DL. Platelet serotonin of hyperactive school age boys. *Br J Psychiatry*, 1974, 125, 138–140.

Retz, W; Thome, J; Blocher, D; Baader, M; Rosler, M. Association of attention deficit hyperactivity disorder-related psychopathology and personality traits with the serotonin transporter promoter region polymorphism. *Neurosci Lett*, 2002, 319, 133−136.

Reuter, M; Kirsch, P; Hennig, J. Inferring candidate genes for attention deficit hyperactivity disorder (ADHD) assessed by the World Health Organization Adult ADHD Self-Report Scale (ASRS). *J Neur Transm*, 2006, 113, 929-938.

Reynolds, B; Ortengren, A; Richards, JB; de Wit, H. Dimensions of impulsive behavior: personality and behavioral measures. *Pers Indiv Differ*, 2006, 40, 305–315.

Ribases, M; Hervas, A; Ramos-Quiroga, JA; Bosch, R; et al. Association study of 10 genes encoding neurotrophic factors and their receptors in adult and child attention-deficit/hyperactivity disorder. *Biol Psychiatry*, 2008, 63, 935-945.

Ridley, RM; Haystead, TA; Baker, HF. An analysis of visual object reversal learning in the marmoset after amphetamine and haloperidol. *Pharmacol Biochem Behav*, 1981, 14, 345–351.

Robbins, TW. Chemistry of the mind: neurochemical modulation of prefrontal cortical function. *J Comp Neurol*, 2005, 493, 140-146.

Rogeness, GA; Javors, MA; Pliszka, SR. Neurochemistry of child and adolescent psychiatry. *J Am Acad Child Adolesc Psychiat*, 1992, 31, 765-781.

Rolls, ET. The functions of the orbitofrontal cortex. *Brain Cogn*, 2004, 55, 11–29.

Roth, JA; Young, JG; Cohen, DJ. Platelet monoamine oxidase in children and adolescents. *Life Sci*, 1976, 18, 919-924.

Ruchkin, VV; Roman, A; Koposov, RA; Britt, AF; Klinteberg, B; Oreland, L; Grigorenko, EL. Platelet, MAO-B, personality, and psychopathology. *J Abnorm Psychol*, 2005, 114, 477-482.

Sagud, M; Pivac, N; Mustapic, M; Nedic, G; Mihaljevic Peles, A; Kramaric, M; Jakovljevic, M; Muck-Seler, D. The effect of lamotrigine on platelet serotonin concentration in patients with bipolar depression. *Psychopharmacology*, 2008, 197, 683-685.

Schalling, D; Edman, G; Asberg, M; Oreland, L. Platelet MAO activity associated with impulsivity and aggressivity. *Person Indiv Diff*, 1988, 9, 597–605.

Schinka, JA; Letsch, EA; Crawford, FC. DRD4 and novelty seeking: results of meta-analyses. *Am J Med Genet*, 2002, 114, 643-648.

Schmitt, J; Jorissen, B; Sobsczak, S; van Boxtel, MPJ; Hogervorst, E; Deutz, NEP; Riedel, W. Tryptophan depletion impairs memory consolidation bur improves focussed attention in healthy young volunteers. *J Psychopharmacol*, 2000, 14, 21-20.

Schmitt, JAJ; Wingen, M; Ramaekers, JG; Evers, JG; Riedel, WJ. Serotonin and human cognitive performance. *Curr Pharmaceut Design*, 2006, 12, 2473-2486.

Schulz, KP; McKay, KE; Newcorn, JH; Sharma, V; Gabriel, S; Halperin, JM. Serotonin function and risk for alcoholism in boys with attention-deficit hyperactivity disorder. *Neuropsychopharmacology*, 2001, 18, 10-17.

Sharp, SI; McQuillin, A; Gurling, HM. Genetics of attention-deficit hyperactivity disorder (ADHD). *Neuropharmacology*, 2009, 57, 590-600.

Shekim, WO; Bylund, DB; Alexson, J; Glaser, RD; Jones, SB; Hodges, K; et al. Platelet MAO and measures of attention and impulsivity in boys with attention deficit disorder and hyperactivity. *Psychiatry Res*, 1986, 18, 179-188.

Shekim, WO; Davis, LG; Bylund, DB; Brunngraber, E; Fikes, L; Lanham, J. Platelet MAO in children with attention deficit disorder and hyperactivity: A pilot study. *Am J Psychiatry*, 1982, 139, 936-938.

Shekim, WO; Hodges, K; Horwitz, E; Glaser, RD; Davis, L; Bylund, DB. Psychoeducational and impulsivity correlates of platelet MAO in normal children. *Psychiatry Res*, 1984, 11, 99–106.

Smalley, SL; Bailey, JN; Palmer, CG; Cantwell, DP; McGough, JJ; Del'Homme, MA; Asarnow, JR; Woodward, JA; Ramsey, C; Nelson, SF. Evidence that the dopamine D4 receptor is a susceptibility gene in attention deficit hyperactivity disorder. *Mol Psychiatry*, 1998, 3, 427–430.

Smolka, MN; Schumann, G; Wrase, J; Grusser, SM; et al. Catechol-O-methyltransferase val158met genotype affects processing of emotional stimuli in the amygdala and prefrontal cortex. *J Neurosci*, 2005, 25, 836-842.

Sobell, JL; Lind, TJ; Hebrink, DD; Heston, LL; Sommer, SS. Screening the monoamine oxidase B gene in 100 male patients with schizophrenia: a cluster of polymorphisms in African-American but lack of functionally significant sequence changes. *Amer J Med Genet. Part B, Neuropsych Genet*, 1997, 74, 44-49.

Solanto, MV. Dopamine dysfunction in AD/HD: integrating clinical and basic neuroscience research. *Behav Brain Res*, 2002, 130, 65-71.

Southam, E; Kirkby, D; Higgins, GA; Hagan, RM. Lamotrigine inhibits monoamine uptake in vitro and modulates 5-hydroxytryptamine uptake in rats. *Eur J Pharmacol*, 1998, 358, 19-24.

Stahl, SM. Platelets as pharmacological models for the receptors and biochemistry of monoaminergic neurons; in Longenecker GL (ed): Platelets: Physiology and Pharmacology. New York, *Academic Press*, 1985, 307-340.

Stuss, DT; Gow, CA; Hetherington, CR. ''No longer Gage'': frontal lobe dysfunction and emotional changes. *J Consult Clin Psychol*, 1992, 60, 349–359.

Suhara, T; Yasuno, F; Sudo, Y; Yamamoto, M; Inoue, M; Okubo, Y; Suzuki, K. Dopamine D2 receptors in the insular cortex and the personality trait of novelty seeking. *Neuroimage*, 2001, 13, 891–895.

Suominen, K; Isometsa, E; Henriksson, M; Ostamo, A; Lonnqvist, J. Hopelessness, impulsiveness, and intent among suicide attempters with major depression, alcohol dependence and both. *Acta Psychiatr Scand*, 1997, 96, 142– 149.

Swann, AC; Bjork, JM; Moeller, FG; Dougherty, DM. Two models of impulsivity: relationship to personality traits and psychopathology. *Biol Psychiatry*, 2002, 51, 988–994.

Swanson, J; Oosterlaan, J; Murias, M; Schuck, S; et al. Attention deficit/hyperactivity disorder children with a 7-repeat allele of the dopamine receptor D4 gene have extreme behavior but normal performance on critical neuropsychological tests of attention. *PNAS*, 2000, 97, 4754-4759.

Swanson, JM; Sunohara, GA; Kennedy, JL; Regino, R; et al. Association of the dopamine receptor D4 (DRD4) gene with a refined phenotype of attention deficit hyperactivity disorder (ADHD): a family-based approach. *Mol Psychiatry*, 1998, 3, 38-41.

Tannock, R; Schachar, RJ; Carr, RP; Chajczyk, D; Logan, GD. Effects of methylphenidate on inhibitory control in hyperactive children. *J Abnorm Child Psychol*, 1989, 17, 473–491.

Taylor, SE; Way, BM; Welch, WT; Hilmert, CJ; Lehman, BJ; Eisenberger, NI. Early family environment, current adversity, the serotonin transporter promoter polymorphism, and depressive symptomatology. *Biol Psychiatry*, 2006, 60, 671-676.

Terracciano, A; Esko, T; Sutin, AR; de Moor, MH; Meirelles, O; Zhu, G; et al. Meta-analysis of genome-wide association studies identifies common variants in CTNNA2 associated with excitement-seeking. *Transl Psychiatry*, 2011, 1, e49.

Uher, R; McGuffin, P. The moderation by the serotonin transporter gene of environmental adversity in the aetiology of mental illness: review and methodological analysis. *Mol Psychiatry*, 2008, 13, 131-46.

Unis, AS; Cook, EH; Vincent, JG; Gjerde, DK; Perry, BD; Mason, C; Mitchell J: Platelet serotonin measures in adolescents with conduct disorder. *Biol Psychiatry*, 1997, 42, 553–559.

Van Gaalen, MM; van Koten, R; Schoffelmeer, AN; Vanderschuren, LJ. Critical involvement of dopaminergic neurotransmission in impulsive decision making. *Biol Psychiatry*, 2006, 60, 66–73.

Van Tol, HH; Wu, CM; Guan, HC; Ohara, K; et al. Multiple dopamine D4 receptor variants in the human population. *Nature*, 1992, 358, 149-152.

Van Tol, HH. The dopamine D4 receptor. NIDA research monograph, 1996, 161, 20-38.

Wade, TR; de Wit, H; Richards, JB. Effects of dopaminergic drugs on delayed reward as a measure of impulsive behavior in rats. *Psychopharmacology* (Berl), 2000, 150, 90–101.

Walderhaug, E; Lunde, H; Nordvik, JE; Landro, NI; Refsum, H. Magnusson. Lowering of serotonin by rapid tryptophan depletion increases impulsiviness in normal individuals. *Psychopharmacology* (*Berl*), 2002, 164, 385-391.

Waldman, ID; Gizer, IR. The genetics of attention deficit hyperactivity disorder. *Clin Psychol Rev*, 2006, 26, 396-432.

Wallis, D. The search for biomarkers for attention deficit/hyperactivity disorder. *Drug News Perspect*, 2010, 23, 438-49.

White, MJ; Morris, CP; Lawford, BR; Young, RM. Behavioral phenotypes of impulsivity related to the ANKK1 gene are independent of an acute stressor. *Behav Brain Funct*, 2008, 4, 54.

Whitfield, JB; Pang, D; Bucholz, KK; Madden, PAF; Heath, AC; Statham, DJ; Martin, NG. Monoamine oxidase: association with alcohol dependence, smoking, and othe rmeasures of psychopathology. *Psychosom Med*, 2000, 30, 443-454.

Winstanley, CA; Eagle, DM; Robbins, TW. Behavioral models of impulsivity in relation to ADHD: translation between clinical and preclinical studies. *Clin Psychol Rev*, 2006, 26, 379-95.

Yu, R. Regional white matter volumes correlate with delay discounting. *PLoS ONE*, 2012, 7, e32595.

Zabetian, CP; Anderson, GM; Buxbaum, SG; Elston, RC; et al. A quantitative-trait analysis of human plasma-dopamine beta-hydroxylase activity: evidence for a major functional polymorphism at the DBH locus. *Am J Hum Genet*, 2001, 68, 515-522.

Zald, DH; Cowan, RL; Riccardi, P; Baldwin, RM; Ansari, MS; Li, R; Shelby, ES; Smith, CE; McHugo, M; Kessler, RM. Midbrain dopamine receptor availability is inversely associated with novelty-seeking traits in humans. *J Neurosci*, 2008, 28, 14372–14378.

In: Psychology of Impulsivity
Editor: Mary C. Olmstead

ISBN: 978-1-63321-879-6

Chapter 8

IMPULSE CONTROL DISORDERS: PROSPECT FOR TREATMENT USING NONINVASIVE BRAIN STIMULATION

Maya Dickler, Antoine Hone-Blanchet and Shirley Fecteau

Canada Research Chair in Cognitive Neuroplasticity,
Centre interdisciplinaire de recherche en réadaptation et intégration sociale,
Centre de recherche universitaire en santé mentale de Québec,
Medical School, Laval University, Canada

ABSTRACT

Impulse control disorders (ICD) are defined by an impaired ability to resist urges and impulses leading to deleterious long-term consequences. ICD affect the general population but may also develop in Parkinson's disease (PD). Indeed, dopaminergic treatments can improve motor symptoms but may also cause ICD, such as hypersexuality and pathological gambling. There is a need for other treatment approaches for ICD as current alternatives still lack conclusive results in terms on long-term treatment efficacy. Conversely, noninvasive brain stimulation (NIBS) is currently studied as an alternative treatment for several psychiatric disorders. The aim of this review is to explore if NIBS may represent an alternative treatment for ICD. Two lines of work are discussed. First, we describe neurocognitive impairments that have been reported in patients with ICD. We mainly focus on risk taking, reward seeking and impulsivity, which have been found to be abnormally higher in patients with ICD with and without PD as compared to healthy subjects. These distinct impairments have been associated with abnormal activity of the prefrontal cortex among other brain regions. Second, we present two NIBS techniques, transcranial magnetic and electric stimulation, and their current use to alleviate symptoms in various neuropsychiatric disorders, including depression and substance use disorders, when targeting the prefrontal cortex. We also discuss proof-of-concept studies modulating cognitive processes such as risk taking, rewars seeking and impulsivity when applying NIBS over the prefrontal cortex in healthy subjects. Although additional studies will be needed on the specific issue of ICD, this short review provides theoretical support for a possible alternative approach to reduce ICD with NIBS.

Introduction

Based on DSM-5 criteria (American Psychiatric Association, 2013), impulse control disorders (ICD) are described as an impaired ability to resist impulses to engage in ultimately self-destructive behavior that may cause harm to oneself or others. Examples of these behaviors include hypersexuality and compulsive buying. ICD are not only found in the general population but also in patients with Parkinson's Disease (PD) (Weintraub et al., 2010). These disorders have deleterious impact on the patients and their families, as well as on their quality of life as they can lead to social, economic and legal issues. Current therapies do not meet medical needs, with only partial and debated success after long cognitive-behavioral therapy and pharmacological treatments (Grant et al., 2003; Potenza et al., 2013). Development of new therapeutic approaches to treat ICD is thus necessary. Recent work suggests that non-pharmacological approaches with non-invasive brain stimulation (NIBS) are clinically beneficial in various neurologic and psychiatric populations (Mondino et al., 2014). Indeed, NIBS such as transcranial magnetic stimulation (TMS) is now approved to treat major refractory depression (O'Reardon et al., 2007). These NIBS approaches may also carry translational benefits as they can modulate cognitive processes, known to be impaired in clinical populations including ICD, such as reducing impulsivity. The aim of this review is to describe the underlying neurocognitive profile of ICD and to explore whether NIBS may represent an alternative avenue to reduce symptoms of patients with ICD.

Impulse Control Disorders

ICD are defined as behavioral impairments characterized by a failure to resist temptation, urges or impulses that may harm oneself or others. These disorders currently include kleptomania, intermittent explosive disorder, trichotillomania, pyromania and impulse control disorders not otherwise specified such as hypersexuality and compulsive shopping (American Psychiatric Association, 2013). Estimated prevalence in North America for compulsive shopping falls between 5 and 6 % (Koranet et al., 2006) and between 3 and 6% for hypersexuality (Kuzma & Black., 2008). Predispositions for the development of ICD include gender (men are more likely to develop hypersexuality), age (younger people are more prone to develop ICD), trait levels of impulsivity or novelty seeking that are above a normal range, and a personal or family history of substance use disorder (Grant et al., 2005). Environmental factors may interact with individual predispositions resulting in the development of this type of behavioral disorders (e.g. a barrage of advertising messages constantly and strongly encouraging consumers to buy and use credit) (Grant & Potenza, 2004).

ICD are also found in PD (PD-ICD). Dopaminergic replacement therapy (DRT), which uses Levodopa (L-DOPA) or dopamine agonists can improve motor symptoms but, in some cases, may unfortunately contribute to the development of ICD in PD patients. Dopaminergic-related ICD can be of different types and co-occur in PD patients. In 2010, the DOMINION multicenter study evaluated that in a large group of PD patients (n=3090), 13.6% presented at least one type of ICD (Weintraub et al., 2010). Specifically, 3.5% of patients exhibited hypersexuality, 5.7% compulsive shopping, and 4.3% compulsive eating behavior. ICD in PD could be explained by the combination of DRT and individual predispositions in patients

(Voon et al., 2011). Predispositions for PD-ICD include gender (e.g. male are more prone to develop hypersexuality), early PD onset, individual high trait impulsivity and novelty-seeking as well as personal or family history of substance use disorders (Voon et al., 2011).

Pathological gambling (PG) was part of the ICD in the DSM-IV-R (American Psychiatric Association, 2001), but was re-classified as a non-substance use disorder in the DSM-5 (American Psychiatric Association, 2013). PG is highly associated with impulsivity (Alessi & Petry, 2003; Dannon et al., 2010). We discuss PG here because we believe it is an important disorder to address in the context of improving decision-making capacities (e.g., suppressing impulsivity) with NIBS, the focus of this review. The prevalence of PG in the general population has been estimated at 1.5% (Ladouceur et al., 2006) and 5.0% for PD patients (Weintraub et al., 2010), highlighting again the importance of further understanding PG and developing new therapeutic approaches.

Triggering factors for the development of ICD may differ for PD and non-PD patients, especially when considering the major role that psychological background and current status play for ICD in non-PD patients (Ladouceur, 2004). However, all patients suffering from ICD (PD or not) share a similar neurocognitive profile including impaired decision-making associated with abnormal activity in the prefrontal cortex. We describe these in the following sections.

Neurocognitive Impairments Associated with Impulse Control Disorders

Risk Taking, Reward Seeking and Impulsivity in Patients with Impulse Control Disorders

Patients with ICD display impairments in cognitive processes involved in decision-making. For instance, patients with compulsive buying disorder showed greater risk taking on the Cambridge Gambling Task as compared to controls (Derbyshire et al., 2014). Patients with PG also show greater risk taking as compared to healthy subjects as measured by various risky decision-making tasks. More specifically, patients with PG showed impaired performance compared to control subjects in the ambiguous decision-making tasks Coin Flipping Task (Brevers et al., 2012) and the Balloon Analogue Risk Task (Xu et al., 2013). Studies have further explored risk taking using functional magnetic resonance imaging (fMRI) to characterize brain activations associated with these cognitive deficits. Two studies demonstrated decreased activation in the ventrolateral prefrontal cortex (vlPFC) in patients with PG as compared to healthy subjects in probabilistic tasks, in which subjects could win or lose money (de Ruiter et al., 2009; Reuter et al., 2005).

Several studies have also found greater level of reward seeking in ICD compared to healthy subjects. Reward seeking has been extensively studied with the Iowa Gambling Task. This task assesses reward-seeking behavior in which subjects must establish an advantageous strategy in order to be more rewarded. A few studies have evaluated this aspect with mixed results in compulsive buyers (Blacket al., 2012; Derbyshire et al., 2014) but patients with PG continuously show abnormal reward seeking as they tend to persist in choosing the less advantageous options in the Iowa Gambling Task (Brevers et al., 2013; Brevers et al., 2013;

Brevers et al., 2012; Dannon et al., 2010; Forbush et al., 2008; Goudriaan et al., 2005; Linnet., 2013; Linnet et al., 2011). fMRI studies have also examined brain activity elicited while patients performed the Iowa Gambling Task . It has been found that patients with PG had decreased activation in the ventromedial prefrontal cortex (vmPFC), orbitofrontal cortex (OFC), and anterior cingulate cortex (ACC) as compared to healthy subjects (Balodis et al., 2012; Potenza, 2013; Tanabe et al., 2007).

Level of impulsivity has also been found to be abnormal in ICD. A widely used questionnaire on impulsivity is the Barratt Impulsiveness Scale (BIS). Its three subscales reflect major components of impulsivity: cognitive impulsiveness, as in making quick decisions; motor impulsiveness, as in acting without thinking, and non-planning impulsiveness, as in lacking forethought (Bayle et al., 2000). Higher scores on the BIS have been reported in patients with compulsive buying disorder (Black et al., 2012) and patients with PG, as compared to healthy subjects (Clarke, 2004; Dannon et al., 2010; Forbush et al., 2008; van Holst et al., 2010). Impulsivity can also be studied with cognitive tasks. A common one is the Delay Discounting Task, which evaluates the future consequences choices (Kirby & Marakovic, 1996). More specifically, impulsivity is reflected as a preference for smaller and immediate reward choices over bigger and delayed ones (Dixon et al., 2009; Petry, 2001, 2012). Patients with PG have shown increased impulsivity levels on Delay Discounting Task as compared to control subjects (Alessi & Petry, 2003; Miedl et al., 2012; Petry, 2001). Importantly, studies have reported a positive correlation between impulsivity level and gambling problem severity in PG (Alessi & Petry, 2003; Kraplin et al., 2014). Finally, patients suffering from hypersexuality were significantly more impulsive at a Go/No-Go task, also designed to assess impulse control (Miner et al., 2009).

Of note, other processes have been found impaired in patients with ICD and those with PG such as cognitive flexibility and working memory as reflected by poorer performance on the Stroop Test and the Wisconsin Sorting Cards Task (Goudriaan et al., 2006). These cognitive processes are intricate in a complex manner and may participate in decision-making deficits observed in PG.

In brief, diminished activation in the prefrontal cortex (particularly vmPFC but also vlPFC and OFC) seems to be associated with impaired performance in decision-making tasks in non-PD ICD patients. However, studies on neurobiological correlates of ICD have mostly been done in PG, and more research exploring neural correlates of other types of ICD is necessary.

Risk Taking, Reward Seeking and Impulsivity in Patients with Parkinson's Disease and Impulse Control Disorders

Similar cognitive impairments have been reported in PD-ICD. First, two studies have reported higher risk taking in PD-ICD compared with PD controls in the Balloon Analogue Risk Task (Claassen et al., 2011; Rao et al., 2010). This task assesses decision-making under uncertainty, as probabilities are neither logically deducible nor can they be inferred from the information presented in the task. In other words, subjects are not aware of the potential gains or losses in advance (Lejuez et al., 2002). Cognitive impairments found in PD-ICD have been further studied using neuroimaging techniques. For instance, fMRI studies have shown that DRT administration increases risk-taking in risky decision paradigms, accompanied by decreased activation of prefrontal cortex and specifically of OFC and ACC (Djamshidian et al., 2010; Rao et al., 2010; Voon, Gao, et al., 2011).

Studies have also shown increased reward seeking and reward sensibility in PD-ICD compared to PD controls as assessed by the Iowa Gambling Task (Pagonabarraga et al., 2007; Poletti & Bonuccelli, 2012). They use the same type of strategy as found in patients with ICD and those with PG, that is continuously choosing the more disadvantageous options throughout the trials (Rossi et al., 2010).

Moreover, patients with PD-ICD show higher impulsivity levels on BIS (Antonelli, Ray, & Strafella, 2011; Isaias et al., 2008; Ray et al., 2012; Voon, Mehta, et al., 2011) as compared to PD controls. They are also more impulsive at the Delay Discounting Task than PD controls. They tend to choose, more frequently, the smaller, immediate amount of money as compared to a greater delayed one (Housden et al., 2010; Voon et al., 2010; Voon, Sohr, et al., 2011). A Positron Emission Tomography (PET) study in PD-ICD patients has shown significantly reduced activity of OFC, ACC and dorsolateral prefrontal cortex (DLPFC) after administration of a dopamine agonist during a card selection game with probabilistic feedback reflecting impulsive choice. This suggests that deactivation of inhibitory pathways localized in these regions may implicate higher impulsivity in probabilistic tasks (van Eimeren et al., 2010).

Finally, patients with PD-ICD seem to present cognitive impairments involving working memory skills, visuo-spatial memory and cognitive flexibility as again reflected by poorer performance in tasks including the Stroop Test and Wisconsin Sorting task (Bentivoglio et al., 2013; Vitale et al., 2011; Voon et al., 2010). These features may also contribute to decision-making deficits observed in these patients.

In summary, there is cumulating evidence pointing towards an impaired inhibitory control network in patients with PD-ICD which is associated with decreased functions of prefrontal structures (particularly the DLPFC, the OFC, and ACC) (Probst & van Eimeren, 2013; Rao et al., 2010; Steeves et al., 2009). Patients with PD-ICD demonstrated decreased functional connectivity between the striatum and ACC as measured by single photon emission tomography. Moreover, this decreased connectivity was associated with significantly lower activity in the ACC (Cilia et al., 2011; Vriend et al., 2014).

In conclusion, decision-making impairments are found in PD and non-PD ICD patients and have been consistently associated with prefrontal dysfunction.

Current Treatments for Impulse Control Disorders

Current treatment for ICD in the general population includes pharmacological and psychological interventions. Antidepressants and opioid receptor antagonists have shown encouraging results (Vitale et al., 2011, Grant et al., 2004) and several clinical trials are underway (Schreiber et al., 2011). There are currently no FDA-approved medications for any ICD. Cognitive-behavioral therapy represents an alternative to pharmacological treatment and has demonstrated positive results for the treatment of PG and other ICDs in the general population. Unfortunately, most of the works using psychological approaches present methodological issues (small sample sizes, lack of randomization, inconsistent provision of treatment, insufficient drop-out and follow-up data, etc.), which do not allow making any conclusions on long-term treatment efficacy (Grant et al., 2003; Grant & Potenza, 2004; Hodgins et al., 2008; Potenza et al., 2013). Another issue is the long duration of the interventions, which is associated with high dropout rates (Hodgins et al., 2008). Plus, the research on the efficacy of cognitive-behavioral therapy has mostly been applied to PG. Few studies have focused on other types of ICD and have found mixed results (Mitchell et al., 2006; Hodgins et al., 2008). More controlled research focusing on treatment of other types of ICDs as well as studies comparing psychological interventions and pharmacotherapies are needed. It is also important to explore novel approaches to treat ICD, which disruptively impact the individual's familial and personal life. These consequences can lead to psychological, social, professional, financial and legal issues, and may in some cases lead to suicide (Okai et al., 2011).

As for PD patients, current treatment for dopamine-related ICD mostly consists of modification of DRT medication. Decrease or discontinuation of dopamine medication (specifically dopamine agonists) is often considered a primary clinical action in reduction of ICD-related symptoms (Okai et al., 2011; Poletti et al., 2013). However, ICD can still persist in some cases and patients may experience difficulties tolerating modifications of medication. A main downside of this intervention is the possible uprising of motor symptoms (Okai et al., 2011; Rabinak & Nirenberg, 2010). It is thus necessary to explore alternative treatments aimed at reducing ICD severity without modifying patients' medication.

New Approaches to Address Neuropsychiatric Disorders with Noninvasive Brain Stimulation

Noninvasive brain stimulation (NIBS) techniques, such as repetitive transcranial magnetic stimulation (rTMS) and transcranial electric stimulation (tES), allow non-invasive modulation of brain activity in living humans. Repetitive sessions of stimulation can induce long-lasting neurophysiological changes and modulate behaviours associated with the targeted area and its connected cortico-subcortical network (e.g., Wagner & Pascual-Leone, 2007; Stagg & Nitsche, 2011). They thus hold promise in reducing symptoms in various clinical populations. For instance, rTMS is an alternative to existing pharmacological treatments in reducing depressive symptoms in major depression disorders (Fitzgerald et al., 2003, 2009; George et al., 2010; George & Post, 2011; O'Reardon et al., 2007; Pascual-Leone et al., 1996; Stern et al., 2007) and in the context of various clinical populations including bipolar disorder (Hadley et al., 2011) and posttraumatic stress disorder (Boggio et al., 2010a). The underlying neurobiological mechanisms of the antidepressant effects of rTMS remain unclear, but efficacy of treatment is predicated by adaptive modulation of the deregulated cortical and subcortical neuronal pathways involving changes in serotonin and dopamine release (George & Post, 2011; Pogarell et al., 2007; Wassermann & Zimmermann, 2012) and activity in the subgenual cingulate cortex (Fox et al., 2012). Similarly, repeated sessions of tES applied over the DLPFC can reduce depressive symptoms in patients with major depressive disorders (Brunoni et al., 2013); this effect can last up to one month and be similar to the effects of fluoxetine (Rigonatti et al., 2008; Boggio et al., 2005).

Studies exploring NIBS as an alternative treatment for depression and disrupted motor function in PD have shown that NIBS is well tolerated among PD patients, which supports the possibility of using NIBS to address other symptoms found in PD, such as ICD. For instance, rTMS over the left DLPFC has a beneficial effect on depression in PD lasting at least 30 days after treatment (Pal et al., 2010). In another study, rTMS over the left DLPFC was proven to be as effective as fluoxetine in the treatment of depression in PD patients (Epstein et al. 2007; Nitsche et al. 2009). Regarding motor functions, many studies using either rTMS or tES over the motor cortex in PD patients have obtained increased motor evoked potentials amplitude as well as improved motor function, illustrated by higher scores in the Unified Parkinson's disease rating scale (Fregni et al. 2006; Boggio et al. 2006). In sum, patients with PD reported improved mood and motor functions with NIBS without any significant side effects.

Of interest, NIBS applied over the DLPFC has also been proven to reduce craving in various substance use disorders, as people with substances use disorders share similar neurocognitive profiles (e.g., higher level of risk taking, reward seeking and impulsivity) (Castellanos et al., 1999; Fernandez-Serrano, Perez-Garcia, Perales, & Verdejo-Garcia, 2010). Studies have reported suppression of craving in individuals addicted to nicotine (Fregni et al., 2008; Amiaz et al., 2009; Boggio et al., 2009; Li et al., 2013), alcohol (Boggio et al., 2008; Mishra et al., 2011; Höppner et al. 2011; De Ridder et al., 2011), marijuana (Boggio et al., 2010b), cocaine (Camprodon et al., 2007), and crack-cocaine (Conti et al., 2014). Based on these results, one can postulate that NIBS might also be beneficial for non-substance use disorders, such as pathological gambling, and ICD.

From a methodological point of view, rTMS is a noninvasive method of neuromodulation based on electromagnetic induction. The magnetic field developed by the rTMS coil induces an electric current within the surface of the cortex and through the skull. This current, depending on the frequency and intensity of stimulation, may either depolarize or hyperpolarize cortical neurons, transiently affecting neuronal activity and transmission associated with the targeted area. Punctual stimulation of the primary motor cortex, or single-pulse TMS, allows the measurement of motor-evoked potentials and is often used to probe cortical excitability in several neurological conditions. On the other hand, repeated trains of stimulation, rTMS, can induce long-lasting neurophysiological changes dependent on cortical plasticity. These long-lasting changes are studied in the context of neuropsychiatric disorders (Wagner et Pascual-Leone et al. 2007). On the other hand, tES is a noninvasive method of neuromodulation based on decades-old observations that neuronal firing is modulated by low amplitude direct current. tES induces a modulatory effect on the cortical excitability that depends on the current direction (Nitsche and Paulus, 2000, Nitsche and Paulus, 2001). When applied to neuronal tissue, *anodal* current leads to increased neuronal firing and facilitates cortical excitability, whereas *cathodal* current leads to decreased neuronal activity. Furthermore, the effects of tES on cortical excitability last beyond the period of stimulation and if applied for several consecutive days they can last for several weeks. The effects of a single session of tES (for 13 minutes) lasts up to 90 minutes (Nitsche and Paulus, 2001). In addition, several consecutive sessions of stimulation induce behavioral effects that last for several weeks (Fregni et al., 2006; Boggio et al., 2007). In sum these techniques (rTMS and tES) are relatively safe, easy to use and carry clinical potential.

Neuromodulation of Cognitive Processes Impaired in Impulse Control Disorders

As described above, ICD patients show impaired decision-making described by increased risk-taking, reward-seeking and impulsivity. Recent compelling evidence suggests that NIBS can modulate decision-making processes in humans by modifying activity in certain brain regions, particularly the DLPFC. More specifically, NIBS over the DLPFC in healthy subjects can induce a more conservative response style in the context of decision-making, optimize decisions, suppress reward seeking, and reduce impulsivity. For instance, active tES, as compared to those who received sham tES, displayed a more cautious response style and were less sensitive to reward in the Risk Task (Fecteau et al., 2007a). Risk taking and reward seeking measured by the Risk Task are abnormally high in individuals with substance use disorders (Roger et al., 1999). In another study (Fecteau et al., 2007b), subjects who received tES over the DLPFC displayed a more conservative response style, as compared to those who received sham tES and were tested on the Balloon Analog Risk Task (Lejuez et al., 2002). Performance on this task correlates with occurrence of real-world risk behaviors (Lejuez et al., 2002, Lejuez et al., 2003), such as risky sexual behaviors (Lejuez et al., 2004), delinquent behaviors (Alkin et al., 2005), as well as self-report measures of risk-related constructs (Lejuez et al., 2002). Patients with addiction to nicotine displayed greater risk taking in the Balloon Analog Risk Task (Lejuez et al., 2002). Finally, NIBS can also reduce impulsivity. In one study, tES over the DLPFC leaded to more careful (less impulsive) driving behaviors using a driving simulator (Beeli et al., 2008). More recently, the effects of NIBS on impulsivity have been measured with the Delay Discounting Task. Levels of impulsivity were suppressed in subjects who received active tES over the DLPFC as compared to sham tES (Hecht, Walsh, & Lavidor, 2013). Similarly, reduced levels of impulsivity were reported after healthy subjects received active rTMS over the DLPFC (Cho et al., 2010).

Finally, NIBS over the DLPFC can also impact attention and memory functions in PD, as demonstrated by improvement of performance in tasks assessing cognitive flexibility and inhibitory skills such as the Stroop task (Boggio et al. 2006). To our knowledge, no studies assessing the effects of NIBS on cognitive function in PD-ICD subjects have taken place yet. The DLPFC is a crucial area for memory, planning, sustained attention and cue-associated anticipation (Petrides, 1994; Cabeza and Nyberg, 2000).

The fact that NIBS can influence decision-making processes such as risk taking, reward seeking, impulsivity or attention challenges existing neuroscience frameworks of cognitive processing. Furthermore, such findings may carry translational value for clinical models and interventions, including substance use disorders and non-substance use disorders such as ICD (Fecteau et al., 2010; Pripfl et al., 2013).

Potential Mechanisms of Action of NIBS on Decision-Making Processes

Several mechanisms might cause these NIBS-induced cognitive and neurobiological changes. We postulate on the main basic neural and cognitive cascade of events, impacted by the modulation of DLPFC that could reduce ICD. At the neural level, the effects of neuromodulation are certainly not only local but spread trans-synaptically across bi-hemispheric cortico-subcortical networks connected with the targeted area (Nahas et al., 2001; Wagner et al., 2007; Valero-Cabré et al., 2007). Targeting the DLPFC with NIBS may co-activate other frontal regions such as the OFC/vmPFC because they are densely interconnected (Ghashghaei and Barbas, 2002). The OFC region appears to be especially involved in inhibitory control functions (Elliot and Deakin, 2005) and is known to have extensive connections to other brain areas such as the striatum and amygdala. Thus, the OFC cortex may serve to integrate cortical and subcortical processing of motivational behavior and reward. According to the model of Ernst and Paulus (2005), the DLPFC is involved in the cognitive process of decision-making, whereas the vmPFC and vlPFC, the striatum and the amygdala are involved in the affective process of decision making; further, an unbalance between these two systems has been suggested in the ICD brain (Vriend et al., 2014). It is possible that neuromodulation may have an impact on this imbalance.

At the cognitive level, the DLPFC appears to be centrally involved in decision-making by integrating cognitive (inhibitory control/executive function) and emotionally relevant information (reward processing/motivation, deliberative systems). Its activity is involved in the cognitive control of the emotional impulse by providing adequate inhibition in a context of seductive options (Groenewegen et al. 2000, Krawczyk et al. 2002, Bechara et al. 2005, Ernst et al. 2005, Evans et al. 2008). Targeting the DLPFC may thus decrease the level of reward seeking and impulsive responses, and increase inhibitory control of prepotent responses, all required capacities for appropriate decision-making behaviors. It may also suppress these memories or attentional-biases, resulting in decreased attention to salient stimuli (Fregni et al. 2007).

Safety Consideration

This kind of brain manipulation also demands careful weighing of ethical and safety consideration. For instance, NIBS may also modulate decision-making, but in the opposite direction as we discussed above. Different parameters of brain stimulation can lead to different behavioral impact, such as increasing risk taking after receiving rTMS (Knoch et al., 2006) or tES (Sela et al., 2012).

Side effects of rTMS include transient neck pain, headaches, local pain and hearing changes. Syncopes, seizures and neuropsychological changes are possible in high frequency rTMS protocols but very rare, and may reflect an epiphenomenon. As for seizures and epilepsy, it has to be mentioned that epilepsy is a strict exclusion criterion for brain stimulation (Rossi et al., 2009).

Side effects of tES (with intensity of 1-2 mA) may include skin redness and sensation of itching under the electrodes, nausea and fatigue. However, these side effects are rare and transient. tES does not induce neural damage and neuropsychological changes, as assessed with behavioral, serum, electroencephalographic and anatomical MRI measurements (Nitsche et al., 2009). Acute stimulation of the scalp is therefore considered safe (Iyer et al. 2005). In sum, no adverse effects of TMS and tES have been consistently reported in more than twenty years of studying brain stimulation. In this regard, delimitation of inclusion and exclusion criteria and strict screening of subjects remain of critical importance in brain stimulation paradigms.

Conclusion

Shared but also differential aspects are important to consider between ICD in the general population and dopamine-related ICD in PD patients. Impaired decision-making and loss of inhibitory control associated with prefrontal dysfunction seem to be the main common traits for the development of this disorder in both populations, but may have different etiologies. It is believed, for example, that non-PD patients with PG suffer from erroneous beliefs that play an important role in the development and maintenance of this type of behavior. Behavioral therapy shows encouraging results in this population as it provides PG patients with the right tools to overcome these false beliefs. As for PD patients, the development of ICD is mainly due to dopaminergic medication prescribed to alleviate motor symptoms. Even though modifying the medication posology can reduce ICD, this can also induce motor complications, which can have an important physical and psychological impact on the patient's quality of life.

Cumulating evidence presented in this chapter shows that NIBS has proven to be an interesting non-pharmacological approach to treat symptoms in several neurological and psychiatric disorders and has shown very encouraging results. When applied over the DLPFC, NIBS can transiently modify decision-making behaviors promoting more cautious, reflective actions. Thus, NIBS may not only represent an alternative non-pharmacological treatment to reduce ICD in PD patients without having to modify their medications but overall, NIBS applied over the DLPFC may represent a new avenue for the treatment of ICD in general.

References

Alessi S. M., & Petry N. M. Pathological gambling severity is associated with impulsivity in a delay discounting procedure. *Behav. Processes*, 64: 345-354 (2003).

American Psychiatric Association. Diagnostic and statistical manual of mental disorders: DSM-IV-TR Washington, DC. *American Psychiatric Association* (2000).

American Psychiatric Association. Diagnostic and statistical manual of mental disorders: DSM-V Washington, DC. *American Psychiatric Association*, (2013).

Amiaz R., Levy D., Vainiger D., Grunhaus L., Zangen A. Repeated high-frequency transcranial magnetic stimulation over the dorsolateral prefrontal cortex reduces cigarette craving and consumption. *Addiction* 104:653-60 (2009).

Antonelli F., Ray N., & Strafella A. P. Impulsivity and Parkinson's disease: more than just disinhibition. *J. Neurol. Sci.*, 310: 202-207 (2011).

Balodis I. M., Kober H., Worhunsky P. D., Stevens M. C., Pearlson G. D., & Potenza M. N. Diminished frontostriatal activity during processing of monetary rewards and losses in pathological gambling. *Biol. Psychiatry*, 71: 749-757 (2012).

Bayle F. J., Bourdel M. C., Caci H., Gorwood P., Chignon J. M., Ades J., & Loo H. Factor analysis of french translation of the Barratt impulsivity scale (BIS-10). *Can J Psychiatry,* 45:156-165 (2000).

Bechara A. Decision making, impulse control and loss of willpower to resist drugs: a neurocognitive perspective. *Nat. Neurosci.*, 8: 1458-1463 (2005).

Beeli G., Koeneke S., Gasser K., Jancke L., Brain stimulation modulates driving behavior. *Behavioral and Brain Functions,* 4:34 (2008).

Bentivoglio A. R., Baldonero E., Ricciardi L., De Nigris F., & Daniele A. Neuropsychological features of patients with Parkinson's disease and impulse control disorders. *Neurol. Sci.,* 34:1207-1213 (2013).

Berridge K. C., Robinson T. E. What is the role of dopamine in reward: hedonic impact, reward learning, or incentive salience? *Brain Research Review* 28:309-369 (1998).

Black D. W., Shaw M., McCormick B., Bayless, J. D., & Allen J. Neuropsychological performance, impulsivity, ADHD symptoms, and novelty seeking in compulsive buying disorder. *Psychiatry Res,* 200:581-587 (2012).

Boggio P. S., Fregni F., Bermpohl F., Mansur C. G., Rosa M., Rumi, D O., Araujo Silva M. T. Effect of repetitive TMS and fluoxetine on cognitive function in patients with Parkinson's disease and concurrent depression. *Mov. Disord.*, 20:1178-1184 (2005).

Boggio P. S., Ferrucci R., Rigonatti S. P., Covre P., Nitsche M., Pascual-Leone A., & Fregni F. Effects of transcranial direct current stimulation on working memory in patients with Parkinson's disease. *J. Neurol. Sci.*, 249:31-38 (2006).

Boggio P. S., Sultani N., Fecteau S., Merabet L., Mecca T., Pascual-Leone A., Basaglia A., Fregni F. Prefrontal cortex modulation using transcranial DC stimulation reduces alcohol craving: a double-blind, sham-controlled study. *Drugs and Alcohol Dependence* 92:55-60 (2008).

Boggio P. S., Liguori P., Sultani N., Rezende L., Fecteau S., & Fregni F. Cumulative priming effects of cortical stimulation on smoking cue-induced craving. *Neurosci. Lett.,* 463:82-86 (2009).

Boggio P. S., Rocha M, Oliveira M. O., Fecteau S., Cohen R. B., Campanhã C., Ferreira-Santos E., Meleiro A., Corchs F., Zaghi S., Pascual-Leone A., Fregni F. Noninvasive brain stimulation with high-frequency and low-intensity repetitive transcranial magnetic stimulation treatment for posttraumatic stress disorder. *J. Clin. Psychiatry.* 71:992-9 (2010a).

Boggio P. S., Zaghi S., Villani A. B., Fecteau S., Pascual-Leone A., & Fregni F. Modulation of risk-taking in marijuana users by transcranial direct current stimulation (tDCS) of the dorsolateral prefrontal cortex (DLPFC). *Drug Alcohol Depend,* 112:220-225 (2010b).

Brevers D., Cleeremans A., Goudriaan A. E., Bechara A., Kornreich C., Verbanc P., & Noel X. Decision making under ambiguity but not under risk is related to problem gambling severity. *Psychiatry Res.*, 200:568-574 (2012).

Brevers D., Bechara A., Cleeremans A., & Noel X. Iowa Gambling Task (IGT): twenty years after - gambling disorder and IGT. *Front Psychol.*, 4:665 (2013).

Brevers D., Cleeremans A., Bechara A., Greisen M., Kornreich C., Verbanck P., & Noel X. Impaired self-awareness in pathological gamblers. *J. Gambl. Stud.*, 29:119-129 (2013).

Brody A. L., Mandelkern M. A., London E. D. Brain metabolic changes during cigarette craving. *Archives of General Psychiatry*, 59:1162-1172 (2002).

Brunoni A. R., Ferrucci R., Bortolomasi M., Scelzo E., Boggio P. S., Fregni F., Priori, A. Interactions between transcranial direct current stimulation (tDCS) and pharmacological interventions in the Major Depressive Episode: findings from a naturalistic study. *Eur. Psychiatry*, 28:356-361 (2013).

Cabeza R., Nyberg L. Imaging cognition II: an empirical review of 275 PET and fMRI studies. *Journal of Cognitive Neuroscience*, 12:1-47 (2000).

Camprodon J. A., Martinez-Raga J., Alonso-Alonso M., Shih M. C., Pascual-Leone A. One session of high frequency repetitive transcranial magnetic stimulation (rTMS) to the right prefrontal cortex transiently reduces cocaine craving. *Drug and Alcohol Dependence,* 86:91-94 (2007).

Castellanos-Ryan N., Rubia K., & Conrod P. J. Response inhibition and reward response bias mediate the predictive relationships between impulsivity and sensation seeking and common and unique variance in conduct disorder and substance misuse. *Alcohol Clin. Exp. Res.*, 35:140-155 (2011).

Cho S. S., Ko, J. H., Pellecchia G., Van Eimeren T., Cilia, R. & Strafella A. P. Continuous theta burst stimulation of right dorsolateral prefrontal cortex induces changes in impulsivity level. *Brain Stimul*, 3:170-176 (2010).

Cilia R., Cho S. S., van Eimeren T., Marotta G., Siri C., Ko J. H., Strafella A. P. Pathological gambling in patients with Parkinson's disease is associated with fronto-striatal disconnection: a path modeling analysis. *Mov. Disord.*, 26:225-233 (2011).

Claassen D.O., van den Wildenberg W. P., Ridderinkhof K. R., Jessup C. K., Harrison M. B., Wooten G. F., & Wylie, S. A. The risky business of dopamine agonists in Parkinson disease and impulse control disorders. *Behav. Neurosci.*, 125:492-500 (2011).

Clarke D. Impulsiveness, locus of control, motivation and problem gambling. *J. Gambl. Stud.,* 20:319-345 (2004).

Conti C. L., & Nakamura-Palacios E. M. Bilateral transcranial direct current stimulation over dorsolateral prefrontal cortex changes the drug-cued reactivity in the anterior cingulate cortex of crack-cocaine addicts. *Brain Stimul.*, 7:130-132 (2014).

Dannon P. N., Shoenfeld N., Rosenberg O., Kertzman S., & Kotler M. Pathological gambling: an impulse control disorder? Measurement of impulsivity using neurocognitive tests. *Isr. Med. Assoc. J.*, 12:243-248 (2010).

Daskalakis Z. J. A randomized trial of rTMS targeted with MRI based neuro-navigation in treatment- resistant depression. *Neuropsychopharmacology*, 34:1255-62 (2009).

De Ridder D., Vanneste S., Kovacs S., Sunaert S., & Dom G. Transient alcohol craving suppression by rTMS of dorsal anterior cingulate: an fMRI and LORETA EEG study. *Neurosci. Lett.*, 496:5-10 (2011).

de Ruiter M. B., Veltman D. J., Goudriaan A. E., Oosterlaan J., Sjoerds Z., & van den Brink W. Response perseveration and ventral prefrontal sensitivity to reward and punishment in male problem gamblers and smokers. *Neuropsychopharmacology,* 34:1027-1038 (2009).

Derbyshire K. L., Chamberlain S. R., Odlaug B. L., Schreiber L. R., & Grant, J. E. Neurocognitive functioning in compulsive buying disorder. *Ann. Clin. Psychiatry*, 26:57-63 (2014).

Dixon M. R., Marley J., & Jacobs E. A. Delay discounting by pathological gamblers. *J. Appl. Behav. Anal.,* 36:449-458 (2003).

Djamshidian A., Jha A., O'Sullivan S. S., Silveira-Moriyama L., Jacobson C., Brown P., Averbeck B. B. Risk and learning in impulsive and nonimpulsive patients with Parkinson's disease. *Mov. Disord.*, 25:2203-2210 (2010).

Elliot R., Deakin B. Role of the orbitofrontal cortex in reinforcement processing and inhibitory control: evidence from functional magnetic resonance imaging studies in healthy human subjects. *International Review of Neurobiology*, 65:89-116 (2005).

Epstein J. A., Bang H., Botvin G. J. Which psychosocial factors moderate or directly affect substance use among inner-city adolescents? *Addictive Behaviors*, 32:700-713 (2007).

Ernst M., Paulus M.P. Neurobiology of decision making: a selective review from a neurocognitive and clinical perspective. *Biological Psychiatry* 58:597-604 (2005).

Evans J. S. Dual-processing accounts of reasoning, judgment, and social cognition. *Annual Review of Psychology* 59:255-278 (2008).

Fecteau S., Pascual-Leone A., Zald D., Liguori P., Théoret H., Boggio P.S., Fregni F. Activation of prefrontal cortex by transcranial direct current stimulation reduces appetite for risk during ambiguous decision making. *Journal of Neuroscience* 27:6212-6218 (2007a).

Fecteau S., Knoch D., Fregni F., Sultani N., Boggio P.S., Pascual-Leone A. Diminishing risk-taking behavior by modulating activity in the prefrontal cortex. A direct current stimulation study. *Journal of Neuroscience*, 27:12500-12505 (2007b).

Fecteau S., Fregni F., Boggio P. S., Camprodon J. A., & Pascual-Leone A. Neuromodulation of decision-making in the addictive brain. *Subst Use Misuse*, 45:1766-1786 (2010).

Fernandez-Serrano M. J., Perez-Garcia M., Perales J. C., & Verdejo-Garcia A. Prevalence of executive dysfunction in cocaine, heroin and alcohol users enrolled in therapeutic communities. *Eur. J. Pharmacol.*, 626:104-112 (2010).

Fitzgerald P.B., Brown T. L., Marston N. A., Daskalakis Z. J., De Castella A., Kulkarni J. Transcranial magnetic stimulation in the treatment of depression: a double-blind, placebo-controlled trial. *Arch. Gen. Psychiatry*. 60:1002-8 (2003).

Fitzgerald P. B., McQueen, S., Herring S., Hoy K., Segrave, R., Kulkarni J., & Daskalakis Z. J. A study of the effectiveness of high-frequency left prefrontal cortex transcranial magnetic stimulation in major depression in patients who have not responded to right-sided stimulation. *Psychiatry Res*, 169:12-15 (2009).

Forbush K. T., Shaw M., Graeber M. A., Hovick L., Meyer V. J., Moser D. J., Black D. W. Neuropsychological characteristics and personality traits in pathological gambling. *CNS Spectr*, 13:306-315 (2008).

Fox M. D., Buckner R. L., White M. P., Greicius M. D., Pascual-Leone A. Efficacy of transcranial magnetic stimulation targets for depression is related to intrinsic functional connectivity with the subgenual cingulate. *Biol. Psychiatry*. 2012.

Fregni F., Boggio P. S., Santos M. C., Lima M., Vieira A. L., Rigonatti S. P., Pascual-Leone A. Noninvasive cortical stimulation with transcranial direct current stimulation in Parkinson's disease. *Mov. Disord.*, 21:1693-1702 (2006).

Fregni F., Orsati F., Pedrosa W., Fecteau S., Tome F. A., Nitsche M. A., Mecca T., Macedo E. C., Pascual-Leone A., Boggio P. S. Transcranial direct current stimulation of the prefrontal cortex modulates the desire for specific foods. *Appetite*, 51:34-41 (2007).

Fregni F., Liguori P., Fecteau S., Nitsche M. A., Pascual-Leone A., Boggio P. S. Cortical stimulation of the prefrontal cortex with transcranial direct current stimulation reduces cue-provoked smoking craving: a randomized, sham-controlled study. *Journal of Clinical Psychiatry*, 69:32-40 (2008).

George M. S., Lisanby S. H., Avery D., McDonald W. M., Durkalski V., Pavlicova M., Anderson B., Nahas Z., Bulow P., Zarkowski P., Holtzheimer P. E 3rd., Schwartz T., Sackeim H. A. Daily left prefrontal transcranial magnetic stimulation therapy for major depressive disorder: a sham-controlled randomized trial. *Arch. Gen. Psychiatry*, 67:507-16 2010.

George M. S., Post R. M. Daily left prefrontal repetitive transcranial magnetic stimulation for acute treatment of medication-resistant depression. *Am. J. Psychiatry*, 168:356-64 (2011).

Ghashghaei H. T., Barbas H. Pathways for emotion: interactions of prefrontal and anterior temporal pathways in the amygdala of the rhesus monkey. *Neuroscience,* 115:1261-1279 (2002).

Goudriaan A. E., Oosterlaan J., de Beurs E., & van den Brink W. Decision making in pathological gambling: a comparison between pathological gamblers, alcohol dependents, persons with Tourette syndrome, and normal controls. *Brain Res. Cogn Brain Res.,* 23:137-151 (2005).

Goudriaan A. E., Oosterlaan J., de Beurs, E., & van den Brink W. Neurocognitive functions in pathological gambling: a comparison with alcohol dependence Tourette syndrome and normal controls. *Addiction*, 101:534-547 (2006) .

Grant J. E., Kim, S. W., & Potenza M. N. Advances in the pharmacological treatment of pathological gambling. *J. Gambl. Stud.*, 19:85-109 (2003) .

Grant J. E., & Potenza M. N. Impulse control disorders: clinical characteristics and pharmacological management. *Ann. Clin. Psychiatry*, 16:27-34 (2004).

Grant J. E., Levine L., Kim D., & Potenza M. N. Impulse control disorders in adult psychiatric inpatients. *Am. J. Psychiatry*, 162:2184-2188 (2005).

Groenewegen H.J., Uylings H.B. The prefrontal cortex and the integration of sensory, limbic and autonomic information. *Progress in Brain Research*, 126:3-28 (2000).

Hadley D., Anderson B. S., Borckardt J. J., Arana A., Li X., Nahas Z., George M. S. Safety, tolerability, and effectiveness of high doses of adjunctive daily left prefrontal repetitive transcranial magnetic stimulation for treatment-resistant depression in a clinical setting. *J. ECT*, 27:18-25 (2011).

Hecht D., Walsh, V., & Lavidor M. Bi-frontal direct current stimulation affects delay discounting choices. *Cogn Neurosci.,* 4:7-11 (2013).

Hodgins D. C., & Peden N. Cognitive-behavioral treatment for impulse control disorders. *Rev. Bras Psiquiatr,* 30 Suppl 1:S31-40 (2008).

Hoppner J., Broese T., Wendler L., Berger C., & Thome, J. Repetitive transcranial magnetic stimulation (rTMS) for treatment of alcohol dependence. *World J. Biol. Psychiatry*, 12:57-62 (2011).

Housden C. R., O'Sullivan S. S., Joyce E. M., Lees A. J., & Roiser J. P. Intact reward learning but elevated delay discounting in Parkinson's disease patients with impulsive-compulsive spectrum behaviors. *Neuropsychopharmacology*, 35:2155-2164 (2010).

Isaias I. U., Siri C., Cilia R., De Gaspari D., Pezzoli G., & Antonini A. The relationship between impulsivity and impulse control disorders in Parkinson's disease. *Mov. Disord.,* 23:411-415 (2008).

Iyer M. B., Mattu U., Grafman J., Lomarev M., Sato S., Wassermann E. M. Safety and cognitive effect of frontal DC brain polarization in healthy individuals. *Neurology,* 64:872-875 (2005).

Kirby K. N., & Marakovic N. N. Delay-discounting probabilistic rewards: Rates decrease as amounts increase. *Psychon. Bull Rev*, 3:100-104 (1996) .

Knoch D., Gianotti L. R., Pascual-Leone A., Treyer V., Regard M., Hohmann M., Brugger P. Disruption of right prefrontal cortex by low-frequency repetitive transcranial magnetic stimulation induces risk-taking behavior. *The Journal of Neuroscience*, 26:6469-72 (2006a).

Knoch D., Pascual-Leone A., Meyer K., Treyer V., Fehr E. Diminishing reciprocal fairness by disrupting the right prefrontal cortex. *Science* 314:829-832 (2006b).

Koran L. M., Faber R. J., Aboujaoude E., Large M. D., & Serpe R. T. Estimated prevalence of compulsive buying behavior in the United States. *Am. J. Psychiatry*, 163:1806-1812 (2006).

Kraplin A., Dshemuchadse M., Behrendt S., Scherbaum S., Goschke T., & Buhringer G. Dysfunctional decision-making in pathological gambling: pattern specificity and the role of impulsivity. *Psychiatry Res*, 215: 675-682 (2014).

Kuzma J. M., & Black D. W. Epidemiology, prevalence, and natural history of compulsive sexual behavior. *Psychiatr Clin. North Am.*, 31:603-611 (2008).

Ladouceur R. Perceptions among pathological and nonpathological gamblers. *Addict Behav,* 29:555-565 (2004).

Ladouceur R., Sylvain C., Sevigny S., Poirier L., Brisson L., Dias C., Pilote P. Pathological gamblers: inpatients' versus outpatients' characteristics. *J. Gambl. Stud.*, 22: 443-450 (2006).

Lejuez C. W., Read J. P., Kahler C. W., Richards J. B., Ramsey S. E., Stuart G. L., Brown, R. A. Evaluation of a behavioral measure of risk taking: the Balloon Analogue Risk Task (BART). *J. Exp. Psychol. Appl.*, 8:75-84 (2002).

Lejuez C. W., Aklin W. M., Jones H. A., Strong D. R., Kahler C. W., Read J. P. The balloon analogue risk task (BART) differentiates smokers and nonsmokers. *Experimental and Clinical Psychopharmacology*, 11:26-33 (2003).

Lejuez C.W., Simmons B.L., Aklin W.M., Daughters S.B., Dvir S. Risk-taking propensity and risky sexual behavior of individuals in residential substance use treatment. *Addictive Behaviors,* 29:1643-1647 (2004).

Linnet J., Moller A., Peterson E., Gjedde A., & Doudet D. Inverse association between dopaminergic neurotransmission and Iowa Gambling Task performance in pathological gamblers and healthy controls. *Scand. J. Psychol.*, 52:28-34 (2011).

Linnet J. The Iowa Gambling Task and the three fallacies of dopamine in gambling disorder. *Front Psychol.*, 4:709 (2013).

Madden G. J., Petry N. M., & Johnson P. S. Pathological gamblers discount probabilistic rewards less steeply than matched controls. *Exp. Clin. Psychopharmacol.*, 17:283-290 (2009).

Miedl S. F., Peters J., & Buchel C. Altered neural reward representations in pathological gamblers revealed by delay and probability discounting. *Arch. Gen. Psychiatry*, 69: 177-186 (2012).

Miner M. H., Raymond N., Mueller B. A., Lloyd M., & Lim K. O. Preliminary investigation of the impulsive and neuroanatomical characteristics of compulsive sexual behavior. *Psychiatry Res*, 174:146-151(2009).

Mondino M., Bennabi D., Poulet E., Galvao F., Brunelin J., & Haffen E. Can transcranial direct current stimulation (tDCS) alleviate symptoms and improve cognition in psychiatric disorders? *World J. Biol. Psychiatry*, (2014).

Nahas Z., Teneback C. C., Kozel A., Speer A. M., DeBrux C., Molloy M., Stallings L., Spicer K. M., Arana G., Bohning D. E., Risch S.C., George M. S. Brain effects of TMS delivered over prefrontal cortex in depressed adults: role of stimulation frequency and coil-cortex distance. *Journal of Neuropsychiatry and Clinical Neuroscience* 13:459-470 (2001).

Nitsche M. A., Paulus W. Sustained excitability elevations induced by transcranial DC motor cortex stimulation in humans. *Neurology* 57:1899-1901 (2001).

Nitsche M. A., Boggio P. S., Fregni F., & Pascual-Leone, A. Treatment of depression with transcranial direct current stimulation (tDCS): A Review. *Experimental Neurology,* 219:14–19 (2009).

O'Reardon J. P., Solvaso H. B., Janicak P. G., Sampson S., Isenberg K. E., Nahas Z., McDonald W. M., Avery D., Fitzgerald P. B., Loo C., Demitrack M, A., George M. S, Sackeim H. A. Efficacy and safety of transcranial magnetic stimulation in the acute treatment of major depression: a multisite randomized controlled trial. *Biol. Psychiatry*, 62:1208-16 (2007).

Okai D., Samuel M., Askey-Jones S., David A. S., & Brown R. G. Impulse control disorders and dopamine dysregulation in Parkinson's disease: a broader conceptual framework. *Eur. J. Neurol.*, 18:1379-1383 (2011).

Pagonabarraga J., Garcia-Sanchez C., Llebaria G., Pascual-Sedano B., Gironell A., & Kulisevsky J. Controlled study of decision-making and cognitive impairment in Parkinson's disease. *Mov. Disord.*, 22:1430-1435 (2007).

Pal E., Nagy F., Aschermann Z. Balazs E., Kovacs N. The impact of left prefrontal repetitive transcranial magnetic stimulation on depression in Parkinson's disease: a randomized, double-blind, placebo-controlled study. *Mov. Disord.* 25:2311-7 (2010).

Pascual-Leone A., Rubio B., Pallardó F., Catalá M. D. Rapid-rate transcranial magnetic stimulation of left dorsolateral prefrontal cortex in drug-resistant depression. *Lancet,* 348:233-7 (1996).

Patton J. H., Stanford M. S., Barratt E. S. Factor structure of the Barratt Impulsiveness Scale. *Journal of Clinical Psychology 51*:768-774 (1995).

Petrides M. Frontal lobes and behaviour. *Current Opinion of Neurobiology*, 4:207-211 (1994).

Petry N. M. Pathological gamblers, with and without substance use disorders, discount delayed rewards at high rates. *J. Abnorm. Psychol.*, 110:482-487 (2001).

Petry N. M. Discounting of probabilistic rewards is associated with gambling abstinence in treatment-seeking pathological gamblers. *J. Abnorm. Psychol.*, 121:151-159 (2012).

Pogarell O., Koch W., Pöpperl G., Tatsch K., Jakob F., Mulert C., Grossheinrich N., Rupprecht R., Möller H.J., Hegerl U., Padberg F. Acute prefrontal rTMS increases striatal dopamine to a similar degree as D- amphetamine. *Psychiatry Res*,156:251-5 (2007).

Poletti M., & Bonuccelli U. Impulse control disorders in Parkinson's disease: the role of personality and cognitive status. *J. Neurol.*, 259:2269-2277 (2012).

Poletti M., Logi C., Lucetti C., Del Dotto P., Baldacci F., Vergallo A., Bonuccelli U. A single-center, cross-sectional prevalence study of impulse control disorders in Parkinson disease: association with dopaminergic drugs. *J. Clin. Psychopharmacol*, 33:691-694 (2013).

Potenza M. N. Neurobiology of gambling behaviors. *Curr. Opin. Neurobiol*, 23:660-667 (2013).

Potenza M. N., Balodis I. M., Franco C. A., Bullock S., Xu J., Chung T., & Grant J. E. Neurobiological considerations in understanding behavioral treatments for pathological gambling. *Psychol Addict Behav.*, 27:380-392 (2013).

Potenza M. N. Non-substance addictive behaviors in the context of DSM-5. *Addict. Behav*, 39:1-2 (2014).

Probst C. C., & van Eimeren T. The functional anatomy of impulse control disorders. *Curr. Neurol. Neurosci. Rep.*, 13:386 (2013).

Rabinak C. A., & Nirenberg M. J. Dopamine agonist withdrawal syndrome in Parkinson disease. *Arch. Neurol.*, 67:58-63 (2010).

Rao H., Mamikonyan E., Detre J. A., Siderowf A. D., Stern M. B., Potenza M. N., & Weintraub D. Decreased ventral striatal activity with impulse control disorders in Parkinson's disease. *Mov. Disord.*, 25:1660-1669 (2010).

Ray N. J., Miyasaki J. M., Zurowski M., Ko J. H., Cho S. S., Pellecchia G., Strafella A. P. Extrastriatal dopaminergic abnormalities of DA homeostasis in Parkinson's patients with medication-induced pathological gambling: a [11C] FLB-457 and PET study. *Neurobiol Dis*, 48:519-525 (2012).

Reuter J., Raedler T., Rose M., Hand I., Glascher J., & Buchel C. Pathological gambling is linked to reduced activation of the mesolimbic reward system. *Nat. Neurosci.*, 8:147-148 (2005).

Rigonatti S. P., Boggio P. S., Myczkowski M. L., Otta E., Fiquer J. T., Ribeiro R. B., Fregni F. Transcranial direct stimulation and fluoxetine for the treatment of depression. *Eur. Psychiatry*, 23:74-76 (2008).

Rossi M., Gerschcovich E. R., de Achaval D., Perez-Lloret S., Cerquetti D., Cammarota A., Leiguarda R. Decision-making in Parkinson's disease patients with and without pathological gambling. *Eur. J. Neurol.*, 17:97-102 (2010).

Rossi S., Hallett M., Rossini P. M., Pascual-Leone A., & Safety of, T. M. S. C. G. Safety, ethical considerations, and application guidelines for the use of transcranial magnetic stimulation in clinical practice and research. *Clin. Neurophysiol.*, 120:2008-2039 (2009).

Sanfey AG., Rilling KJ., Aronson JA., Nystrom LE., Cohen JD. The neural basis of economic decision making in the Ultimate Game. *Science* 300:1673-1675 (2003).

Schreiber, L., Odlaug, B. L., & Grant, J. E. Impulse control disorders: updated review of clinical characteristics and pharmacological management. *Front Psychiatry*, 2:1 (2011).

Sela T., Kilim A., & Lavidor M. Transcranial alternating current stimulation increases risk-taking behavior in the balloon analog risk task. *Front Neurosci*, 6:22 (2012).

Stagg C. J., & Nitsche M. A. Physiological basis of transcranial direct current stimulation. *Neuroscientist*, 17:37-53 (2011).

Steeves T. D., Miyasaki J., Zurowski M., Lang A. E., Pellecchia G., Van Eimeren T., Strafella A. P. Increased striatal dopamine release in Parkinsonian patients with pathological gambling: a [11C] raclopride PET study. *Brain,* 132:1376-1385 (2009).

Stern W.M, Tormos J.M, Press D.Z, Pearlman C, Pascual-Leone A. Antidepressant effects of high and low frequency repetitive transcranial magnetic stimulation to the dorsolateral prefrontal cortex: a double-blind, randomized, placebo-controlled trial. *J. Neuropsychiatry Clin. Neurosci.*, 19:179-86 (2007).

Tanabe J., Thompson L., Claus E., Dalwani M., Hutchison K., & Banich M. T. Prefrontal cortex activity is reduced in gambling and nongambling substance users during decision-making. *Hum Brain Mapp*, 28:1276-1286 (2007).

Valero-Cabré A., Payne B.R, Pascual-Leone A. Opposite impact on 14C-2-deoxyglucose brain metabolism following patterns of high and low frequency repetitive transcranial magnetic stimulation in the posterior parietal cortex. *Experimental Brain Research,* 176:603-615 (2007).

van Eimeren T., Pellecchia G., Cilia R., Ballanger B., Steeves T. D., Houle S., Strafella A. P. Drug-induced deactivation of inhibitory networks predicts pathological gambling in PD. *Neurology*, 75:1711-1716 (2010).

van Holst R. J., van den Brink W., Veltman D. J., & Goudriaan A. E. Why gamblers fail to win: a review of cognitive and neuroimaging findings in pathological gambling. *Neurosci. Biobehav. Rev.,* 34:87-107 (2010).

Vitale C., Santangelo G., Trojano L., Verde F., Rocco M., Grossi D., & Barone, P. Comparative neuropsychological profile of pathological gambling, hypersexuality, and compulsive eating in Parkinson's disease. *Mov. Disord.*, 26:830-836 (2011).

VoonV., Reynolds B., Brezing C., Gallea C., Skaljic M., Ekanayake V., Hallett, M. Impulsive choice and response in dopamine agonist-related impulse control behaviors. *Psychopharmacology* (Berl), 207:645-659 (2010).

Voon V., Gao J., Brezing C., Symmonds M., Ekanayake V., Fernandez, H., . . . Hallett, M. Dopamine agonists and risk: impulse control disorders in Parkinson's disease. *Brain,* 134:1438-1446 (2011).

Voon V., Mehta A. R., & Hallett M. Impulse control disorders in Parkinson's disease: recent advances. *Curr Opin Neurol,* 24:324-330 (2011).

Voon V., Sohr M., Lang A. E., Potenza M. N., Siderowf, A. D., Whetteckey J., Stacy M. Impulse control disorders in Parkinson disease: a multicenter case--control study. *Ann. Neurol.*, 69:986-996 (2011).

Vriend C., Pattij T., van der Werf Y. D., Voorn P., Booij J., Rutten S., van den Heuvel O. A. Depression and impulse control disorders in Parkinson's disease: two sides of the same coin? *Neurosci. Biobehav. Rev.*, 38:60-71 (2014).

Wagner T., Valero-Cabre A., & Pascual-Leone A. Noninvasive Human Brain Stimulation. *Annual Review of Biomedical Engineering*, 9: 527–565 (2007).

Wassermann E.M, Zimmermann T. Transcranial magnetic brain stimulation: therapeutic promises and scientific gaps. *Pharmacol. Ther.* 133:98-107 (2012).

Weintraub D., Koester J., Potenza M. N., Siderowf A. D., Stacy, M., Voon, V., Lang, A. E. Impulse control disorders in Parkinson disease: a cross-sectional study of 3090 patients. *Arch. Neurol.*, 67:589-595 (2010).

Xu S., Korczykowski M., Zhu S., & Rao, H. Assessment of risk-taking and impulsive behaviors: A comparison between three tasks. *Soc. Behav. Pers.*, 41:477-486 (2013).

EDITOR CONTACT INFORMATION

Dr. Mary C. Olmstead, Professor
Department of Psychology
Dept. of Biomedical and Molecular Sciences
Centre for Neuroscience Studies
Queen's University
Kingston, ON Canada K7L 3N6
Tel: 613-533-6208
Fax: 613-533-2499
E-mail: olmstead@queensu.ca

INDEX

A

abuse, 4, 65, 96, 122, 131
academic performance, vii
access, 25, 62, 70
accessibility, 24
acid, 97, 103
acute stress, 139
AD, 127, 138
adolescent boys, 108, 110
adolescent development, 80
adolescent female, 6
adrenaline, 99, 100
adulthood, 19, 53, 59, 120, 135
adults, 12, 18, 45, 59, 65, 73, 74, 78, 79, 81, 122, 123, 124, 126, 131, 156
adverse effects, 149
aetiology, 139
affective disorder, 59, 96
African-American, 138
age, 18, 30, 35, 36, 37, 44, 51, 53, 58, 65, 72, 96, 99, 102, 105, 110, 111, 114, 115, 116, 118, 119, 120, 121, 122, 123, 133, 134, 137, 142
aggression, vii, x, 4, 44, 49, 50, 55, 56, 57, 58, 59, 60, 78, 83, 87, 97, 123, 124, 126, 129, 131, 135, 136
aggressive behavior, 53, 57, 95, 97, 98
aggressive personality, 129
aggressiveness, 46, 58
agonist, 157
alcohol consumption, 63, 64, 68, 72, 75, 80, 81, 91
alcohol dependence, 133, 138, 139, 154
alcohol use, 2, 65, 68, 73, 88, 89, 91, 153
alcoholics, 98, 129
alcoholism, 20, 89, 120, 128, 131, 135, 136, 138
alertness, 94
allele, 83, 98, 99, 100, 104, 105, 107, 108, 114, 115, 116, 117, 118, 120, 123, 124, 125, 127, 129, 130, 133, 139
alternative treatments, 146
ambivalence, 65
American Psychiatric Association, x, 29, 30, 45, 61, 62, 65, 66, 68, 69, 71, 142, 143, 150
American Psychological Association, 126, 132
amine(s), 58, 121, 127
amplitude, 103, 104, 147
amygdala, 81, 82, 88, 120, 131, 136, 138, 149, 154
anatomy, 157
anger, x, 49, 53, 54, 55, 56, 57, 58, 87
annealing, 104
anorexia nervosa, 46
ANOVA, 102, 105, 106, 107, 108, 109, 110, 111, 112, 113, 114, 115, 118
anterior cingulate cortex, 94, 98, 144, 152
anticoagulant, 103, 104
antidepressant(s), 122, 134, 146
antisocial behavior, 89, 127, 129
antisocial personality, 50, 95
antisocial personality disorder, 95
anxiety, 4, 16, 19, 51, 54, 58, 60, 65, 78, 79, 83, 96, 99, 120, 133
anxiety disorder, 19, 51, 54, 65, 96
APA, 20, 44, 65, 70, 90, 95, 101, 102
appetite, 153
appraisals, 14
Argentina, 49
arousal, 65, 87, 127
arrest, 95
Asian countries, 2
assertiveness, 42
assessment, vii, viii, 2, 7, 8, 9, 12, 14, 16, 17, 18, 22, 23, 28, 29, 31, 35, 46, 47, 51, 52, 53, 59, 63, 70, 71, 73, 74, 75, 97
assessment tools, vii, 14
athletes, 74

Attention Deficit Hyperactivity Disorder (ADHD), 23, 29, 30, 31, 95, 96, 97, 98, 99, 100, 101, 102, 105, 106, 107, 110, 111, 112, 113, 114, 115, 116, 117, 118, 119, 121, 122, 123, 124, 125, 126, 128, 129, 130, 131, 132, 133, 135, 137, 138, 139, 140, 151
attitudes, 10, 36
autism, 135
aversion, 85
avoidance, 13, 66, 72, 84, 85, 88, 121
awareness, 4, 13

B

Barratt Impulsiveness Scale (BIS), 144
barriers, 57
basal ganglia, 82
base, 98
base pair, 98
BD, 57, 133, 139
Beck Depression Inventory (BDI), x, 49, 52, 58
Beck Hopelessness Scale (BHS), 52
behavior of children, 30
behavior therapy, 16, 17, 71
behavioral aspects, 24
behavioral assessment, 14
behavioral dimension, 95
behavioral disorders, 29, 95, 122, 142
behavioral dysregulation, 74
behavioral problems, 24, 120
behavioral sciences, 26
behaviors, vii, viii, x, xi, 2, 4, 8, 9, 16, 21, 22, 23, 24, 25, 26, 28, 30, 31, 50, 52, 53, 57, 58, 60, 61, 62, 63, 64, 65, 66, 67, 68, 69, 71, 72, 77, 78, 79, 80, 81, 83, 84, 86, 87, 94, 95, 97, 99, 103, 121, 142, 148, 149, 150, 154, 157, 158
Belgium, 33, 35
beneficial effect, 147
benefits, 9, 142
bias, viii, 21, 29, 31, 68, 81, 82, 84, 152
bilateral, 152
binge eating, vii, x, 61, 62, 63, 68, 69, 72, 73, 75, 79, 80, 81, 88, 90
biochemistry, 138
biological markers, 136
biological processes, xi, 94
biological psychiatry, 133
biomarkers, xi, 94, 95, 101, 125, 139
bipolar disorder, vii, 1, 58, 59, 134, 146
blood, 98, 99, 100, 104, 118, 134
blood vessels, 100
borderline personality disorder (BPD), vii, ix, 1, 18, 49, 50, 53, 58, 60, 65, 87, 95, 102
brain, vii, xi, xii, 57, 60, 77, 81, 82, 83, 85, 89, 94, 97, 98, 99, 120, 132, 134, 141, 142, 143, 144, 146, 148, 149, 151, 153, 155, 158
brain activity, 98, 144, 146
brain functions, 97
brain stem, 82
brain structure, 60, 134
bulimia, x, 48, 61, 63, 75, 90
bulimia nervosa, x, 48, 61
burdensomeness, 4
Butcher, 36, 45, 46
buyers, 143

C

candidates, 124
cascades, 74
catecholamines, 100
catechol-o-methyl transferase (COMT), xi, 94
categorization, 44
Caucasians, 51, 102
CDC, 50
central nervous system (CNS), 97, 99, 100, 134, 153
cerebrospinal fluid, 58, 97
challenges, 3, 5, 6, 13, 148
childhood, 22, 23, 28, 59, 65, 87, 88, 90, 96, 133, 135
childhood aggression, 87
children, vii, viii, xi, 21, 22, 23, 24, 29, 31, 45, 53, 54, 58, 78, 79, 80, 81, 85, 94, 95, 99, 101, 102, 105, 106, 107, 108, 110, 111, 112, 113, 114, 115, 116, 117, 118, 119, 121, 122, 123, 124, 127, 128, 129, 131, 132, 133, 135, 137, 138, 139
cholesterol, 132
chromatograms, 104
chromosome, 98, 99, 100
cigarette smoke, 134
cigarette smokers, 134
cigarette smoking, 75, 80, 130
City, 105
clarity, 3, 9
classes, 63
classification, 44, 46, 47
classroom, 30, 31
clients, 71
clinical application, 20
clinical assessment, 8
clinical diagnosis, 29, 96
clinical psychology, 74
clinical trials, 145
clozapine, 122, 129
cluster analysis, ix, 33, 37
clustering, ix, 33, 35, 43

clusters, ix, 33, 36, 37, 38, 40, 41, 42, 95
cocaine, 128, 130, 147, 152, 153
codon, 100, 126
codon 158, 100
coercion, 58
cognition, 4, 18, 88, 95, 123, 124, 152, 156
cognitive deficit(s), 143
cognitive dimension, 29
cognitive dysfunction, 99
cognitive flexibility, 144, 145, 148
cognitive function, 4, 97, 98, 101, 123, 148, 151
cognitive impairment, 129, 144, 145, 156
cognitive level, 149
cognitive performance, 138
cognitive process, xii, 97, 141, 142, 143, 144, 148, 149
cognitive processing, 148
cognitive style, 135
cognitive tasks, 144
cognitive therapy, 5, 17, 18
cognitive-behavioral therapy, 142, 146
college students, 6, 18, 66, 71, 72, 75
communication, 57
communities, 50
community, 19, 51, 74, 120, 131
comorbidity, 23, 29, 30, 73
competitiveness, 42
complement, 29
complexity, 97, 103
compliance, 9
complications, 150
comprehension, 51
compulsiveness, ix, 33
computed tomography, 132
conceptualization, vii, xi, 6, 68, 77, 79, 81
conduct disorder, 51, 83, 96, 100, 102, 127, 129, 139, 152
configuration, 43
conflict, 14
confrontation, ix, 34, 41
connectivity, 132, 145, 153
conscientiousness, 90
consent, 51
consolidation, 138
construct validity, 47
construction, 75
consulting, 74
consumers, 142
consumption, 63, 80, 150
control group, 112
controlled research, 146
controversies, 91
convergence, 81
conversations, 8, 29
cooperation, 102
coping strategies, 16
correlation(s), 6, 29, 51, 55, 56, 57, 78, 84, 98, 105, 106, 114, 119, 121, 128, 134
correlation coefficient, 114
correlational analysis, 55
cortex, xii, 82, 94, 98, 100, 123, 124, 132, 137, 138, 141, 144, 146, 147, 149, 151, 153, 156, 158
cortical neurons, 147
craving, 147, 150, 151, 152, 154
criminal behavior, 95
criminality, 96
critical analysis, 31
Croatia, 93, 101
cross-sectional study, 158
CSF, 97, 127, 130
CT, 105, 115, 117
cultural norms, 62
culture, 73
CV, 126, 128
cycles, 104
cysteine, 103

D

daily living, 3
deaths, 3, 18
decision-making process, 15, 16, 148
deconstruction, 4
deficiency(s), 5, 16, 97, 100
deficit, 22, 28, 95, 121, 122, 126, 127, 128, 129, 130, 131, 132, 133, 134, 135, 136, 137, 138, 139
degradation, 97, 100, 123
Deliberate Self-harm Inventory (DSHI), 52
delinquency, 45
delinquent behavior, 148
delusions, 119
dementia, 134
denaturation, 104
dependent variable, 25, 26, 53, 105, 110, 115
depression, ix, x, xii, 2, 3, 4, 6, 17, 19, 34, 41, 45, 49, 52, 54, 55, 56, 57, 58, 59, 63, 74, 78, 79, 80, 81, 83, 84, 86, 87, 89, 90, 102, 120, 127, 128, 132, 134, 136, 137, 141, 142, 146, 151, 152, 153, 154, 156, 157
depressive symptomatology, 80, 81, 139
depressive symptoms, 6, 13, 55, 81, 83, 146
depth, 9
destruction, x, 61, 62, 65
detection, 103, 104
developmental disorder, 96
developmental psychopathology, 59, 85, 86

Diagnostic and Statistical Manual of Mental Disorders, 29, 71, 125
diagnostic criteria, xi, 66, 93, 95
dieting, 69, 73
direct observation, 8, 22
disclosure, 16
disorder, x, 3, 29, 46, 47, 50, 51, 54, 58, 61, 63, 66, 74, 75, 89, 90, 95, 96, 97, 102, 103, 123, 125, 126, 127, 128, 129, 130, 131, 132, 133, 134, 135, 136, 137, 138, 139, 142, 143, 144, 146, 150, 151, 152, 155
disposition, x, 61, 62, 78, 81, 84
dissociation, 70, 71
distress, xi, 5, 62, 63, 64, 65, 66, 68, 69, 70, 77, 79, 80, 81, 82, 85, 86, 121
distribution, 51, 108, 109, 114, 118, 127, 130
DNA, 104, 134
doctors, 101
domestic violence, 95
dominance, 82
dopamine, xi, 83, 89, 94, 98, 99, 100, 121, 123, 124, 126, 127, 128, 129, 130, 132, 133, 138, 139, 140, 142, 145, 146, 150, 151, 152, 155, 156, 158
dopamine agonist, 142, 145, 146, 152, 158
dopamine-beta-hydroxylase (DBH), xi, 94
dopaminergic, xi, xii, 83, 94, 95, 97, 98, 100, 101, 115, 121, 123, 125, 130, 135, 139, 141, 150, 155, 157
dorsolateral prefrontal cortex, 145, 150, 151, 152, 156, 158
dosage, 51
DRD4 gene, 100, 115, 126
drinking, x, xi, 61, 62, 63, 64, 66, 68, 69, 71, 72, 73, 74, 75, 77, 79, 80, 86, 90, 122
drug addict, 46
drug treatment, 119
drugs, 87, 130, 139, 151, 157
DSM, 55
DSM-IV-TR, 150
dysthymic disorder, 51

E

eating disorders, 19, 34, 35, 44, 46, 47, 48, 65, 73, 74
EEG, 152
elaboration, 4
electric current, 147
electrodes, 149
electromagnetic, 147
electrophoresis, 104
emergency, 83
emission, 130, 132, 145
emotion, xi, 8, 22, 65, 77, 78, 79, 80, 81, 82, 83, 84, 86, 88, 154
emotion regulation, 83
emotional cascade theory, 66
emotional disorder, 17
emotional dysregulation, ix, 33, 50, 65
emotional experience, 66
emotional problems, vii
emotional reactions, 8
emotional responses, 82
emotional state, 66, 123
emotional stimuli, 120, 138
emotionality, 86
empathy, 85
encoding, xi, 94, 101, 124, 125, 135, 137
environment, 75, 90, 120, 128
environmental factors, 96, 120
environmental influences, 128
environmental stress, 120
enzyme(s), 99, 100, 124, 127
epilepsy, 149
equilibrium, 105
Estonia, 93, 101
ethical standards, 102
ethics, 51
ethnicity, 99, 122
etiology, xii, 73, 85, 94, 96, 101, 125, 128
Europe, 2, 59
everyday life, 75
evidence, vii, ix, x, xi, 1, 3, 14, 23, 28, 33, 35, 43, 47, 61, 62, 63, 64, 66, 68, 71, 77, 82, 86, 102, 127, 129, 137, 140, 145, 148, 150, 153
evoked potential, 147
excitability, 147, 156
excitation, 124
exclusion, 66, 119, 149
executive function, viii, 21, 22, 23, 24, 26, 28, 29, 57, 100, 123, 125, 149
executive functioning, viii, 21, 22, 23, 24, 28, 29
Executive Functioning Scale, viii, 21, 22, 24, 25, 30
executive functions, viii, 21, 22, 26, 28, 100, 125
expectancies, x, 61, 62, 63, 67, 68, 69, 70, 71, 72, 73, 75, 88
expertise, 9, 23
exposure, 4, 85, 95, 110, 130
externalizing behavior, 23, 28, 31, 78, 79, 80, 86, 90
externalizing disorders, 78
externalizing dysfunction, 78, 79, 80, 81, 83, 84, 85

F

factor analysis, 25
Fairbanks, 97, 130

fairness, 155
false belief, 150
families, 24, 25, 26, 27, 28, 142
family environment, 94, 120, 139
family history, 142, 143
family relationships, 96
fasting, 103
FDA, 145
fear, 4, 53, 57
feelings, 6, 16, 36, 53, 65, 66, 70, 133
financial, 15, 146
five-factor model, 126
fixation, 5
flexibility, viii, 21, 22, 28
fluorescence, 103, 104
fluoxetine, 130, 146, 147, 151, 157
fMRI, 89, 143, 144, 152
Ford, 13, 18
formation, 23, 30
frontal cortex, 99, 100, 127
frontal lobe, 126, 129, 138
functional approach, 74
functional changes, xi, 94, 95

G

gambling, vii, xi, xii, 64, 72, 73, 77, 79, 81, 88, 95, 99, 126, 141, 143, 144, 147, 150, 151, 152, 153, 154, 155, 156, 157, 158
gel, 104
gender differences, 18, 97, 122
gene expression, 100
gene promoter, 135
generalizability, 14
genes, xi, 94, 97, 99, 101, 115, 124, 125, 126, 129, 131, 132, 133, 135, 137
genetic factors, xi, 93, 95
genetic marker, vii, xi, 94, 101, 125
genetics, 128, 130, 139
genome, 139
genotype, 98, 100, 105, 107, 108, 109, 110, 114, 115, 116, 117, 118, 120, 123, 125, 129, 130, 131, 138
Gestalt, 23, 28, 29
globus, 100
goal-directed behavior, 22
grades, 29, 70, 86
gravity, 15
gray matter, 57, 134
grounding, 70, 71
guidelines, 74, 157
guilt, 57, 65

H

habituation, 5, 19
halo effect, viii, 21, 22, 23, 24, 28, 29, 30, 31
halos, 31
haplotypes, 131, 132
harmful effects, 4
head injuries, 4
health, 20, 63
heavy drinking, x, xi, 61, 62, 68, 77, 79, 80
helplessness, 36
heroin, 153
heterogeneity, 97, 123
higher education, 50
Hispanics, 51
history, x, 5, 10, 12, 13, 18, 44, 50, 51, 61, 62, 66, 68, 78, 127, 131, 155
HIV, 95
HM, 127, 128, 131, 132, 138
homeostasis, 157
hopelessness, x, 5, 6, 17, 18, 49, 50, 52, 55, 56, 57, 58
hospitalization, 44
hostility, 97
human, xi, 83, 91, 93, 94, 99, 100, 102, 126, 127, 133, 134, 136, 138, 139, 140, 153
human behavior, xi, 93, 94
human brain, 126, 127
human subjects, 153
hyperactivity, ix, 22, 23, 28, 31, 95, 96, 99, 100, 102, 105, 106, 112, 115, 118, 119, 121, 122, 123, 124, 126, 127, 128, 129, 130, 131, 132, 133, 134, 135, 136, 137, 138, 139
hyperactivity-impulsivity, 96, 112, 123
hypothesis, x, 28, 57, 61, 70, 75, 91, 101, 115, 119, 123, 125, 127

I

ID, 130, 139
identification, vii, 6, 50, 63, 78, 95, 125
illegal drug use, 75, 91
illicit drug use, 122
impairments, vii, xii, 141, 142, 143, 144, 145
improvements, xii, 9, 94, 95, 101, 125
impulses, xii, 15, 141, 142
impulsive action, x, xi, 61, 64, 67, 74, 77, 78, 80, 81, 82, 83, 85, 86, 90, 95
impulsive inaction, xi, 77, 80, 82, 83, 85, 86
impulsiveness, x, 10, 12, 14, 15, 18, 20, 49, 50, 55, 56, 57, 58, 59, 98, 99, 103, 108, 119, 130, 138, 144

in vitro, 138
inattention, 22, 94, 95, 96, 99, 102, 105, 106, 110, 111, 112, 115, 118, 119, 121, 122, 123, 124
independent variable, 25, 115
individual differences, 62, 68, 81, 84, 85, 86, 87
individuals, vii, x, 1, 3, 4, 5, 6, 9, 13, 14, 15, 16, 17, 61, 62, 64, 66, 68, 69, 79, 84, 85, 95, 98, 104, 114, 121, 139, 147, 148, 155
induction, 147
infancy, 87
infants, 86, 89
information processing, 91, 135
informed consent, 35, 51, 102
inhibition, 19, 22, 89, 95, 97, 98, 120, 126, 128, 149, 152
initiation, 22, 72, 88
injury(s), vii, x, 19, 57, 58, 59, 61, 62, 63, 65, 70, 71, 72, 73, 74, 75, 90, 126
insertion, 98
instinct, 13
integration, vii, 65, 75, 95, 154
intentionality, 29
interaction effect(s), 118, 125
internal consistency, 13, 24, 52, 53
internalizing, xi, 44, 77, 78, 79, 80, 81, 82, 83, 84, 85, 86, 89, 90
internalizing dysfunction, 78, 79, 80, 81, 82, 83, 84, 85, 86
International Classification of Diseases, 51
interpersonal relations, 15, 16
interpersonal relationships, 15, 16
interpersonal skills, 44
intervention, 9, 12, 16, 17, 18, 50, 51, 60, 63, 85, 146
intervention strategies, 9, 85
intron, 104, 116, 118, 125, 130, 136
introversion, ix, 34, 41
Iowa, 143, 145, 151, 155
Israel, 47, 87
issues, 47, 90, 145

J

joints, 45
Jordan, 58, 62, 67, 74, 90

K

kidney, 100
kill, 5, 15, 16
kindergartens, 102, 122
KOH, 104

L

language development, 95
languages, 137
lead, vii, xii, 4, 9, 23, 29, 62, 63, 64, 67, 69, 79, 94, 95, 101, 120, 125, 142, 146, 149
leadership, 42
learning, x, 61, 62, 68, 70, 83, 97, 151, 153, 154
legal issues, 142, 146
legs, 65
leisure, 96
lens, 9
life experiences, 7
lifetime, 2, 3, 15, 51, 52, 53, 54, 56, 57, 65, 134
light, 70, 82
Likert scale, 12, 13, 14, 36, 52, 53
limbic system, 100, 124
localization, 99
loci, 128
locus, 98, 127, 128, 130, 140, 152
loneliness, 57
longitudinal study, 59, 71, 73, 102, 132, 136
love, 122

M

magnetic field, 147
magnetic resonance, 143, 153
magnetic resonance imaging, 143, 153
magnitude, 86
MAI, 52, 54, 55, 56
major depression, 65, 132, 134, 138, 146, 153, 156
major depressive disorder, ix, 49, 50, 59, 60, 146, 154
man, 15
management, 22, 154, 157
mania, 95, 134
manic, 98
manipulation, 149
MANOVA, 37, 55
mapping, 44
marijuana, 147, 151
marital status, 35, 36, 37
Maryland, 1
materials, 22
MB, 126, 132
Means-Ends Problem-Solving Procedure (MEPS), 12
measurement(s), viii, 2, 12, 58, 81, 103, 133, 147, 149
measurement bias, 81
median, 84

medical, 35, 142
medication, 75, 91, 102, 122, 134, 146, 150, 154, 157
medicine, 58, 73
medulla, 100
melatonin, 99
membership, 37
memory, 28, 73, 97, 138, 148
memory function, 148
mental disorder, 30, 45, 50, 150
mental health, 5, 6, 60
mental illness, 36, 42, 139
mental retardation, 51
messages, 142
meta-analysis, 28, 31, 73, 87, 88
metabolic changes, 151
metabolism, 135, 158
metabolites, 58, 97, 127
methodology, 123
methylphenidate, 132, 139
midbrain, 98, 129
Minneapolis, 45, 46, 47
Minnesota multiphasic personality inventory, 46
misuse, 152
models, 4, 65, 80, 83, 85, 87, 90, 97, 138, 139, 140, 148
modifications, 146
modules, 16
monoamine oxidase type B (MAO-B), xi, 94
mood disorder, 50, 54, 96
morbidity, 51
motif, 100
motivation, 7, 9, 22, 43, 71, 88, 149, 152
motor control, 130
MRI, 134, 149, 152
mRNA, 127
multidimensional, 4, 52, 54, 56, 74
Multidimensional Anger Inventory (MAI), 52
multiple factors, 86
multivariate analysis, 55
mutilation, 72, 74

N

nausea, 149
negative affectivity, 79
negative consequences, vii, 1, 2, 12, 81, 94
negative emotions, xi, 77
negative mood, 64
negative outcomes, 84
negative reinforcement, x, 61, 62, 63, 64, 66, 68, 69, 70, 71, 79, 80
negative urgency, x, 14, 61, 62, 64, 65, 67, 68, 69, 71, 72, 73, 78, 79, 86, 88
nerve, 100
nervous system, 97
Netherlands, 47
neurobiology, 94, 97, 127, 133
neurodegenerative disorders, 99
neuroimaging, xi, 93, 94, 128, 144, 158
neuronal circuits, 123
neurons, 98, 138
neuropharmacology, 136
neuropsychiatry, 127
neuropsychological tests, 139
neuroscience, 81, 82, 90, 138, 148
neuroticism, 90, 99, 120, 132
neurotransmission, 83, 139, 155
neurotransmitter(s), 83, 95, 97, 98, 99, 125
neurotrophic factors, 137
nicotine, 73, 147, 148
non-invasive brain stimulation (NIBS), 142
nonsmokers, 110, 155
non-smokers, 121, 122, 134
non-suicidal self-injury (NSSI), x, 61, 62
normal children, 136, 138
North America, 2, 142
novelty seeking, 98, 99, 137, 138, 142, 151
null, 105
null hypothesis, 105

O

observational learning, 68
obstacles, 13
obstruction, 122
ODD, 29, 30, 31
offenders, 119, 129, 136
opportunities, 7, 8
Oppositional Defiant Disorder (ODD), 29
optimism, 42
orbitofrontal cortex, 82, 94, 137, 144, 153
outpatient(s), 17, 51, 55, 155
overlap, 29, 81, 84

P

pain, 4, 16, 66, 72, 149
parallel, viii, 21, 25, 28
paranoia, 128
parental pressure, 70
parenting, 60
parents, viii, 22, 23, 24, 31, 51, 101, 102, 122
parietal cortex, 158

paroxetine, 137
participants, x, 35, 49, 50, 51, 53, 54, 55, 57, 58, 66, 101, 102, 103, 104, 108, 109, 110, 112, 113, 114, 115, 116, 120, 121, 123
path model, 152
pathology, 34, 35, 36, 44, 46, 47, 78
pathophysiology, 131
pathways, 3, 5, 74, 88, 90, 125, 145, 146, 154
PCR, 104
Pearson correlations, 56
peer group, 58
percentile, 25, 26, 27, 110
peripheral blood, 104
peripheral nervous system, 100
permission, 102
pernicious anemia, 99
perseverance, 14, 42, 64, 67, 103
personal life, 146
personality characteristics, 46
personality dimensions, ix, 33, 35, 47
personality disorder, 46, 47, 59, 60, 65, 95, 96, 119, 128, 129
personality prototypes, ix, 33, 34, 35, 43, 45
personality scales, 44
personality traits, x, 14, 44, 47, 53, 61, 64, 67, 78, 91, 99, 121, 130, 131, 134, 137, 139, 153
personality type, 34, 36, 45
pessimism, 36, 58
PET, 145, 152, 157, 158
pH, 104
pharmacogenetics, 132
pharmacological treatment, 142, 145, 146, 150, 154
pharmacotherapy, 99
phenol, 133
phenotype(s), 47, 124, 127, 136, 139
Philadelphia, 19
physicians, 73
Physiological, 157
pilot study, 138
placebo, 87, 153, 156, 158
plasticity, 98, 147
platelets, 98, 99, 110, 111
platform, 9
playing, 96
polarization, 155
polygenic disorder, 97
polymerase, 104, 105
polymerase chain reaction, 104, 105
polymorphism(s), 82, 83, 87, 89, 97, 98, 99, 100, 104, 114, 115, 116, 118, 123, 124, 125, 126, 127, 128, 129, 130, 131, 133, 134, 135, 136, 137, 138, 139, 140
population, ix, xii, 18, 19, 33, 34, 35, 43, 50, 59, 72, 97, 126, 127, 139, 141, 142, 143, 145, 150
positive correlation, 119, 144
positive mood, 64, 79, 81
positive reinforcement, 64, 70, 79, 80
positron, 130
posttraumatic stress, 132, 136, 146, 151
post-traumatic stress disorder, 65, 135
potential benefits, 4, 16
preadolescents, 122, 134
predictor variables, 26
prefrontal cortex(PFC), xii, 81, 82, 100, 121, 123, 124, 127, 128, 138, 141, 143, 144, 145, 152, 153, 154, 155, 156
premenstrual syndrome, 131
preparation, 10, 12, 103
preparedness, 72, 75, 88, 90
preschool, 31
preschool children, 31
prestige, 31
prevalence rate, 65
prevention, 5, 17, 18, 20, 50, 63, 71, 85
primary school, 102
priming, 151
principles, 75
prisoners, 34, 46
probability, 26, 75, 155
probands, 128
probe, 147
problem behavior(s), viii, 21, 63, 89, 123, 125
problem drinking, 62, 63, 64, 73, 79, 86, 90
problem solving, 17, 18, 19
problematic alcohol use, 72
problem-solver, 5, 10, 13
problem-solving, viii, 1, 2, 3, 4, 5, 6, 8, 9, 10, 12, 13, 14, 15, 16, 17, 18, 19
problem-solving skills, 5, 13, 15
problem-solving strategies, 4, 9
project, 14
promoter, 89, 98, 100, 126, 130, 131, 134, 137, 139
protective factors, 20
proteins, 97, 99
prototype(s), vii, ix, 33, 34, 35, 43, 45
psychiatric diagnosis, 89, 91
psychiatric disorders, xi, xii, 65, 88, 93, 95, 96, 99, 101, 121, 125, 131, 141, 150, 156
psychiatric patients, 19, 47, 119
psychiatry, 137
psychological assessments, viii, 2, 7, 8, 9
psychological instruments, 7
psychological processes, 4
psychologist, 35, 101
psychology, 59, 85, 90

psychopathology, ix, xi, 31, 34, 35, 41, 43, 44, 46, 48, 77, 78, 80, 82, 83, 84, 85, 88, 90, 91, 121, 131, 133, 134, 137, 139
psychopathy, 46
psychosocial factors, 153
psychotherapy, 9
psychotic symptoms, 19, 119, 136
psychotropic drugs, 99
puberty, 122, 131
public health, 2, 50
punishment, 57, 68, 70, 71, 84, 152

Q

quality control, 105
quality of life, 142, 150
questionnaire, 25, 52, 54, 103, 144

R

race, 99, 122
radio, 104
rash, x, 61, 62, 63, 64, 67, 68, 69, 71, 72, 77, 78, 79, 80, 81, 84, 85, 86, 88
rating scale, viii, 21, 22, 23, 24, 25, 28, 29, 147
reactions, 8, 12, 15, 94
reactivity, 66, 84, 152
realism, 42
reality, ix, 34, 41, 44
reasoning, 14, 153
receptors, 90, 98, 100, 137, 138
recommendations, viii, 2, 9, 14, 15, 17
reflexive responsivity to emotion (RRE), xi, 77, 79, 86
regression, viii, 22, 25, 26, 110, 115, 118, 124
regression analysis, viii, 22, 25, 26
regression model, 26, 110
reinforcement, x, 61, 62, 68, 69, 70, 71, 79, 80, 88, 153
rejection, 44
relevance, ix, 34, 35, 43, 46
reliability, 13, 53, 59
relief, x, xi, 61, 62, 63, 64, 66, 68, 69, 70, 77, 80, 81
remediation, vii
replication, 35, 45
reputation, 31
researchers, 65, 66, 84, 85
residuals, 105, 115, 118
resilience, 16, 70, 95
resources, 70
response, viii, x, 5, 11, 12, 14, 19, 21, 24, 25, 29, 41, 45, 61, 62, 63, 64, 66, 67, 68, 69, 71, 80, 82, 86, 89, 95, 126, 128, 131, 148, 152, 158
responsiveness, 84
reversal learning, 137
rewards, 150, 155, 156
risk assessment, vii, 1, 20
risk factors, vii, xi, 1, 6, 17, 50, 59, 65, 67, 69, 70, 75, 77, 79, 136
risk profile, 85
risks, 14, 50, 94, 121
risk-taking, 148
room temperature, 103

S

sadness, 65
safety, 70, 149, 156
savings, 15
schizophrenia, 51, 54, 96, 102, 129, 132, 138
school, viii, 21, 22, 23, 24, 25, 26, 28, 29, 58, 96, 122, 129, 137
scope, 73
seasonality, 119
self-awareness, 4, 151
self-confidence, ix, 34, 41
self-control, 3, 103
self-destructive behavior, 142
self-efficacy, 6, 16
self-harm, vii, 52, 53, 57, 59, 60, 62, 65, 66, 67, 68, 69, 70, 71, 72, 73, 74, 81, 129
self-injury, vii, 19, 57, 58, 59, 63, 70, 71, 72, 73, 74, 75, 90
self-monitoring, 22
self-mutilation, 72, 74
self-organization, 22
self-reflection, 22
self-regulation, 22, 87
self-reports, 23, 64
sensation, 64, 67, 71, 99, 121, 149, 152
sensation seeking, 67, 71, 99, 121, 152
sensitivity, 84, 90, 120, 124, 152
serotonergic dysfunction, 121
serotonin, xi, 81, 82, 83, 89, 90, 91, 94, 97, 98, 99, 120, 126, 127, 128, 129, 130, 131, 132, 133, 134, 135, 136, 137, 139, 146
serotonin (5-HT), xi, 94
sertraline, 136
serum, 149
sex, 31, 42, 64, 72, 79, 85, 88, 90, 96, 105, 108, 110, 121
sex differences, 85, 88, 90, 108, 121
sex role, 42

sexual behavior, 64, 72, 75, 81, 91, 95, 148, 155, 156
sham, 148, 151, 154
shape, 83
shortage, 45
showing, 44, 109, 118, 119, 121, 122, 123, 124, 125
side effects, 147, 149
signal transduction, 100
skin, 65, 149
skin picking, 65
smoking, x, xi, 61, 62, 63, 64, 65, 66, 68, 69, 72, 73, 75, 77, 80, 88, 99, 102, 110, 119, 121, 122, 126, 130, 131, 132, 139, 151, 154
smooth muscle, 100
SNAP, 102, 110, 111, 114, 115
SNP, 105, 115, 126
social behavior, 90
social cognition, 90, 153
social competence, 18
social environment, 58
social group, 4
social influence(s), 89
social learning, 73
social situations, 70
social skills, 16
social support, 4, 16
social support network, 16
socialization, 85
software, 104
solution, 5, 12, 13, 18
Spain, 21, 24, 25
spatial memory, 145
species, 98
SS, 98, 104, 109, 110, 120, 128, 138
stability, 134
stabilization, 51, 127
stabilizers, 104
standard deviation, 37, 105
state(s), ix, 2, 4, 5, 15, 25, 34, 41, 44, 57, 69, 70, 72, 121
statistics, 20, 130
stimulation, vii, xii, 64, 70, 141, 142, 146, 147, 149, 150, 151, 152, 153, 154, 155, 156, 157, 158
stomach, 65
stratification, 97
stress, 2, 4, 5, 16, 18, 29, 75, 90, 120, 127, 131
stressful events, 69
stressful life events, 103, 105, 109, 120
stressors, viii, 2, 5, 15, 17
striatum, xi, 81, 94, 145, 149
structure, 9, 19, 24, 35, 47, 52, 59, 136, 156
style, viii, 2, 4, 6, 8, 14, 17, 19, 88, 148
subdomains, 99
substance abuse, vii, 2, 4, 51, 78, 98
substance use, xii, 65, 71, 75, 95, 134, 141, 142, 143, 147, 148, 153, 155, 156, 158
substitution, 100
substrate(s), xi, 93, 99, 103
suicidal behavior, ix, 11, 14, 18, 19, 49, 50, 52, 55, 57, 58, 59, 95, 133
suicidal ideation, 3, 17, 51, 52, 54, 60
suicide, vii, 1, 2, 3, 4, 5, 6, 10, 12, 13, 14, 15, 16, 17, 18, 19, 20, 50, 51, 52, 53, 54, 55, 56, 57, 58, 59, 60, 73, 97, 98, 120, 127, 138, 146
suicide attempters, 18, 19, 20, 51, 57, 58, 59, 60, 98, 138
suicide attempts, 3, 4, 6, 13, 15, 16, 17, 20, 50, 51, 53, 57
suicide rate, 50
suppression, 147, 152
survivors, 3
susceptibility, 4, 128, 136, 138
symptomology, 80, 81, 82
symptoms, xii, 6, 28, 29, 30, 36, 41, 43, 52, 53, 54, 58, 88, 95, 96, 99, 101, 102, 105, 106, 107, 112, 113, 114, 118, 119, 121, 122, 123, 124, 125, 129, 131, 135, 141, 142, 146, 147, 150, 151, 156
synapse, 83, 98
syndrome, 128, 154, 157
synthesis, 97

T

tandem repeats, 100, 115
target, 69, 71, 99
target response, 69
TCC, 104
teachers, viii, 22, 23, 24, 25, 26, 27, 28, 29, 31, 101
techniques, viii, xii, 8, 21, 22, 29, 141, 144, 146, 147
temperament, 15, 83, 84, 85, 130
terminals, 100
testing, ix, 34, 41, 44
testosterone, 85
test-retest reliability, 52
theoretical support, xii, 141
therapeutic approaches, 142, 143
therapeutic communities, 153
therapeutic interventions, 34
therapist, 70
therapy, vii, 9, 17, 19, 20, 71, 74, 142, 145, 150, 154
thoughts, 4, 5, 8, 51, 52, 54
threats, 9
thrombocyte, 132
tissue, x, 61, 62, 65, 147
tobacco, 126, 133
tobacco smoking, 126
tonic, 124, 127

TPA, 42, 43
training, 22, 23, 28
traits, 9, 19, 20, 47, 50, 51, 53, 56, 57, 58, 64, 67, 73, 74, 79, 80, 97, 133, 140, 150
trajectory, 2, 81
transactions, 86
translation, 36, 140, 151
transmission, 128, 129, 131, 147
trauma, 50
treatment, vii, viii, ix, xii, 2, 6, 7, 8, 9, 14, 16, 17, 18, 19, 22, 25, 34, 35, 36, 42, 43, 46, 47, 55, 63, 71, 87, 94, 95, 97, 101, 125, 129, 131, 136, 141, 145, 146, 150, 151, 152, 153, 154, 155, 156, 157
trial, 19, 152, 153, 154, 156, 158
trichotillomania, 142
tricyclic antidepressant(s), 87
Trinidad, v, 21
tryptophan, 97, 98, 128, 135, 139
twins, 96
tyramine, 99

U

UK, 130
uniform, 122
United States (USA), 2, 58, 74, 104, 105, 129, 135, 155
unstructured interviews, 22
urban, 102
urgency, 15, 62, 64, 67, 68, 69, 72, 74, 75, 78, 79, 80, 81, 82, 83, 86, 90, 91
Urgency, Premeditation, Perseverance, and Sensation Seeking Impulsive Behavior Scale (UPPS), 11, 13

V

validation, 44, 47, 53, 73, 75, 90
variables, 26, 28, 37, 38, 40, 52, 54, 55, 56, 65
variations, 47, 83, 125
vein, 103
velvet, 130
ventromedial prefrontal cortex, 81, 82, 127, 144
violence, 2, 3, 4, 5, 6, 9, 14, 15, 17, 58, 97, 120
violent behavior, 99, 131
violent criminals, 97
vomiting, 75, 90
vulnerability, 2, 57, 69, 87, 99, 121
vulnerability to depression, 87

W

Washington, 20, 30, 87, 89, 125, 126, 132, 150
water, 103, 104
weakness, 36, 42
white matter, 134, 140
Wisconsin, 144, 145
withdrawal, 64, 157
withdrawal symptoms, 64
working memory, viii, 21, 22, 28, 123, 144, 145, 151
workload, 25
workplace, 96
World Health Organization (WHO), 2, 20, 59, 137
worry, 41
wound healing, 65

X

X chromosome, 99

Y

yield, 80, 121
young adults, 17, 19, 72, 73, 96